IS IT OK TO LAUGH ABOUT IT?

I0883765

This research was supported by
The Open University of Israel Research Fund

Language Editor: Jean Vermel

Is it Ok to Laugh About It?

Holocaust Humour, Satire and Parody in Israeli Culture

Liat Steir-Livny

VALLENTINE MITCHELL
LONDON • CHICAGO, IL

First published in 2017 by Vallentine Mitchell

Catalyst House,
720 Centennial Court,
Centennial Park, Elstree, WD6 3SY, UK

814 N. Franklin Street,
Chicago,
IL 606010, USA

www.vmbooks.com

Copyright © 2017 Liat Steir-Livny

British Library Cataloguing in Publication Data:
An entry can be found on request

ISBN 978 1 910383 35 3 (Cloth)
ISBN 978 1 910383 49 0 (Paper)
ISBN 978 1 910383 36 0 (Ebook)

Library of Congress Cataloging in Publication Data
An entry can be found on request

All rights reserved. No part of this publication may be reproduced in any form or by any means, electronic, mechanical, photocopying, reading or otherwise, without the prior permission of Vallentine Mitchell & Co. Ltd.

Contents

Preface

Holocaust humour, satire and parody deal with issues and matters that are connected to the Holocaust: Hitler, Nazism, Holocaust, Holocaust memory, Holocaust survivors and their offspring, and are very sensitive and complex issues. For many years, Israeli culture recoiled from dealing with the Holocaust from these perspectives. The perception was that a humourous approach to the Holocaust might threaten the sanctity of its memory, or evoke feelings of disrespect towards the subject and hurt survivors' feelings. Official agents of Holocaust memory continue to follow this approach, but from the 1990s, a new unofficial path of memory began taking shape in tandem. It is an alternative and subversive path that seeks to remember, albeit differently. Texts that combine the Holocaust with humour, satire and parody are a major aspect of this new memory.

This book focuses on the new humouristic, satiric and parodic representations of the Holocaust in Israeli culture.[1] It analyzes alternative ceremonies, films, TV shows, art, books, poetry, jokes and internet videos and memes. The book explores these new cultural expressions of the Holocaust through theories of humour, and of individual and collective post-trauma.

Often, the public debate as well as the academic debate regarding Holocaust humour, satire or parody in the western world and in Israel claim that Holocaust humour is part of a dangerous historical, social and cultural process that normalizes Nazism and Hitler. Holocaust humour still often provokes anger and is considered as cheapening the trauma and degrading the pain of the survivors. Those who use Holocaust humour often receive complaints and are subject to invectives because of what is considered, by many, an inappropriate approach to the memorialization of the Holocaust.[2]

This book claims that the perception of Holocaust humour as dangerous is an arguable point when dealing with Holocaust commemoration in the world.[3] However, since Israel is a unique sphere of Holocaust awareness,[4] Holocaust humour of Jewish-Israelis has particular legitimate functions. In Israel, a post-traumatic society, whose problematic security situation strengthens constant anxiety, and where canonic memory agents increase the acting out of the trauma and encourage unending victimization, Holocaust humour is a much-needed defence mechanism. It is the way for some of the second and third generation Holocaust survivors to work against the victimization, to protect the individual and collective soul, even briefly, to protest against the blend of the past in the present, and to dismantle the factors of fear. In that sense, Holocaust humour in Israel also reflects two additional major functions: a vent for frustration; and a mechanism for social cohesion.[5]

Moreover, the book will claim that Holocaust humour, satire and parody which rebel against the way Israeli society lives the trauma in the present by deconstructing the fear factor, paradoxically, unknowingly (and probably unwillingly) simultaneously strengthen, in other ways, the dominance of the trauma in the present by inserting it even more into everyday life and popular culture.

Thus, Holocaust humour, satire and parody in Israel are a double-edged sword: on the one hand, they function as an attempt to fight the acting out of the trauma but, on the other, they strengthen certain elements of acting out. With the help of humour, while the fear factors are much less frightening, they are more present. This is a contradictory process of removal and assimilation at the same time.

The first part of the book, the *Introduction*, offers a theoretical substructure. The first chapter, *Jewish and Israeli Humour* explains the various definitions of Jewish humour and Israeli humour. The second chapter, *Holocaust Humour: from Taboo to Debate in the Western World*, explores the way Holocaust humour has changed from being unmentionable and unacceptable to coming out in the open for discussion in popular culture in the western world. The third chapter, *Holocaust Awareness and Holocaust Humour in Israel*, shows the developments regarding Holocaust humour in Israel over the years, explains why Israel is a separate sphere regarding Holocaust awareness, and what the functions of Holocaust humour within this unique society are.

The second part of the book, *Holocaust Humour, Satire and Parody in Israeli Culture*, looks at different types of Holocaust humour. The fourth chapter, *Laughter through Pain: the Intergenerational Transmission of the Holocaust*, analyzes the way in which the second- and third-generation Holocaust survivors deal with the trauma. The chapter explores the terms, 'second-generation Holocaust survivor' and 'third-generation Holocaust survivor', and shows that these terms are both biological and cultural. The chapter analyzes films, books, poetry and skits that reflect how these two generations use humour as a defence mechanism, and the way these texts show how the trauma entered their lives, and influenced their identity - both individually and collectively.

The fifth chapter, *Black Humour in Alternative Holocaust Remembrance Day Ceremonies in Israel,* delineates the characteristics of the official ceremonies marking Holocaust and Heroism Remembrance Day, explains how the alternative ceremonies undertake to subvert these characteristics, and focuses on the humouristic aspects of the *Tmuna* ceremonies (1999-to the present), the *Remembrance in the Living Room* ceremonies (2011- to the present) and the *Beit Lihiot* ceremonies in Holon (1999-2012).

The sixth chapter, *Satirizing the Instrumentalization and Commercialization of the Holocaust,* shows how television satire uses skits in order to protest, among other issues, the way collective memory agents exploit the Holocaust by instrumentalizing and commercializing it. Diverging from arguments that the satirical skits trivialize the Holocaust and Nazism, the chapter maintains that they instead articulate the powerful position the Holocaust holds as a constituting event in the consciousness and identity of younger generations in Israel who try to fight the way the memory of the Holocaust in Israel has become a commodity or a way to achieve personal profit.

The seventh chapter, *Holocaust Satire and Parody as a Part of a Political and Social Protest,* analyzes the way Holocaust humour, satire and parody are used to protest against political and social ills in Israel. In a society where the Holocaust resides as an ongoing trauma, it is mainly leftists who use Holocaust humour, satire and parody in order to vent frustration, and protest against right-wing government policy and right-wing politicization of the Holocaust. Holocaust humour, satire and parody is also analyzed as a tool for social cohesion among left-wingers in Israel. The chapter also maintains that those who use humour, satire and parody in order to protest against the use of the Holocaust by the right-wing, sometimes use the Holocaust themselves in satirical texts that present their political and social agenda.

The eighth chapter, *Holocaust Humour from the Perspective of the Ethnic Conflict,* traces the way Mizrahim[6] use Holocaust humour and satire in order to participate in the Holocaust remembrance arena in Israel, and simultaneously protest against the way they were marginalized for many years. The chapter explores how young Mizrahim use Holocaust humour and satire as a social protest against the canonic memory of the Holocaust as well as against wider orientalist conceptions and cultural marginalization. The texts in the chapter reveal a complex encounter between Mizrahim and Ashkenazim[7], an encounter whose harsh echoes can also be found in the arena of Holocaust commemoration.

The ninth chapter, *The Downfall of the Führer: Lampooning Hitler's Image*, explores the humouristic use of Hitler's image. Jokes about Hitler existed and were told underground during the 1930s, after the Nazis came to power, as well as appeared in some films and books during the Second World War and in its aftermath.[8] In recent decades, the mocking of Hitler has become a wide-range phenomenon, especially on the internet, which has become a wide cultural field for Hitler jokes, satire and parody. The chapter analyzes the various humouristic, satiric and parodic uses of Hitler's image in Hebrew.

The tenth chapter, *Holocaust Jokes in Contemporary Israeli Websites: Characters and Developments*, analyzes Holocaust jokes found on contemporary Israeli websites. The other chapters in the book demonstrate that most humouristic, satiric and parodic texts in Israel engage in the memory of the Holocaust in Israel and criticize it, and/or lampoon the Nazis. For the most part, Holocaust humour, satire and parody avoid touching the dark core of the Jews in the Holocaust. This chapter shows how Holocaust jokes in Hebrew are a separate genre. The chapter compares the narratives of Holocaust jokes in Hebrew with Holocaust jokes that were told by Jews during the Holocaust (and have previously been analyzed).[9] The chapter attempts to uncover whether there is any observable continuity from the Jewish black humour formed during the Holocaust, or whether there are any differences demonstrating the unique aspects of Israeli Holocaust jokes.

Even though Holocaust remembrance in Israel is a flourishing research subject, the new humouristic cultural representations of the Holocaust have not yet been researched in depth. There are few articles that analyze specific skits and satire,[10] and I have addressed several aspects of the subject in my previous book.[11] However, there is no comprehensive analysis that addresses the multiple humouristic facets of Holocaust humour, satire and parody in Israel. The analysis of the new memory and its functions in this book is innovative, intriguing and challenges the canonic borders of Holocaust research and memory.

Notes

1. The book analyzes texts written by Jewish-Israelis. The representation of the Holocaust among Arab-Israelis is not discussed in the book.
2. For example, G. D. Rosenfeld, *Hi Hitler: How the Nazi Past Is Being Normalized in Contemporary Culture* (Cambridge University Press, 2015); A. Rosenfeld, *The End of the Holocaust* (Indiana: Indiana University Press, 2013); A. Casher, 'Haim satira beyom hashoah hi legitimit?' ['Is Holocaust satire on Holocaust Remembrance Day legitimate'?] *Retro-tik tikshoret*, 5 May, 2016. https://www.youtube.com/watch?v=QKcLzLcMjLA

Accessed 2 June 2016. [Hebrew]. The Second Authority for Television and Radio often receives complaints regarding Holocaust-related skits which are presented as satire. See L. Steir-Livny, *Har hazikaron yizkor bimkomi* [*Let the Memorial Hill Remember: Holocaust Representations in Israeli Popular Culture*] (Tel Aviv: Resling, 2014) [Hebrew].

3. For example, see an opposing perception of Holocaust humour, especially of Jews in the world in A. Atlani, *The Ha-Ha Holocaust: Exploring Levity Amidst the Ruins and Beyond in Testimony, Literature and Film*, a thesis submitted in partial fulfillment of the requirements for the degree in Doctor of Philosophy, The University of Western Ontario, 2014 http://ir.lib.uwo.ca/cgi/viewcontent.cgi?article=3776&context=etd Accessed 2 October 2015.
4. See Chapter 1.
5. A. Ziv, *Personality and Sense of Humor*, (Tel Aviv: Papyrus, 1996) [Hebrew].
6. Mizrahim - Jews who immigrated to Israel from Asia and North Africa, and their offspring.
7. Ashkenazim – Jews who immigrated from Europe and the USA, and their offspring.
8. R. R. Wisse, *No Joke: Making Jewish Humor* (Princeton: Princeton University Press, 2013), pp. 143-181; I. Levin, *Mi'ba'ad la'dmaot [Through the tears: Jewish humor under the Nazi regime*] (Jerusalem: Yad Vashem, 2004) [Hebrew], pp. 37–69; H. Ostrower, *Lelo humor hayinu mitabdim* [*Without humor we would have killed ourselves*] (Jerusalem: Yad Vashem, 2009) [Hebrew], pp. 49-97
9. Ibid.
10. E. Zandberg 'Critical laughter: Humor, popular culture and Israeli Holocaust commemoration', Media, Culture & Society, (28(4), 2006), pp.561-579; E. Zandberg, 'Ketchup Is the Auschwitz of Tomatoes': Humor and the Collective Memory of Traumatic Events', *Communication, Culture & Critique*, 2014, pp. 1–16.
11. Steir-Livny, *Let the Memorial Hill Remember*, pp.37–78.

PART 1

INTRODUCTION

1

Jewish and Israeli Humour

Jewish Humour in Research: Definitions

Researchers have endeavoured to define the traits and characteristics of the multiple definitions of Jewish humour. The broad definition regarding the concept of Jewish humour shared by most researchers is that the uniqueness of Jewish humour is based on two core components: first, the unique Jewish literacy (including the *Midrash*,[1] and *pilpul*[2]). The second is Jewish history with its particularly difficult experiences - persecution, expulsion, exile, and pogroms[3] - culminating in the Holocaust.[4]

Sigmund Freud saw Jewish humour as humour created and told by Jews, dealing with Jewish figures and characteristics, and intended especially for Jewish people. He particularly focused on self-deprecating humour as a Jewish trait. He saw Jewish humouristic culture as a culture with self-irony which ridicules not only non-Jews but also Jewish society's most sacred values. He claimed that he did not know whether there were other instances of a people making fun of its own character to such a degree.[5]

Christie Davies disagrees with Freud's argument - that there are none who can laugh at themselves like the Jews - by drawing attention to the Scots, in particular, as well as other minorities who also use self-deprecating humour to repudiate negative stereotypes directed against them by majority groups. However, Davies claims that Jewish self-deprecating humour is richer and deeper than the self-deprecating humour of other minorities. It illustrates the ability to combine the paradox of the achievements of the Jews, on the one hand, and the negative stereotypes of the often hostile environment, on the other.[6]

Hershey H. Friedman and Linda Weiser-Friedman find the origins of Jewish humour in the Bible, *Talmud*,[7] and *Midrash*. The authors argue that satire, irony and self-deprecating humour can be found in these canonic writings.[8] Others claim, on the contrary, that apart from *Purim* celebrations,[9] the Jewish religion treats humour with suspicion.[10]

Avner Ziv claims that Jewish humour can be defined as humour created by Jews intended mainly for Jews, and which reflects particular aspects of Jewish life. Even though some claim that humouristic expressions can be found among Jewish writers in western Europe in the thirteenth and fourteenth centuries, Ziv and other researchers of Jewish humour concentrate on nineteenth century eastern Europe,[11] where Jews lived in very poor conditions and were constantly in physical danger. Under these demographic and socio-economic terms, a special type of humour developed that helped the Jews survive their hardships as well as deal with their misery and distress as an oppressed minority. According to these scholars, the humour that developed under these conditions had particular characteristics that helped the Jews survive. A great part of this humour is enveloped in great sadness and wit, and enables dealing with pain and hardship.[12]

Ziv sees three major characteristics of this Jewish humour: first, making fun of the tragic reality and thereby undermining the fear, distorting the tragic reality, and making it laughable and thus less threatening. Black humour and intellectual humour which emphasize the absurd elements of reality can be found in this humour. In this sense, Jewish humour is a defence mechanism which helps in dealing with a harsh life. The second characteristic is the focus on the uniqueness of the Jewish people, the way they differ from the surrounding society and feel superior to it. In Ziv's opinion, Jewish humour stems from the dissonance between the self-perception of the Jews themselves as the chosen people, on the one hand, and their life at the bottom of the social scale in nineteenth century Eastern Europe, on the other.[13] In this sense, Jewish humour has a social aspect. The third characteristic is self-deprecating humour that is expressed in knowing one's weaknesses and having the ability to laugh at them. These three traits can be found among people who are not Jewish, but most Jewish humour is marked by these three features.[14]

Theodor Reik developed a theory that sees Jewish humour as humour with masochistic (deriving pleasure from humiliation and self-abuse) traits. He claims that history turned the Jews into marionettes; they were unable to decide regarding their faith. The self-deprecating humour and its masochism enabled them to rise above their powerless, and many times, tragic lives, and has been essential to Jewish survival in the diaspora.[15] Martin Grotjahn links the concept of Jewish self-deprecating humour and masochism with the Jewish religion. In his opinion, since the Jews perceived suffering throughout the generations as an outcome of God's will, they were not able to be angry at God. This aggression was directed through humour, towards the Jews themselves.[16]

Nathan Ausubel claims that although all good humour is universal, there are differences produced by particular conditions of life and patterns of culture. In addition, many Jewish jokes revolve around adversity because there is an instinct for self-preservation. By laughing at the absurdities and cruelties of life, these jokes relieve much of the sting. Among Jews, laughter and tears, comedy and tragedy are all mixed up together: it is laughter through tears. Jewish humour is a calculated method for ridiculing out of existence the foibles and incongruities in the Jewish character. Moreover, in Jewish humour there is a great amount of self-criticism, disguised as irony, satire and caricature, and it aims at making the listeners think.[17]

Henry Eilbirt claims that a Jewish joke is a joke that stems from Jewish life, reflects real Jewish characteristics or stereotypes of Jews, and uses spoken, everyday language.[18] Arie Sover claims that Jewish humour is an amazing survival tool. It was the expression of a powerless minority expected to deal with hardships, persecutions and the need to find instant solutions to distress. It is the power of the powerless who always need to adjust themselves.[19]

Another claim is that, in regard to self-deprecating humour, the development of Jewish humour has to do with the political, social and cultural emancipation in the nineteenth century in western Europe and to Jewish assimilation in these times. In this case, the Jews, who went through a secularization processes and tried to assimilate in the non-Jewish society, told jokes about Jews, not in order to laugh at themselves but to laugh at other Jews - the 'Old Jews' - the traditional, religious Jews who did not change their lives, and from whom the emancipated secular Jews wished to separate themselves. In these cases, Jewish humour is a source for non-identification with Jewish tradition and does not function as self-deprecating.[20]

Ruth R. Wisse claims that, on the one hand, since comedy drives off sadness and fear, humour enabled European Jewry to deal with its endemic powerlessness. Laughter is a wonderful way of dealing with crises, when you have no political power. The humour in Yiddish was the humour of the weak - those who were unable to change their situation - and so they laughed about it.[21]

Mizrahi Jews[22] also had a special type of humour that developed under the influence of the Jewish experience in the various countries in which they lived. In Ziv's opinion, since life in these countries was not as bad as in eastern Europe, humour did not develop the same characteristics as the Jewish humour in eastern Europe.[23] Recent studies regarding humour of Jews in the Jewish centers in North Africa and Asia show that the Jews there developed a type of humour in which one can find both similarities to European Jewish humour (such as, self-deprecating humour, black humour, etc), and also differences. For example, North African Jewish humour reflects the differences between the various Jewish communities in North Africa, the relationship between Jews within the Jewish communities, their relationship with their Muslim neighbors, the status of women, and more.[24]

Contrary to these attempts to define Jewish humour, some researchers argue that there is no categorical evidence to support the fact that it is the Jewish experience that gave birth to Jewish humour, or that there is such a thing called 'Jewish humour'.[25] For example, Dan Ben-Amos claims that the concept of 'Jewish humour' is a myth. It is not a characteristic of the Jewish people but it is the result of specific socioeconomic factors.[26] Elliott Oring argues that many scholars attribute to the 'People of the Book' the title of 'People of the Joke', but the meaning of Jewish humour is deeper than any simple formula can explain. According to him, conceptualizations of the Jewish joke are merely crystallizations of conceptualizations of the Jewish people, their history, and their identity.[27]

Israeli Humour Versus Jewish Humour: Similarities and Differences

There is a dispute among researchers regarding the question as to what happened to Jewish humour in Eretz Israel and after 1948 – in Israel. Amos Eilon claims that traditional Jewish humour with its incisive self-irony has disappeared among Israelis.[28] Ofra Nevo also claims that one of the best known traits of Jewish humour – self-deprecating humour - was lost in Israel when the Jews became a majority.[29] Ziv claims that in Israel, Jewish humour changed. The Jews went from being a minority to a majority. Their life circumstances changed and this called for different kinds of humour, for example, military humour. The characteristics of Jewish humour that helped the Jews survive as a minority in often hostile environments became irrelevant. In Israel, due to the different conditions of life, humour fulfills other functions.[30] Ziv claims that while the major characteristic of Jewish humour was the ability of self-deprecation, the major characteristic of Israeli humour is *hutzpa:* cheekiness. In his opinion, Israeli humour is often characterized by aggressiveness, when a preferable form would be satire. Israeli satire often laughs at Jews, but these are 'other Jews' who belong to the 'wrong' political, economic or ethnic group. However, self-deprecating Israeli humour also still exists.[31]

According to Sover, immigration to Israel over the years has changed Jewish humour. In Israel, the Jews are no longer the oppressed minority. They are the ruling majority, and therefore do not need many aspects of the type of Jewish humour that developed in the Jewish *shtetl*[32] under persecutions, in the pogroms and the Holocaust. According to him, Israeli humour is less self-deprecating, and much more straightforward. It appears a lot when dealing with politics and war in order to discharge tension.[33] Ruvik Rozenthal also claims that Israeli humour is blunter than Jewish humour and therefore less 'Jewish' than the humour in the Diaspora. In Israel, instead of laughing about weakness, jokes are about power. 'We've lost a world of Yiddish humour that didn't succeed in immigrating to Israel,' he says.[34]

Opposed to the claims that immigration to Israel changed the basis of Jewish humour and opposed to the notion that living in an independent country stopped the need for self-deprecating humour, Wisse analyzes the Jewishness of Israeli humour. She claims that the perception that Israelis do not laugh as Jews did in the past, and especially do not laugh at themselves as much, is based on two related assumptions: the relation of Jewish humour to powerlessness and the relation of Israel to power. She claims that professional humourists who immigrated to Israel imported Jewish humour to Israel. They continued their performances and, now free of fear, had every opportunity to express themselves. In addition, Jews in the State of Israel were indeed no longer a minority, but they did not and do not live peacefully in a safe environment. The hostilities by Arab nations towards Israel have never stopped, and Israelis were and are constantly threatened by this situation. According to Wisse, the unrealized hopes for political normality that accompanied Jews in the Diaspora continue to accompany Jews in Israel. Political abnormality continues, even in a sovereign State, and therefore influences humour. Also, Jewish humour is affected by anti-Jewish politics. The Jews in the Diaspora suffered from it and the Jews in Israel do as well. Therefore, Israeli humour has Jewish traits – the humour of the persecuted is still a part of the Jewish State.[35] This conclusion leads Wisse to criticize Israeli humour: laughter is a wonderful way of dealing with crises when you have no political power, but it is not the way to solve them in the real world. In this way, she believes, laughter can hold back political action and turn to passivity.[36]

Notes

1. *Midrash* - [Hebrew] an early Jewish interpretation of or commentary on a Biblical text. See: 'Midrash', http://www.dictionary.com/browse/midrash
2. *Pilpul* - [Hebrew] Critical analysis, casuistic argumentation especially among Jewish scholars on Talmudic subjects. See: 'Pilpul', http://www.dictionary.com/browse/pilpul?s=t
3. Pogrom – an organized massacre of Jews by non-Jews.
4. A. Ziv, 'Psycho-social aspects of Jewish humor in Israel and in the Diaspora'. In A. Ziv (ed), *Jewish Humor* (New Brunswick and London: Transaction Publishers, 1998), pp.47-74.
5. S. Freud, *Jokes and Their Relation to the Unconscious* (The Standard Edition) (New York: W. W. Norton & Company, 1990).
6. C. Davies, 'Exploring the Thesis of the Self-Deprecating Jewish Sense of Humor', in A. Ziv & A. Zajdman (eds) *Semites and Stereotypes: Characteristics of Jewish Humor*

(London: Greenwood Press, 1993), pp.29-46; C. Davies, *The Mirth of Nations* (New Brunswick, NJ: Transaction, 2010).

7. *Talmud* - the collection of Jewish law and tradition consisting of the Mishnah and the Gemara.One edition was produced in Eretz Israel, ca 400AD and another was produced in Babylonia, c. 500AD. http://www.dictionary.com/browse/talmud?s=t
8. H. H. Friedman & L. Weiser-Friedman. *God Laughed: Sources of Jewish Humor* (New Brunswick, NJ: Transaction, 2014).
9. *Purim* - A Jewish holiday in which the Jews dress up in costumes, and mock the Jewish communities' leaders and rabbis.
10. A. Sover, 'Jewish humor'. *Oxford Bibliographies* (2015). http://www.oxfordbibliographies.com/view/document/obo-9780199840731/obo-9780199840731-0117.xml Accessed September 30, 2015.
11. Ziv, *Jewish Humor.*
12. A. Ziv, 'Psycho-social aspects of Jewish humor'; Ziv, *Personality and Sense of Humor.*
13. Ibid.
14. A. Ziv, 'Introduction', in A. Ziv (ed), *Jewish humor* (Tel-Aviv: Papyrus, 1986), pp.7-18; Ziv, 'Psycho-social aspects of Jewish humor'.
15. T. Reik, *Jewish Wit* (New York: Gamut Press, 1962).
16. M. Grotjahn, 'Jewish jokes and their relation to masochism', in M.W. Mendel (ed), *A celebration of laughter* (Mara Books, 1970).
17. N. Ausubel, *A Treasury of Jewish Humor* (New York: M. Evans and Company, 1951).
18. H. Eilbirt, 'Jewish Humor: The Logic of Jewish Humor', *World Humor and Irony Membership Serial Yearbook* (1987), pp.178-180.
19. A. Shani, 'Hoker hahumor hayehudi Arie Sover' ('Jewish Humor Researcher Arie Sover: Israeli Humor is less clever than the Jewish Humor'), 11 February 2016 http://www.haaretz.co.il/magazine/ayelet-shani/.premium-1.2848505 Accessed 12 February 2016. [Hebrew]
20. S. Juni, B. Katz and M. Hamburger, 'Identification with the Aggression vs. Turning against the self: an empirical study of the turn of the century European Jewish humor', *Current Psychology* 14 (4, 1996), pp.313-328.
21. R. R. Wisse, *No Joke: Making Jewish Humor* (Princeton: Princeton University Press, 2013).
22. Mizrahi Jews *(Mizrahim)* – Jews from Asia and North Africa and their offspring.
23. Ziv, 'Introduction'.
24. For example: I. Ben-Ami, '*Hahumor hayehudi hamarokayi*', ['Jewish Moroccan Humour'], *Moroccan Jewry: Chapters in the research of their Culture* (Jerusalem: Reuven Mas, 1976), pp.127-135 [Hebrew]; N. Pinto-Abecasis, *Hatavas, hamegohatz vehazi haIsha* [*The Peacock, the Ironed Man and the Half-Woman*] (Jerusalem: Ben-Zvi Institute, 2014) [Hebrew]; A. Knafo, *Te im Nana* [*Tea with Na'na: The Jokes of Moroccan Jews*] (Tel-Aviv: Bimat Kedem, 2014) [Hebrew]; I. Elias , 'Lama marokaim ohavim lizchok al azmam', ['Why Moroccans love to laugh about themselves'], http://www.haaretz.co.il/gallery/.premium-1.2854321 [Hebrew] Accessed 19 February 2016.
25. Sover 'Jewish humor'.
26. D. Ben-Amos, 'The 'Myth' of Jewish Humor.' *Western Folklore* 32.2 (1973), pp.112–131.
27. E. Oring, 'The People of the Joke: On the Conceptualization of a Jewish Humor.' *Western Folklore* 42.4 (1983), pp.261–271.
28. A. Eilon, *Haisraelim* [*The Israelis*] (Tel-Aviv: Schocken, 1970) [Hebrew].

29. O. Nevo, 'Do Jews in Israel still laugh at themselves?' in A. Ziv (ed), *Jewish humor*, (New Brunswick and London: Transaction Publishers, 1998), pp.191-202.
30. Ziv, 'Introduction'.
31. Ziv, *Personalityand Sense of Humor*. Regarding Israeli satire, see also L. Shifman, *Haars, Hafreha vehaima hapolaniya*[*Televised Humor and Social Cleavages in Israel, 1968-2000*] (Jerusalem: Magnes Press, 2008) [Hebrew], pp. 1-9.
32. *Shtetl* – a Yiddish word for a small town with a large Jewish population in eastern Europe from thw 16th century. The shtetl's Jews lived a traditional orthodox life. The shtetl as a way of life was terminated in the Holocaust.
33. Shani, Arie Sover'
34. Y. Nativ, 'Tishmeu bdiha' [Listen to a joke'], *Mako*, 24 September 2013 http://www.mako.co.il/weekend-articles/Article 7779cbe186f4141006.htm Accessed 2 February 2016.
35. Wisse, No Joke; Nativ, 'Listen to a joke'. [Hebrew]
36. Ibid.

2

Holocaust Humour: From Taboo to Debate in the Western World

The combination of the Holocaust and humour was taboo for several decades after the Holocaust in the western world. It was seen as a threat to the sacredness of the memory of those who perished in the Holocaust, and a disrespectful provocation. Between the 1930s and the 1990s, only few texts addressed Nazism and the Holocaust from humouristic perspectives.

In *The Great Book of Jokes* by Alter Droyanov (1938), an author who collected Jewish jokes, a number of jokes about Hitler appeared.[1] During the Second World War, a few films addressed the Nazi persecutions from a humouristic perspective [*The Great Dictator*, (Charlie Chapin, 1940), *You Nazty Spy!* (Jules White, 1940); *To Be or Not To Be* (Ernst Lubitsch, 1942)]. Bertolt Brecht's 1941 satire, *The Resistible Rise of Arturo Ui,* presented an absurd account of Hitler as Ui, a faux hoodlum in 1930s Chicago bullying his way into a monopoly in the vegetable market.[2]

After the Second World War, in the DP (displaced persons) camps, Israel Kaplan (1902-2003), a Holocaust survivor[3] and a Hebrew and Yiddish teacher, published a book in Yiddish called *Dos folksmoil in Natsi klem* [*The peoples' voice in the grip of the Nazis*], in which he wrote about the importance of Jewish Holocaust humour under the Nazis, and referred to it as elixir.[4]

Another Holocaust survivor who engagedin the aftermath of the Second World War in the importance of humour for Jews during the Holocaust was Viktor Frankl, a Jewish psychiatrist. In his book, *Man's Search for Meaning*, he unfolds his personal experience during the war, analyzes the psychological processes undergone by the prisoners in the camp, and argues that life in the camps gave the prisoner a choice between two courses of action.[5] As Frankl saw it, in the difficult reality of the camps, the loss of values symbolized the loss of the self. People who accepted the weakening of their moral and spiritual selves, who fell prey to the degenerating effects of the camp and lost their faith in a better future were doomed. On the other hand, those who even under the atrocious circumstances of the concentration camps tried to continue nurturing their souls and spirits had a better chance to rise above the horrible conditions and even to survive. Prisoners who were capable of experiencing their internal world had a place to escape to, they were able to flee their environment into the spiritual freedom of their internality, thus finding shelter from the emptiness, desolation and spiritual poverty of life in the camps. According to Frankl, he and his friends made an agreement to tell each other a funny tale every day. Other prisoners joined in on the activity as well. They laughed about general subjects, but also used self-deprecating humour and laughed at their condition as prisoners. For example, when they were sent to take a shower, not knowing what would happen to them, one way to endure the anxiety (they did not know whether these were real showers or gas) was to laugh at the occasion and make fun of each other: '...We knew that we had nothing to lose except our so ridiculously naked lives. When the showers started to run, we all tried very hard to make fun, both about ourselves and about each other. After all, real water did flow from the sprays!'[6]

Between the end of the Second World War and the 1990s, very few books dared to touch on the trauma in a humourous way. In 1969, Romain Gary published *The Dance of Genghis Cohn*. The book is a black humour Holocaust story in which the ghost of Genghis Cohn, an unsuccessful Jewish comedian from Warsaw, enters the body of Herr Schatz, the Nazi officer who has given the command to execute Cohn and others.The book was adapted into a film, directed by Elijah Moshinsky, in 1993. *Jacob the Liar* (Jurek Becker, 1969) - follows the life of Jacob Heym in the Łódź ghetto, Poland, who lies he has a radio, and he hears that the Red Army is approaching, in order to encourage the Jews of the ghetto. In his satiric book, *The Ghost Writer* (1979), writer Philip Roth described an encounter in the 1970s between the protagonist Nathan Zuckerman (one of Roth's literary alter egos) and a mysterious woman who Nathan suspects to be Anne Frank who actually survived the war and lives under an alias in the USA.

From the cinematic perspective, *The Producers* (Mel Brooks, 1968), is a satire in which a failed Broadway producer who tries to avoid a bankruptcy produces a musical about Hitler and the Nazis, and because of the audience's stupidity, it becomes a huge hit. *Jacob the Liar* was adapted twice into films (Frank Beyer, 1975 and Peter Kassovitz,1999).[7]

The Intensification of Holocaust Humour in the Western World since the 1980s

A worldwide debate about combining the Holocaust with humour began in the 1980s. Disagreements on the subject broke out over Art Spiegelman's graphic novel *Maus: A Survivor's Tale* (1986), in which Spiegelman rendered his Holocaust survivor father's biography into a world of cats versus mice.

The graphic novel which uses a great deal of black humour achieved tremendous success, and was the first graphic novel to win a Pulitzer Prize (1992).[8]

From the 1990s on,[9] combining the Holocaust with humour appeared more and more freely.[10] The texts address the past and the present. For example, only from the 1990s onward did scholars start to work on serious comprehensive research regarding Holocaust humour during the Holocaust. In 1993, Steve Lipman, an American Reform rabbi, published his book, *Laughter in Hell: The Use of Humor during the Holocaust*. The many examples in the book indicate that humour in the ghettos and the camps served as a weapon for those who were helpless and incapable of uprising or resisting. Other American researchers, such as Louis Kaplan[11] and John Morreall[12] dedicated their studies to humour during the Holocaust and discussed humour as a way of invoking critical thought, bringing people together, and helping them pull through tragic situations. Their studies indicate that humour served as a subversive force: a way to oppose the Nazi regime where criticism was forbidden, where a joke at the expense of Hitler was thought as undermining the Führer, and where telling an anti-Nazi joke or even listening to one was considered treason. In addition, these studies depict humour as a cohesion-creating mechanism of victims against their attackers, forming solidarity among oppressed individuals and allowing victims to try and endure what could be described as hell, without losing their sanity.

From the 1990s, filmmakers have also dismantled the sanctity of the Holocaust, and have introduced Holocaust memory into mundane comic situations. The film, *Life is Beautiful* (Roberto Benigni, 1997), spearheaded the way towards a deeper debate on the topic. The film tells the story of an Italian Jew, Guido Orefice, and his son Joshua, who are deported to an extermination camp in 1943. Guido tells his son that they are playing a complicated game, which they can ultimately win by using their imaginative powers. Guido relies on deception, humour, pretense and fast wit to save his son's life. In debates about the film, some argued that Benigni 'made a joke of the Holocaust.' Still others held that Benigni managed to instill a touching tragic-comic aspect into the film generating a powerful sense of the absurdity of the Jewish race theory by the Nazis and highlighting the important role of humour in the concentration camps.[13]

Later films that returned to the past and addressed the Holocaust from a humouristic perspective [such as, *Train of Life* (Radu Mihăileanu, 1998) and *Inglourious Basterds* (Quentin Tarantino's 2009)] were also perceived with mixed emotions.[14] Some films deal with Nazism from a humourous science-fiction angle, shattering the 'sanctity' of the Holocaust. One example is *Dead Snow*, a semi-comic slasher film, directed by Tommy Wirkola that was released in 2007 in Norway. It describes a group of medical students on a skiing trip in a beautiful region during the Second World War. Taken as prisoners by the Nazis, they manage to escape. In the present, the Nazi zombies return to slaughter the young Norwegians. This film did not achieve a marked success nor did it arouse controversy. *Iron Sky* (Timo Varensula 2011) is a wild science-fiction comedy that was highly successful worldwide, but also failed to ignite controversy. It tells the story of Nazis who fled to the moon at the end of the Second World War and, in the present, return to Earth in order to take it over.[15]

The documentary film *The Last Laugh* (Ferne Pearlstein, 2016) is an overview on the way western culture, especially cinema, deals with Holocaust humour. The film combines scenes from films, rare archival footage of cabarets from Theresienstadt, Holocaust survivors who talk about their black humour during the Holocaust, scenes of comedians telling Holocaust jokes, interviews with comedians, Jewish leaders and Auschwitz survivor Renee Firestone, whose sense of humour is an integral part of her identity. The interviewees, who ponder the question whether the Holocaust is an absolutely off-limits topic for comedy, give varied answers, and the director chooses to leave it as an open question. Her ambition is to provoke debate and discussion, to stimulate a conversation about freedom of speech, collective memory and ways to remember the past.[16]

Moreover, in the last decades, a growing number of stand-up comedians have dared to relate to the subject, while blending it with texts that represent the present. For instance, in 1999, Lisa Lipkin and Rabbi Moshe Waldoks, both second-generation Holocaust survivors, put on a joint stand-up show in New York whose subject was the Holocaust. They had spent years rummaging through their families' traumatic past, an experience that Lipkin describes as 'swimming through a sea of skeletons'. Humour, she says, is the rescue boat which took them to the safety of sanity. The two claim that second-generation Holocaust survivors have always told Holocaust jokes, but did so amongst themselves and felt ashamed about it. But by the late 1990s, it was already possible to proudly 'come out' with it. 'Mourning with laughter is as Jewish as a dill pickle', they said.[17]

This combination can be found from the 1990s also on the radio, TV skits and TV sitcoms such as *Seinfeld, Curb your Enthusiasm, South Park, Family Guy*, *Extras* and more. Some of them are written by Jews and some by non-Jews.[18] For example, in an episode of *Seinfeld*, Jerry wants to differentiate between the two kinds of salutes that the Nazis used: 'And I noticed that the Nazis in those movies always had, like, two separate Heils. They had the regular Heil that they would do, and when they were around the offices, they had this casual Heil.' (Episode 318). In another episode (Season 5, Episode 19, 'the Raincoats', Part II) Jerry relates that he and his girlfriend were making out in the cinema while *Schindler's List* was being screened, and paid homage to a famous scene in the film where Schindler gives a touching monologue regarding the way he could have saved more Jews. In *Seinfeld*, that monologue with its exact physical nuances was converted to Elaine's boyfriend who thinks he could have done more for Jerry's parents when they visited New York: he could have taken them to more museums, more restaurants etc.

Larry David, who created *Seinfeld* together with Jerry Seinfeld, used Holocaust humour also in his own series, *Curb your Enthusiasm*. It is a semi-documentary that follows the life of Larry David as he makes his way in show business, his relationships with his wife and friends, and represents episodes from his apparent life. In March 2004 (Season 4, Episode 39, "The Survivor"), Larry and his wife, Cheryl, are planning to renew their vows. In honour of the event, they invite family and friends to celebrate with them. Larry's father invites his friend who is a Holocaust survivor and another guest who has just participated in the *Survivor* reality TV show; the two guests quickly start arguing about who the 'real survivor' who suffered the most is. Each one relates horror stories from their biography: while the Holocaust survivor tries to explain what he went through, for the young man it is clear that what he underwent while the reality show was being shot on the island is worse than what the Jews suffered in the Holocaust, therefore he is the 'real survivor'. In this episode, David states his repulsion with reality shows that, for participants and viewers alike, blur the differences between fantasy and reality, and also his disappointment at the younger generation's total incomprehension of what happened in the Holocaust.

Trey Parker and Matt Stone created *South Park*, the animation series for adults, fabled for its snide humour and deliberate lack of political correctness. They used Holocaust humour several times in order to protest the social and political ills of American society, for example, showing political correctness that causes blindness to the other and acceptance of every extreme act performed by the other ("Death Camp of Tolerance, 2002) as well as against the Christian audience's blind acceptance of ridiculous historical tales dramatically shown on the movie screen ("The Passion," 2004).

In the TV series *Extras*, Ricky Gervais plays a second-rate actor who, in each episode, finds himself cast in a minor role on the set of a different film. In a 2005 episode, he is an extra in a Holocaust film in which Kate Winslet stars as a modest nun. Winslet is presented as a loud-mouthed and vulgar woman who spends much of the day complaining about having missed out on winning an Oscar four times because she was never cast in a Holocaust film. She thinks out loud that now, with this film, her time will come. The disparity between her vulgarity and the scenes in which she plays the role of a virtuous nun creates hallucinatory situations that question the representation of the Holocaust in popular culture.[19]

All these representations as well as other representations of Holocaust humour receive mixed responses when now and then an uproar breaks out. For example, in 2009, Jewish comedian Roseanne Barr caused a turmoil when she was photographed on the cover of *Heeb* magazine with a Hitler moustache, taking out a tray of burned men cookies from the oven.[20] In 2013, a controversy broke out when the late Joan Rivers, also a well-known Jewish performer, said of the supermodel Heidi Klum, 'The last time a German looked this hot was when they were pushing Jews into the ovens'.[21]

In addition, video clips uploaded to the internet and viewed by many viewers around the world offer proof that Holocaust humour is a part of some survivors' lives as well.[22] For example, a humouristic representation that set off a worldwide storm is a clip filmed in Auschwitz-Birkenau (German Nazi Concentration and Extermination Camp) Memorial and State Museum, featuring Adolek Kohn, a Jewish survivor of Auschwitz who lived in Australia together with members of his family. Kohn was a child during the Holocaust, and was deported with his mother in a cattle car from Lodz to Auschwitz, a journey that lasted three days. Mengele sent his mother to her death and Kohn to forced labour. He survived and, at the end of the war, immigrated to Australia. In 2010, he returned to Auschwitz with his daughter and four grandchildren. On the same railroad track where he was separated forever from his mother, as happened to many others, his daughter, Jane Korman, filmed the 89-year-old Kohn dancing with his grandchildren to the soundtrack of Gloria Gaynor singing 'I will survive'. Korman, an Australian artist, had the idea of making the video with the hope of presenting a different angle on Holocaust memory. The initiative triggered a range of reactions across the world.[23]

Ridiculing Hitler and Nazism in Germany

Even in Germany, where Holocaust humour was taboo, by the 1990s, Germans, especially young adults, seemed ready to laugh at Hitler and the Nazis,[24] and this type of humour can be found in some stand-up comedy acts, TV series, comics and films.

Ofer Ashkenazi claims that, in contemporary Germany, two forms of humour can be found: there are grotesque TV game shows that include imitations of Nazis and there is also sophisticated Holocaust satire in which there is a parallel drawn between contemporary Germany and what happened in Germany prior to the Second World War, as a kind of a warning sign. Through the grotesque humour, the Germans say: look at them, it is not us, and through the sophisticated humour they say: look at them, we don't want to become them. The shared perception of these two kinds of humour is the outer perspective. Nazism is represented as a far foreign phenomenon that other people are responsible for, 'God forbid not us'.[25] In his opinion, the mocking of Hitler and Nazism has a dual function in the current memory discourse: on the one hand, it emphasizes the sense of detachment from the Nazi past, marking the Germany of the present as completely different. On the other hand, it perpetuates the presence of the Nazi past in contemporary discourse, making it an inseparable part of this discourse. This is extremely important because it challenges the victimization discourse which has intensified in Germany in recent decades.[26]

For example, Walter Moers's comics about Hitler's postwar resurrection are published since the late 1990s and in recent years are adapted into a film; Kai Wessel's TV film, *Goebbels und Geduldig* (2000), borrows the central concept from Chaplin's *The Great Dictator*, that of a Jewish *doppelgänger* impersonating a Nazi leader. The film presents a comedy of errors, as Goebbels and Harry Geduldig, both played by the same actor, exchange roles in a double intrigue. The film aired on Germany's major television network, ARD, with seemingly only minor protests.[27]

A mainstream Holocaust comedy feature, was Dani Levy's, *Mein Führer: Die wirklich wahrste Wahrheit über Adolf Hitler* (2006). In the film, Levi deconstructs Hitler's charismatic mystique, suggesting that the German leader's oratory greatness was a charade, the creation of his great Jewish teacher. The film was funded by the German film industry, and was directed by a Swiss filmmaker. Reviews of the film suggest a three-way division of opinion. Some critics felt that treating Hitler and the Nazis as comic figures trivialized the Holocaust. Other critics held that satire was appropriate for any material, but they found that Levi failed to create a true comedy. Still other critics thought the film succeeded in getting viewers to laugh at the past without obscuring history's lessons.[28] A 2007 German comedy, entitled *Mein Führer: The Truly Truest Truth about Adolf Hitler,* portrays Hitler as an impotent man who plays with battleships in the bathtub and wets his bed.[29] The novel, *Er ist wieder da* [*Look Who's Back*] by Timur Vermes, published in 2013, was translated into more than thirty languages and made into a film in 2015. Vermes' narrative claims that Hitler did not kill himself. He wakes up, after seventy years, his clothes still soaked in petrol, in present-day Berlin. Exploring the twenty-first century German metropolis, he sees everything through Nazi eyes, with predictably comical consequences.[30]

Since the end of the 1990s, more and more parodies have appeared on German TV shows. For example, the successful Austrian-German comedy duo Stermann & Grissemann have created many skits that mock the Nazis; TV comedians like Ralf Schmitz and Anke Engelke (in her show *Ladykracher*) mock the Nazis and Nazi sympathizers; 'Obersalzberg' is an ongoing skit in *Switch Reloaded*, a late night comedy show, which premiered in 2008 and immediately gained much popularity. It parodies Hitler's day-to-day operations in the office, positioning him as a ruthless yet gullible boss. Hitler's Nazi soldiers are depicted as chaotic drones following a loony leader.

Germans have greeted these parodies with mixed emotions: some believe that the past can be treated also with humour, while others find any comic accounts of the Nazi regime grotesque and unethical. Either way, Hitler parodies in Germany are creating controversy and stimulating public discourse.[31] Giuliana Sorce[32] explains that these parodies do not mock or trivialize the actual horrors of the Holocaust. They mostly mock Hitler and sometimes his staff. Images such as those of concentration camps, gas chambers, or dying individuals are not a part of these parodies. In this environment the stand-ups of the Jewish-German comedian Oliver Polak are an exeption. Polak integrates Holocaust Jokes in his shows, that broaden the humor beyond lampooning the Nazis and also deals with the Jews.[33]

Racism and Anti-Semitism in Holocaust Humour

A different, very problematic and dangerous genre of Holocaust humour is anti-Semitic and racist Holocaust humour. Opposed to the other examples that were mentioned above, this genre mostly contains racist jokes that ridicule the Holocaust, minimize it and often support Holocaust denial. This genre appears in the Muslim world, but also in the western world, not only amongst neo-Nazi groups. For example, in recent years, the Iranian government has arranged a yearly international Holocaust caricatures exhibition. The caricatures mainly support Holocaust denial, deal with the Holocaust as a 'myth' invented by Jews and Zionists, and represent the Jewish-Israelis as Nazis.[34] Another example is the racist and anti-Semitic French stand-up comedian Dieudonné M'bala M'bala. Dieudonné was convicted in court several times on anti-Semitism charges. He hosted on one of his shows, Holocaust denier Robert Faurisson and awarded him an 'insolent outcast' prize. Dieudonné invented the 'quenelle', a hand gesture that imitates the Nazi salute in order to express his racist opinions. People around the world use this gesture when they want to express their harsh opinions towards Jews and Israel, and to ridicule the Holocaust. In recent years, neo-Nazis and radical right-wingers around the world photograph themselves doing the 'quenelle' in various places in the world, as a homage to Dieudonné's racist and anti-Semitic messages.[35]

The Critique on Holocaust Humour

A debate has been going on for many years regarding the question of whether the Holocaust can be represented in art and in popular culture. This question has not been resolved[36] and, as noted, in addition in the last decades, the humoristic representation of the Holocaust had intensified. The change in attitude towards Holocaust humour in the western world and the growing number of texts that address the Holocaust through comedy, satire or parody worries many. As often noted, Holocaust humour is perceived as cheapening the trauma and as trivializing the Holocaust. For example, Gavriel D. Rosenfeld[37] claims that until the turn of the millennium, the Nazi era was viewed as an exceptional period in history. In the last two decades, however, this view has been challenged by what he calls a powerful wave of normalization. Rosenfeld claims that in contemporary western intellectual, political and cultural life, the Nazi era is being relativized, universalized, and aestheticized. The representation of the depiction of the Second World War, the Holocaust, and the figure of Adolf Hitler have undergone a major process of trivialization in the United States and Europe. Rosenfeld defines this as a move away from moralizing approaches. In his opinion, normalization threatens to blunt the horrors, annul the singularity of the Nazi past and the Second World War. The humouristic ubiquity of Hitler and the Nazis (which he considers bad taste) has given them the appearance of normality. Rosenfeld claims that Holocaust humour is part of the problematic changes that trivialize the trauma, and could turn the Nazis, Hitler, and the Holocaust into empty signifiers.

According to him, for increasing numbers of people, the Nazi era has lost its historical specificity. Hitler and the Nazis are no longer the absolute symbols of extreme and radical evil, and the Holocaust's unquestioned status as the greatest trauma of the twentieth century is not a consensus anymore. Rosenfeld claims that the more the Holocaust and Hitler's image are presented in humourous and ironic ways, the more they undermine the terrible reality of the Holocaust. Through these representations, he says, the Nazi era becomes banal and even entertaining. He believes that laughing at Hitler and Nazism runs the risk of aestheticizing the Nazi past, and of relativizing its criminality.

Alan Rosenfeld, in his book *The End of the Holocaust*,[38] sees the dominance of the Holocaust in American popular culture as destructive and wrong. He claims that these representations bring a shallowness to the memory of the trauma, blunt the possibility of feeling empathy towards the victims of the Holocaust, and trivialize the mass murder. Rosenfeld also turns against humouristic representations of the Holocaust. He sees these kinds of texts as dangerous expressions, on the verge of anti-Semitism that will lead to 'the end of the Holocaust'. He claims that there is a big difference between black humour that was practiced during the Nazi era by its victims (which he sees as a legitimate response) and current Holocaust humour which he sees as merely cruel. He is amazed to learn that second-generation Holocaust survivors can bring themselves to crack jokes regarding the Holocaust, and is repelled by stand-up comedians or Holocaust jokes on the internet, which he sees as tasteless, vile and mean-spirited expressions that ridicule Jewish suffering. He sees Holocaust humour as odious, deriding the Jewish victims of Hitler, and claims that the impulses that give rise to this degenerate humour are hard to fathom. He believes that to expose oneself to it is to be immediately soiled. For him, Holocaust humour indicates that a point has been reached where, at least for some people, it is now acceptable to reduce the horrors of the Holocaust to sick jokes. This development, he asserts, helps to trivialize and vulgarize the mass murder.[39]

But can we project the same perceptions on Jewish-Israeli Holocaust humour, satire and parody in Hebrew?

Notes

1. B. Mar, 'Mendy Cohn limed Yiddish et sahkaney haben shel shaul' ['Mendy Cohn taught Yiddish to the actors of 'The Son of Saul"], *Haaretz*, 18 March 2016 http://www.haaretz.co.il/gallery/cinema/.premium-1.2884632 Accessed 18 March 2016. [Hebrew]
2. C. J. Gilbert, 'Playing With Hitler: Downfall and Its Ludic Uptake', *Critical Studies in Media Communication* Vol. 30, No. 5, December (2013), pp.407-424.
3. The definition of 'Holocaust survivor' has changed over the years. The current definition has been in existence since 2009, and is considered to be the most widely accepted today, stating that a Holocaust survivor is: 'A person who lived in one of the countries that were conquered or were under direct influence of the Nazi regime for any period of time between 1933 and 1945. It also includes people who had been forced to leave their homes because of the Nazi regime'. See Y. Boginski, 'Skira historit shel hamusag nitzol shoah' ['A Historical Overview of the Concept of a Holocaust Survivor'] 1/24/2013, *The Knesset*, http://www.knesset.gov.il/mmm/data/pdf/m03154.pdf [Hebrew]
4. Mar, 'Mendy Cohn'.
5. V. E. Frankl, *Man's Search for Meaning: An Introduction to Logotherapy* (New York: Simon & Schuster, 1984), p.88.
6. Frankl, *Man's Search for Meaning*, pp.34-35.
7. E. Pfefferkorn, 'The Art of Survival: Romain Gary, 'The Dance of Genghis Cohn', *Modern Language Studies*, Vol. 10, No. 3 (Autumn, 1980), pp.76-87; J. Kauffman 'Gallows humor and Jewish humor: A reading of 'The Dance of Genghis Cohn' by Romain Gary', in A.

Ziv (ed), *Jewish humor* (New Brunswick and London: Transaction Publishers, 1998), pp.99-110.

8. In 1992 Spiegelman published a sequel *Maus II: And Here My Troubles Began*. See, for example, T. Des Press. 'Holocaust Laughter?', in Berel Lang (ed):*Writing and the Holocaust* (New York: Holmes and Meier, 1988), pp. 216-233; H. Andreas, 'Of Mice and Mimesis: Reading Spiegelman with Adorno,' in Barbie Zelizer (ed.) *Visual Culture and the Holocaust* (Rutgers University Press, 2001), pp.28-44.
9. Preliminary research had been conducted in the 1980s, for example, regarding anti-Semitic Holocaust jokes in western Germany. See, A. Dundes & T. Hauschild, 'Auschwitz Jokes', *Western Folklore*, Vol. 42, No. 4 (Oct., 1983), pp.249-260.
10. L. Kaplan, 'It will get a terrific laugh: On the problematic pleasures and politics of Holocaust Humor,' in H. Jenkins, T. McPherson & J. Shattuc (eds), *Hop on pop: the politics and pleasures of popular culture* (Duke University Press Books, 2003), pp. 343-356; J. Morreall, 'Humor in the Holocaust: Its Critical, Cohesive, and Coping Functions', *Holocaust TRC*, 22.11.2001; http://www.holocaust-trc.org/humor-in-the-holocaust/ Accessed 2 October 2008.
11. Kaplan, 'It will get a terrific laugh'.
12. Morreall, 'Humor in the Holocaust'.
13. For example, R. Ben-Ghiat, 'The Secret Histories of Roberto Benigni's Life Is Beautiful,' in J. D. Zimmerman (ed), *Jews in Italy under Fascist and Nazi Rule1922-1945*, (Cambridge: Cambridge University Press, 2005), pp.330-350; S. Ezrahi, 'After Such Knowledge, What Laughter?' *Yale Journal of Criticism, special issue on the Holocaust and Interpretation*, 14.1 (2001), pp.287-317; K. Niv, *Ahaim yafim aval lo leyehudim* [*Life Is Beautiful but Not for Jews*] (Tel Aviv: N.B. Sfarim Hagut, 2000) [Hebrew]; S. Zand, *Kolnoa vehistoria* [*Cinema as History*](Tel Aviv: Am Oved, 2002) [Hebrew]; O. Bartov, *Hayehudi bakolnoa [The Jew in Cinema*] (Tel Aviv: Am Oved, 2008) [Hebrew]; L. Baron, *Projecting the Holocaust into the present: the changing focus of Contemporary Holocaust Cinema* (Maryland: Rowman & Littlefield, 2005). See especially pp.135-170; J. H. Egerton, *'Kush mir in tokhes!': Humor and Hollywood in Holocaust Films of the 1990s*, A Ph.D dissertation, submitted to The University of Texas at Austin, (2006) http://www.lib.utexas.edu/etd/d/2006/egertond25518/egertond25518.pdf Accessed 1 November, 2015; A. Ben-Dat, *Bein humor letrauma bein etica leestetica (Between Humor and Trauma* [*Between Ethics and Aesthetics*], (Tel-aviv: Resling, 2015) [Hebrew].
14. On Holocaust comedies see also: A. Kerner, *Film and the Holocaust: New Perspectives on Dramas, Documentaries and Experimental Films* (New York: Continuum Books, 2011), pp. 79-100; H. Gonshak, *Hollywood and the Holocaust* (Maryland: Rowman & Littlefield Publishers, 2015), pp.229-250, 299-310.There are also films that focus in a humouristic-bitter manner on the aftermath of the Holocaust. For example: *Mendel* (Alexander Røsler, 1997). See: Egerton, *Kush mir in tokhes!* pp.140-178.
15. 'Zikaron 2:0: *Ha'shoah ka'movila tarbutit*' ('Memory 2.0: Holocaust in culture'), *City Maus* 18 April 2012 http://www.mouse.co.il/CM.articles_item,610,209,67612,.aspx Accessed 3 September 2013 [Hebrew]. The Nazis also appeared in other science fiction movies before these movies, such as *They saved Hitler's Brain* (David Bradley, 1968), *Shock Waves* (Ken Wiederhorn, 1977), *Zombie Lake* (Jean Rollin, 1981), and as surfers in *Surf Nazis must Die* (Peter George, 1981). See P. Askal, 'KsheHitler matza hania' ('When Hitler Found a Parking Space'), *Liberal*, 23, March 2016, pp.78-83.
16. L. Berger, 'Tribeca 2016 Women Directors: Meet Ferne Pearlstein – 'The Last Laugh', *Indiewire*, 18 April, 2016 http://www.indiewire.com/2016/04/tribeca-2016-women-directors-meet-ferne-pearlstein-the-last-laugh-288342/ Accessed 1 May 2016.

17. In the United States, about a quarter million people are defined as second-generation survivors. The expanding, shifting remembrance of the Holocaust in the United States is greatly associated with their work in the field. See S. Oster, 'Holocaust Humor', *UTNE Reader – The Best of the Alternative Press*, September-October 1999. http://www.utne.com/mind-and-body/holocaust-humor.aspx Accessed on 21 May 2013. For further discussion of the second-generation Holocaust survivors in the United States, see, for example, A. L. Berger, & N. Berger, *Second Generation Voices: Reflections by Children of Holocaust Survivors and Perpetrators.* (Syracuse University Press, 2001).
18. J. Demsky, 'Searching for Humor in Dehumanization: American Situational Comedies and Second/Third Generation Holocaust Representation', *Film and History Conference*, November 2015, Madison WI.
19. The humourous way in which Gervais handled Holocaust films received even greater significance when life imitated art: in 2008 Winslet played a Nazi in *The Reader* and won an Oscar. Gervais who hosted the Golden Globe ceremony that year joked on stage that his Holocaust prediction had come true. 'I told you, do a Holocaust movie and the awards come, didn't I?'
20. D. Berrin, 'Roseanne plays Hitler for Heeb magazine', 3 August 2009, http://www.jewishjournal.com/hollywoodjew/item/roseanne_plays_hitler_for_heeb_magazine_20090803 Accessed 20 January 2010.
21. CNN Stuff, 'Joan Rivers not apologizing for Holocaust joke', 1 March 2013 http://edition.cnn.com/2013/02/28/showbiz/joan-rivers-holocaust-joke/ Accessed 2 July 2016.
22. See Chapter 5.
23. N. Launstein, 'Nitzolei show' ['The Show of the Shoah'], *Yediot Aharonot*, 8 September 2010, pp.22-24 [Hebrew]; B. Trezise, *Performing Feeling in Cultures of Memory,* (Palgrave Macmillan Memory Studies, 2014), pp. 28-55. For an analysis of this clip and other examples of Holocaust humour in Australia see: D. Slucki, 'Trivialization or Commemoration: Holocaust Humor in Australia,' in: E. Lederhendler & G. N. Finder(eds), *A Club of their Own: Jewish Humorists in the Contemporary World* (New York: Oxford University Press, 2016), pp.204-229.
24. C. J. Gilbert, 'Playing with Hitler: Downfall and Its Ludic Uptake', *Critical Studies in Media Communication* Vol. 30, No. 5, December (2013), pp.407-424. The video has been removed as Jane Korman did not have copyright for the song. It can be found on her personal site: http://www.janekormanart.com/janekormanart.com/16.Dancing_Auschwitz/16.Dancing_Auschwitz.html Accessed 2 May 2016
25. O. Ashkenazi, 'Ridiculous Trauma: Comic Representations of the Nazi Past in Contemporary German Visual Culture', Cultural Critique, 78 Spring 2011, pp. 88-118.
26. Askal, 'Hitler found'; Ashkenazi, 'Ridiculous Trauma'.
27. R. C. Reimer, 'Does Laughter Make the Crime Disappear?: An Analysis of Cinematic Images of Hitler and the Nazis, 1940-2007,' September (2009) Issue 52, http://sensesofcinema.com/2009/feature-articles/does-laughter-make-the-crime-disappear-an-analysis-of-cinematic-images-of-hitler-and-the-nazis-1940-2007/ Accessed 8 February 2016.
28. Ibid.
29. Gilbert, 'Playing With Hitler'.
30. G. D. Rosenfeld, *Hi Hitler: How the Nazi Past Is Being Normalized in Contemporary Culture* (Cambridge University Press, 2015), pp.234-291, especially pp.219-225
31. Ibid.

32. G. Sorce, 'Hitler and Humor: Coming to Terms with the Past Through Parody', *Global MediaJournal*, German Edition, Vol. 5, No.2, Autumn/Winter 2015 http://www.globalmediajournal.de/2015/12/18/hitler-and-humor-coming-to-terms-with-the-past-through-parody/ Accessed 1 January 2016
33. For comparison of Holocaust awareness in Israel, Germany and the USA see: Sznaider, N. and Levy, D. *The Holocaust and Memory in the Global Age* (Philadelphia: Temple University Press, 2006).
34. I. Eichner, 'Taharut karikaturot shoah beiran' ('Holocaust caricatures contest in Iran), *YNET*, 12 January 2016 http://www.ynet.co.il/articles/0,7340,L-4752001,00.html Accessed 12 January 2016 [Hebrew]
35. G. Miller, 'Zarfat: antishemiut bazerem hamercazy' ('France: Mainstream Antisemitism'), *CFCA*, 1 November, 2013 http://antisemitism.org.il/article/82729/%D7%A6%D7%A8%D7%A4%D7%AA-%D7%90%D7%A0%D7%98%D7%99%D7%A9%D7%9E%D7%99%D7%95%D7%AA-%D7%A2%D7%9B%D7%A9%D7%99%D7%95-%D7%91%D7%96%D7%A8%D7%9D-%D7%94%D7%9E%D7%A8%D7%9B%D7%96%D7%99 Accessed 1 July 2016 [Hebrew]; J. Lichfield, 'Anti-semitic' comedian Dieudonné M'bala M'bala had his show cancelled in France after Nicolas Anelka's inverted Nazi salute', 7 January 2014 http://www.independent.co.uk/news/world/europe/quenelle-comedian-dieudonn-mbala-mbalas-show-is-banned-in-france-9044504.html Accessed 1 July 2016
36. It is a part of a wider debate regarding the representation of the Holocaust in art and in popular culture. See for example, T. W. Adorno, *Negative Dialectics* (London: Routledge, 2000); Godfrey Mark, *Abstraction and the Holocaust* (New Haven: Yale University Press, 2007); E. Wiesel, 'Art and the Holocaust: Trivializing memory', *The New York Times*, 11 June 1989, http://www.nytimes.com/1989/06/11/movies/art-and-the-holocaust-trivializing-memory.html?pagewanted=all Accessed 2 October, 2012; A. Rosenfeld, *The End of the Holocaust* (Indiana: Indiana University Press, 2013).
37. Rosenfeld, *Hi Hitler*.
38. Rosenfeld, *The End of the Holocaust*, pp.11, 243-244.
39. Ibid.

3

Holocaust Awareness and Holocaust Humour in Israel

In the reflexive skit, 'Crusader Skit-Writers' ['Kotvei Maarchonim Zalbanim'] (2012), three crusaders meet in order to discuss 'the plague'. They are in a distant field, a remote fortress is seen in the background. 'You cannot do such things', the leader (Dvir Benedek) reprimands the other two. His two friends vehemently reply, 'No, no, it's not like we're laughing at the plague, we're not saying it's a good thing or that it didn't happen; on the contrary, we're condemning society's stereotypical and simplistic attitude toward the plague'. The leader refuses to accept their views, pointing at the remote fortress: 'Do you know how many people in the fortress lost their relatives in the plague'? he reproachfully asks the two, 'Entire families'! His subordinates are not satisfied with his argument. 'I would like to tell you', says one of them, 'that I actually do know a lot of people who are second-generation plague survivors, and they are coping with the disease through humour'. 'But I don't understand what you're trying to say', the leader becomes angry, 'it's just like a young child breaking eggs without making an omelet, what are you trying to say?' 'That's open to interpretation', they reply. 'Had we wanted to dictate a message, we would have written it on a piece of paper'. They decide to resolve the problematic situation with a compromise: instead of writing a skit on the plague, they are to write an historical skit which will be a parable on the plague, 'say about the eruption of Mount Vesuvius in Pompeii'.

In this skit, young Jewish-Israelis protest the way the pathos ridden canonic memory of the Holocaust is the mainstream (the fortress), while those seeking to address the trauma with humour are marginalized, sent outside the borders of the fortress, even though it is a basic tool for struggling with trauma. The young writers wish to infiltrate the consensus which is not willing to accept a humourous discussion of the Holocaust, forcing them into the arms of the parable, against their will. The skit mirrors the current debate on the commemoration of the Holocaust in Israel, and the attempts made by the second and third generations to cope with the postmemory that shaped their identity through humour. They wish to give this alternative form of remembrance a legitimate place inside the consensus, and to open Israeli society to another way of dealing with the trauma.

Indeed, in Israel, Holocaust humour that has changed slowly over the decades from taboo to debate is still far from being in the consensus.

Holocaust Humour in Israel

The combination of Holocaust and humour was almost taboo until the 1990s.[1] Joseph Bau (1920–2002) was one of the exceptions: a Holocaust survivor who dared to deal publicly with Nazism and the Holocaust from the perspective of black humour. Bau survived the Płaszów Nazi concentration camp. He was a graphic artist, a writer and a poet, a joke teller and a painter. He and his wife Rebeca were a part of the famous Schindler's List. Their unbelievable wedding (Joseph dressed up as a woman and snuck into the women's blocks in Płaszów) was reenacted in the famous film *Shindler's List* (Steven Spielberg, 1993). His friends say that the jokes he told them in the camp helped them to survive. After liberation, he returned to Poland and was, amongst other things, a successful caricaturist whose caricatures were published in many newspapers in Poland. In some of his caricatures, he addressed Nazism through black humour. For example, he fought the perception that after the Germans were defeated, Nazism disappeared and 'a new Germany appeared'. In a caricature, he drew a German building from a bird's-eye view. The perspective showed that the building was in the shape of a swastika. In another caricature, he ridiculed the Germans who claimed they had completely changed. The caricature portrays such a German who returns home. His son tells him not to disturb him: he is busy playing 'concentration camp', beating a doll with a whip, and the slogan 'Heil Hitler' is written on the wall.[2]

In 1950, he and his wife immigrated to Israel, where he became a well-known graphic artist and was of the animation pioneers in Israel. Bau wrote books, poetry, painted and created animated short films (most of them humorous). His memoir *Dear God! Have you ever gone Hungry?* [*Shnot Tarzah* (Hebrew, 1982, English, 1998)] in which he recounts his and Rebeca's life story, especially during the Holocaust, includes black humour. The book contains stories and drawings that describe the hardship and atrocities in dramatic and humoristic perspectives combined. For example, on a piece of toilet paper Bau drew Hitler and a drawing of a Jewish transport in which an inmate suggest 'innocently' to a German officer: 'come with us'. His Holocaust lithographs are very dramatic, showing scenes from the inmates' lives, such as hunger, massive killings, getting beaten with a whip, etc. In some of the lithographs he designed, he dealt with the Holocaust through black humour. 'A swing', he wrote on one of the posters that was all black. Just the feet of a prisoner in a striped prisoner's uniform are swaying in the upper left side. In another poster, he drew a zebra behind bars with a number tattooed on its body.[3]

From the 1990s, the approach towards Holocaust humour began to change slowly. It was a part of a broader change in Israeli Holocaust awareness in the 1980s and the 1990s. In those decades, the Holocaust's place in Israeli collective identity had intensified. It became an important part of Israeli everyday discourse. It was made a permanent feature of both the high school curriculum and matriculation exams. At the same time, more and more Holocaust survivors began to publish their memoirs while the second- and third-generation Holocaust survivors – the children and grandchildren of Holocaust survivors – began to discuss the ways in which the trauma affected their lives, and showcase the relationship with their parents and grandparents through art.[4] Humoristic texts regarding the Holocaust began to infiltrate the cultural arena.

In 1997, Israelis fumed when it transpired that on Holocaust and Heroism Remembrance Day, people swapped Holocaust jokes on the internet. The reactions were divided into two groups: those who saw it as a healthy way of coping with the Holocaust in the present, and others who took issue with breaking the final taboo on the subject.[5] The screening of *Life is Beautiful* in Israel (1997) again placed the subject on the public agenda, reactions in Israel were varied. Some viewers walked out of the film demonstratively. Others maintained that representations of the Holocaust do not have to be realistic or possess documentary qualities. Those who supported the humouristic approach of the film contended that the angry critics of *Life is Beautiful* apparently were not acquainted with the tradition of Jewish humour and its ties to pain and persecution, or with the unique role of humour and fantasy in attempts to survive or, at least, preserve a semblance of normality and humanity during the Holocaust. In the 1990s and the first decade of the new millennium, the humoristic, satiric and parodic representations of the Holocaust grew in various cultural fields, and in the last decade the phenomenon has intensified. Holocaust humour has increasingly been trickling into films, prime time television, art, internet video and memes, alternative ceremonies, theatre, poetry books and more, though criticism on this phenomenon persists.[6] These various representations will be analyzed in the book.

This gradual entrance of Holocaust humour into the mainstream is also apparent in research. In the last two decades, Israeli scholars began addressing the topic of Holocaust humour under Nazism. Adir Cohen in his book *Living Life with Laughter* [*Haim bizhok*],[7] analyzed, among other subjects, Jewish jokes that were told by Jews in the ghettos and concentration camps. In his *The Great Jewish Humor Book* [*Sefer hahumour hayehudi hagadol*],[8] a collection of Jewish jokes, he also presents self-deprecating jokes made by Jews during the Holocaust.

In 2002, Ruth Bondi, a Holocaust survivor who documents the Jews of Czechoslovakia under Nazi occupation, addressed the contribution of humour and satire by Jews in the Theresienstadt camp-ghetto. She described the songs, skits, cabaret shows, and the satirical newspapers that were an integral part of life there.[9] In another book written in 2008, she addressed the subject again:

> In humour there was consolation, a momentary victory over reality, a touch of illusion, a trace of freedom. Humour helped the inmates hold out as long as they could, to maintain the integrity of their personalities, to cast off fear, to chuckle instead of giving in, to disguise the dread, to view the present as temporary, a bridge to tomorrow.[10]

Itamar Levin, author of *Through the Tears* [*Miba'at ladmaot*],[11] wrote about self-deprecating and black humour in the ghettos and concentration camps. Levin recounts that, at first, he was hesitant about the issue with which his book engages, having reservations about linking the Holocaust with humour, but after having seen that the book was received favorably, he understood that the Israeli public had advanced in its outlook on the matter. He asserts that discovering the humour used during the Holocaust attests to the ability to mentally resist the Nazis and serves as an historical source of information, providing a look into the attitudes and states of mind of Jews at that time.

Researcher Chaya Ostrower sees Holocaust humour under Nazism and in the ghettos and concentration camps as a survival mechanism. In her book, *Without Humor we would have Killed Ourselves* [*Lelo humor haino mitabtim*][12], she describes humour as one of the highest and most efficient psychological mechanisms in the hierarchy of defence mechanisms. In the horrifying conditions of the ghettos and concentration camps, laughter was a genuine rebellion against reality – a spiritual rebellion. In the preface to her book, Ostrower confesses that when the idea to connect humour and the Holocaust came to her, she was both enthusiastic and apprehensive, as such a combination was a kind of sacred taboo. That apprehension was also present when she contacted Holocaust survivors and asked them for information about the issue. She was afraid that the survivors would think that the study sought to disparage the scope of the Holocaust or diminish the trauma and suffering. When the first interviewees told her about the jokes they came up with during the Holocaust and said that without humour, they could not have survived, she decided to delve deeper into the research. As noted, in addition to the research which deals with Holocaust humour during the Holocaust, in recent years, scholars have started working on research regarding contemporary Holocaust humour in Israel.[13]

Israel as a Unique Place of Holocaust Awareness

Research discusses various ways of dealing with trauma as a collective. Trauma in the mental-psychological sense was first cited in the late nineteenth-century. Freud, the founder of psychoanalysis, was among the first to develop it. Freud considered that one of the central concepts in trauma was 'repetition compulsion' - returning to a trauma while blurring the boundaries between past and present, and thus re-experiencing the trauma. This repetition causes suffering and works against the desire of the sufferer.[14]

Freud's disciples broadened the debate on trauma, and its immediate and later symptoms. Post-Traumatic Stress Disorder (PTSD) entered the DSM [The Diagnostic and Statistical Manual of Mental Disorders, published by the American Psychiatric Association (APA)], in 1982. It is considered an extremely common mental disturbance among people who have undergone traumatic incidents. Its sufferers continue to experience the traumatic events after the traumatic event. One of its main characteristics is that the trauma is relived by the individual through intrusive, recurrent recollections of the past in the present.[15] According to research, trauma can affect wider circles and post-traumatic like syndromes can appear among people who did not experience the trauma themselves.

Examining how groups confront their collective traumas, Ron Eyerman claims that 'cultural trauma' is an historic event in the consciousness of every member of the collective. This memory undergoes constant reinterpretation. Different generations have different perspectives on the event because of both emotional and temporal distance as well as altered circumstances and needs, but all generations interpret the event as a primal part of their identity.[16] Jeffrey Alexander claims that any event – as horrendous as it may be – will turn into a trauma for the collective only if members of the elite define and construct it as such. He explains that collective trauma is constructed by 'memory agents' – members of the hegemony who feel this event will affect the collective memory and identity in the present and in the future. These 'memory agents' construct the trauma as 'collective' through a long cultural process of narration and signification.[17]

The Holocaust was and remains a central trauma in Israel's national consciousness. The memory of the trauma does not fade over the years; on the contrary, Holocaust representations and the public discourse regarding the Holocaust have only grown stronger in recent decades. Studies in Israel have shown that Holocaust memory has a very powerful presence, does not have just a one-generational impact, and is a cross-generational defining trait of the Jewish population in Israel.[18] Alon Gan refers to it as a 'victimization discourse' and 'victimized awareness' that shapes the Israeli identity; Adi Ophir claims that Holocaust memory in Israel went through a process of 'sanctification'; Avraham Burg refers to it as 'the religion of trauma'.[19] Researchers claim that the Israeli media, educational and cultural fields, and public discourse in Israel frame the Holocaust as a current, ongoing local trauma rather than an event that ended decades ago in another place.[20]

In Israel, where there is massive use of Holocaust rhetoric by politicians, journalists and educators,[21] surveys reveal that among the Jewish-Israeli population in general, since the 1940s, the Holocaust has been assimilated as a central event, and young Jewish-Israelis perceive the Holocaust as the historical event that has had the greatest impact on them and their future, even more than the founding of the State.[22] Other research has shown that the knowledge the second- and third-generation Holocaust survivors have about the Holocaust in Israel, and the way the Holocaust has shaped their identity is similar to those Israelis of the same age who are not biological offspring of Holocaust survivors. This phenomenon is very different from other places in the world, where there is a huge gap in knowledge and perception of the Holocaust between biological offspring of Holocaust survivors and other Jewish people their age.[23]

Moreover, in Israeli collective memory, the trauma of the Holocaust is not focused solely on events that occurred in the past. The sensitive relationships between Israel and the Arab nations, the decades-long Jewish-Israeli-Palestinian conflict, the threat of annihilation, the continuing terrorist attacks and intifadas - all these have created an atmosphere of constant vigilance and ongoing anxiety. The ongoing problematic security situation in Israel, which is accompanied by politicization of the Holocaust, have caused the trauma of the Holocaust to be integrated with Israeli present-day reality and replicated within it.[24] For example, a recent survey from 2015 shows that 43% of Jewish-Israelis believe that the danger of a second Holocaust exists by another perpetrator – the Palestinians. They think that the long-term aspirations of the Palestinians are to conquer Israel and murder its Jewish citizens.[25]

Israel as a unique sphere of Holocaust awareness also affects the meaning of the terms 'second-generation Holocaust survivors' and 'third-generation Holocaust survivors'. The term 'second-generation Holocaust survivor' was coined by Canadian psychoanalysts as a clinical concept, and today is common terminology for children of Holocaust survivors. Since the 1960s, research has dealt with the effects of the trauma on the children of Holocaust survivors and, from the 1980s, research also deals with its effects on the grandchildren of Holocaust survivors. A number of interpretations of the term 'second-generation and third-generation Holocaust survivor' can be found in research: the first interpretation refers to the children and grandchildren of immigrants from Germany (and after the 1938 annexation, also Austria) who fled to the land of Israel after the rise of Nazism but before the Second World War. The second interpretation refers to the children and grandchildren of Jews who were in Europe during the Second World War and who survived. A third interpretation addresses the terms second-generation and third-generation Holocaust survivor as cultural, and refers to Jews who were born after the Holocaust.

Some claim that, in a broad sense, the terms include everyone in the world who was born after the Holocaust. Others expand on the definition within the borders of the Jewish nation: the terms can define people who are not biological offspring of Holocaust survivors but express cognitive and emotional identification with the descendants of Holocaust survivors, arising out of a sense of a shared destiny. Others claim that 'second generation' and 'third generation' are cultural terms, especially in Israel, where Holocaust awareness is intensive and comprehensive, much more than other places in the world. Therefore, in Israel, the terms 'second-generation Holocaust survivors' and 'third-generation Holocaust survivors' refer not only to the offspring of Holocaust survivors, but can be perceived as cultural terms, representing the Jewish-Israelis who were born after 1945 in Israel (second generation) and in the late 1960s and the beginning of the 1970s (third generation), and grew up in an environment that was soaked in Holocaust awareness, anxiety and stress.[26]

Freud considered melancholy and mourning as two contradictory forms of coping with trauma: an individual in a melancholic state identifies with the lost object, obscuring the differences between the individual and the object, thereby damaging the ego. In mourning, in contrast, the mourner undergoes a healthy process of internalization; s/he can deal with the past by creating distance from it. Mourning brings with it the possibility of starting a new life, and any disturbance of that process can become harmful.[27]

Dominic LaCapra claims that the danger inherent in the disintegration of distinctions between different times and the merging of the traumatic past with the present is relevant not only for those who experienced the trauma themselves but also for groups and societies that are linked to those traumas. Both groups and societies can become trapped in a situation that commingles past and present, and reconstructs the trauma, or certain aspects of it, in different ways. Such post-traumatic symptoms can affect the group's behavior in the societal and political spheres.

Following Freud, LaCapra distinguishes between two forms of collective memory of the Holocaust. The first is 'acting out': the past is not construed as remote events that are long gone or as a distant memory, but is reborn and experienced as if integral to present-day social and cultural life. The second form is 'working-through': clear boundaries are maintained between past and present, and there is awareness of the differences between 'then' and 'now'. There is less identification with the assimilation of the traumatic period. While there is also a return to the past in 'working-through', it is accompanied by conscious control of the past, a critical distance from it, and a gaze at it from a distant perspective.[28] Amos Goldberg contends, in the footsteps of LaCapra, that the way Holocaust memory was shaped in Israel provides evidence for Israeli society being post-traumatic and existing in the condition of *acting out*.[29]

Another term that can be used to describe Holocaust memory in Israel is 'Secondary Traumatic Stress': indirect exposure to the trauma which affects those who were not involved in the traumatic events. Secondary Traumatic Stress can be found in friends and relatives of the traumatized persons as well as in wider circles. Research claims that indirect exposure to a trauma through an intense cultural and media debate (television, radio, journalism, internet, etc.) can affect people who were not involved. PTSD symptoms, such as stress and anxiety, can appear in people who suffer from Secondary Traumatic Stress, albeit less intensely.[30]

Humour as a Defence Mechanism: Black Humour and Self-deprecating Humour

There are techniques that the 'I' uses in dealing with post-trauma or Secondary Traumatic Stress symptoms. Freud coined the psychological term 'defence mechanism'. This phrase describes the struggle of the 'I' with ideas or actions which cause the individual unbearable pain.[31] The study of defence mechanisms shows that they are meant to help the 'I' with its struggle with the development of anxiety. Defence mechanisms are directed at protecting the 'I', and saving it from experiencing sorrow.[32] Defence mechanisms are automatic psychological processes, subconscious means of self-defence that, by distortion of reality, protect the individual from inner or outer pressure – thoughts, memories or feelings that cause anxiety or threaten the 'I'. Mostly, the individual is not aware of the use of this mechanism.[33]

Freud saw humour as a pivotal defence mechanism. He believed that when people use humour in situations that provoke their fear and anxiety, they gain a new perspective on the situation that helps them avoid experiencing negative emotions.[34] With the help of humour, people can thus deal with difficult situations, and avoid or reduce their emotional suffering and grief.[35]

Later studies address humour as a defence mechanism that helps individuals alleviate stress, cope with negative feelings and tough situations, mitigate suffering, dissipate feelings of anxiety - at least for a certain time - and gain some sense of power and control in situations of helplessness. Humour can help those coping with unpleasant memories and aid trauma victims in reducing their tension and anxiety.[36]

Humour can also help those people who are surrounded by traumatized persons, as humour is also a vaccination against over-identification. Too much pity can cause tremendous suffering, pain and depression. In order to reduce the pain, the individual must create a wall of defence against the identification, a temporary emotional numbness.[37]

As a defence mechanism, humour has two aspects: black humour and self-deprecating humour.[39] The therapeutic importance of black humour and self-deprecating humour for traumatized individuals has frequently been studied, and in a wide range of contexts (among victims of abuse, crime, disasters, and more), and particularly in the context of Jewish humour. Black humour has been presented as an effective tool for oppressed minorities to withstand attacks by their oppressors. In the Jewish context, it constitutes the defence mechanism of an entire people.[40]

There are three main motifs for the use of self-deprecating humour: the first is the will to prevent aggression – if a person laughs at his own foibles, he prevents others from doing so; the second is the will to achieve appreciation. An individual who uses self-deprecating humour knows that his/her ridiculous character can be found in others, and it allows others to identify with him/her. The third motif of self-deprecating humour is an active struggle with fear, and it is an attempt to minimize fear: if the individual can laugh at a situation, then it might not be that bad.[41]

Black humour deals with anxiety-producing subjects: attesting to this are its alternative terms - horror humour, sick humour, gallows humour, and grim humour. Black humour is deliberately used in order to cope with particularly difficult situations. Ziv claims that black humour revolving around war, injuries and death helps soldiers who are at war and wounded soldiers to cope in the battlefield as well as with the memories and injuries they carry with them. For example, black jokes were prevalent among injured combat soldiers lying in hospitals during Israel's Yom Kippur War (October 1973). Through taking serious matters not seriously, they take off the edge, neutralize the horribleness and even try to rise above it. In this manner, they also manage to encourage their friends. The harsh reality cannot be changed, but the attitude toward that reality can.[42]

But those who use black humour can be also persons who were not traumatized directly, but are a part of the group in which the trauma happened (secondary traumatic stress). For example, Aliza Ruth Florenthal has found representations of black humour in obituaries, eulogies and on tombstone epitaphs.[43] This is the way the family members deal with their pain. During the 1982 Lebanon War, black humour evolved further in Israel, not only amongst soldiers, reflecting the ambivalent feelings of the Israeli public toward that war. In the Gulf War (1991), black humour developed even further to also include the home front, as the war turned the entire country into a frontier. The most popular show of the time was *Zehu Ze*! (Israeli Educational Television, 1978-1998), which featured many funny skits about typical Gulf War situations.[44] More recently, Karin Keidar Cohen, Shir Ben-Ishay and Shir Dimri examined how humour, black humour and self-deprecating humour today influences the coping of Gaza envelope residents with the trauma inflicted by *Operation Protective Edge* [*Tzuk Eitan* (2014)], during which many rockets were launched at that area. They concluded that humour has a significant role in maintaining physical and mental health, and that it comprises an important mechanism for dealing with many of the psychological-mental stress factors. Humour enables people to rise above situations and influences their mental resilience. Exposure to humour reduces the level of stress hormones in the blood cycle even after the traumatic events have ended. Humour is correlated with lower levels of anger, anxiety, depression and melancholy. It not only reduces the negative effect, but also increases the levels of the positive effect. It appears that this increase in the positive effect serves as a key mechanism through which humour contributes to mental resilience.[45] Moreover, research shows how jokes about the horrors of hospitals and operation rooms might appall those who are not part of the system, but for doctors who are involved in human tragedies on a daily basis, humour can serve as a mechanism of balance, allowing them to adopt a different outlook on the situation, while maintaining their mental equilibrium and preventing them from sinking into depression, which is natural considering the circumstances in which they work.[46]

Another example of how humour defends the soul against fear and anxiety of death can be found in the study carried out by Haya Milo on folk songs of Israeli soldiers. These songs are usually written by groups of soldiers and are based on famous, popular tunes. The songs are distributed and sung by soldiers, and are only for soldiers during their military service. The songs' creators are anonymous and the songs are a central part of military folklore which appears spontaneously and without guidance from above. According to Milo, folk songs speaking of death and war are parodic songs aimed at contradicting the heroic messages assimilated in popular Hebrew war songs. The main strategy for dealing with death in the soldiers' folk songs is black humour: the sublime heroic death and the glorified national victim who appear in Israeli popular songs undergo a process of diminution and ridiculing, created through reversing the meaning of the original songs. The songs which illustrate death through descriptions of the shattering and dismantling of the warrior's material body serve as a subversive form of protest, acting against the element of glorifying death in the national ethos. Army folk songs also have an important role in letting off steam, regulating the soldiers' emotions of frustration and anger towards the military system, often burdensome and stressful. The marginality of the genre permits it to become the voice of the soldiers, a channel of expression for subversive and non-normative contents, without fearing disciplinary public-moral punishment.

According to Milo, despite protest being an important function of this kind of songs, it is preceded by the primary and more fundamental need to deal with the fear of death, and conquer it by using black humour. The songs are a 'verbal mask', partitioning between the soldiers and the acknowledgement of death, in occurrences which are beyond the scope of control. Yet, masks inherently cover up and expose at the same time. As a strategy of protest and provocation, the subversion of the songs responds to a repressed layer of emotions which do not coincide with the act of glorifying death. The songs peel off the refined cultural mask of turning the victim into a symbol, into a sort of living-dead, in order to reveal the cruel truth hiding under it.

In this sense, these group songs can be seen as a form of psychological treatment, bringing together the patient and the object of anxiety, in a gradual manner and in a safe, protected environment in order to gradually reduce fears. In their own way, the songs attempt to 'digest' the anxiety caused by battle, and to overcome the destructive elements of facing death. Humour allows soldiers to continue bearing the burden against which they rebel and accept at the same time. The songs are a form of an outlet of feelings of frustration and desperation as well as a defence mechanism in the face of death. As such, they comprise a powerful therapeutic psychological mechanism.[47]

With this understanding, this book claims that in Israel, where Holocaust awareness is unique and more intense than other places in the world, and where the Holocaust is perceived and represented as an ongoing trauma, Holocaust humour, satire and parody in Hebrew should not be perceived as a disturbing process that could damage Holocaust memory, but rather as a healthy defence mechanism of a post-traumatic society.

Some of the texts that are analyzed in this book were written by biological children and grandchildren of Holocaust survivors, and others were written by those who are considered second and third generation culturally. The book will claim that since the Jewish-Israeli society is submerged in Holocaust memories and associations, the younger generations use Holocaust humour, satire and parody in order to deal with the trauma, defend their souls and move from acting out to working through. The book will show how Holocaust humour also helps them criticize Holocaust collective memory agents and, in a society which looks upon reality through Holocaust glasses, also criticize different phenomena in Israel as well as create social cohesion among the groups who oppose the way Israeli collective memory agents use the memory of the Holocaust. These critical texts are their way of fighting the blend of past and present. Therefore, even the use of Holocaust humour to protest against various phenomena in Israeli society is not only a way to vent frustration and to create social cohesion, but also serves as a defence mechanism. Humour, satire and parody enable the taking of a step back and looking at the Israeli reality in a detached way that, in turn, neutralizes the acting out of the trauma.

In addition, the book will claim that these defence mechanisms, in a way, subvert themselves and their goals. While inserting Holocaust humour, satire and parody in debates in multiple fields (politics, economics, ethnic conflicts, etc.), while interpreting everyday trivialities through Holocaust humour, and by protesting through humour against the manipulations in Holocaust commemoration, the second- and third-generations turn into collective memory agents in double and contradictory forms: on the one hand, they are fighting against the acting out of the trauma in the Israeli present and, on the other, they are creating yet another layer of acting out, by integrating the Holocaust into their everyday life. With humour' help, the fear factors are much less frightening, but they are more present. In other words, in a paradoxical manner, while fighting the acting out of the Holocaust, these texts add to the acting out of the trauma by turning it into an integral part of the present.

Notes

1. An exception is a paragraph in Israel Gutman's book from the 1960s. Gutman, an historian and a Holocaust survivor who participated in the Warsaw Ghetto uprising, chronicled his memories of the ghetto. In one chapter, he writes about a seminar for counselors of *Hashomer Hatzair (*a socialist-Zionist, secular Jewish youth movement) in January of 1942, in which he took part. A comic routine performed at a party held as part of this seminar, and which included many jokes about the Nazis, was a great success. See: I. Gutman, R*esistance: The Warsaw Ghetto Uprising* (Boston: Houghton Mifflin, 1994).

2. L. Steir-Livny, an interview with Clila and Hadassah Bau, who operate the Josef Bau Museum, 25 November 2016.
3. Josef Bau's Homepage http://www.josephbau.com/ Accessed 1 September 2016; S. Giuseppe, 'Josef Bau: Israel's Walt Disney and Mapmaker of Hell', The Krakow Post, 7 September 2012 http://www.krakowpost.com/5785/2012/09/josef-bau-israels-walt-disney-and-mapmaker-of-hell Accessed 2 September 2016.
4. Porat, *The Smoke-Scented Coffee*, pp.357-378; L. Steir-Livny, *Shtei panim bamarah: Yezug Nitzolei haShoah bakolnoa haIsraeli* [*Two Faces in the Mirror: the representation of Holocaust survivors in Israeli cinema*] (Jerusalem: Eshkolot-Magness, 2009) [Hebrew], pp. 96-204; I. Milner, *Kirey avar* [*A Torn Past*] (Tel Aviv: Am Oved, 2003) [Hebrew], pp.19-35; Y. Loshitzky, *Identity Politics on the Israeli Screen* (Texas: University of Texas Press, 2001), pp.15-71.
5. Y. Loshitzky, 'Post-Memory Cinema: Second-Generation Israelis Film the Holocaust,' *Identity Politics on the Israeli Screen* (University of Texas Press, 2001), pp.32-71.
6. Steir-Livny, *Let the Memorial Hill Remember*, pp. 37-78.
7. A. Cohen, *Haim bizhok[Living Life with Laughter*] (Haifa: Amazia, 1994) [Hebrew]
8. A. Cohen, *Sefer hahumour hayehudi hagadol* [*The Great Jewish Humor Book*] *(*Or Yehuda: Kinneret, 2004) [Hebrew].
9. R. Bondi, *Shorashim akurim: prakim ba'toldot yahadut czechia, 1939-1945* [*Torn Roots*] (Yad Vashem u'beit terezinpp, 2002)], pp.69-70 [Hebrew].
10. R. Bondi, R. C. Naor, *Trapped: Essays on the History of the Czech Jews, 1939-1945*. (Jerusalem: Yad Vashem Publications, 2008), p.89.
11. Levin, *Through the Tears.*In the film *Beyond the Tears* (Hedva Galili-Smolinsky, 2009) which engages in humour as a coping mechanism during the Holocaust, Holocaust survivors recount how humour served as a central, significant mechanism of coping with the horrors they experienced.
12. Ostrower, *Without Humor we would have killed ourselves*. Especially pp. 63-104.
13. Ostrower, *Without Humor we would have killed ourselves*, pp. 11-16.
14. S. Freud, *Meever laoneg vemasot aherot* [Beyond the Pleasure and other Works], (Tel Aviv: Dvir, 1978) [Hebrew]; S. Freud, *Hatipul ha-psichoanaliti* [Psychoanalysis Treatment], (Tel Aviv: Am Oved, 1988) [Hebrew].
15. J. L. Herman, Trauma vehachlama [Trauma and Healing], (Tel Aviv: Am Oved, 1994) [Hebrew]; 'PTSD', Diagnostic and Statistical Manual of Mental Disorders (5th ed.) (Arlington, VA: American Psychiatric Publishing, 2013). pp. 271–280.
16. R. Eyerman, *Cultural Trauma: Slavery and the Formation of African-American Identity* (Cambridge: Cambridge University Press, 2002).
17. J. C. Alexander, 'Toward a Theory of Cultural Trauma, in J. C. Alexander (ed), *Cultural Trauma and Collective Identity* (Berkeley: University of California Press, 2009), pp.1-30; J. C. Alexander, 'On the Social Construction of Moral Universals: The 'Holocaust' from War Crime to Trauma Drama,' in J. C. Alexander(ed), *Cultural Trauma and Collective Identity* (Berkeley: University of California Press, 2009),pp. 196-263.On the role that the media plays in the production and circulation of cultural memories, and how it can redefine or transform what is collectively remembered, see also, for example: A. Erll & A. Rigney (eds),*Mediation, Remediation, and the Dynamics of Cultural Memory* (Berlin and New York: de Gruyter, 2009); B.A. Kaplan, *Landscapes of Holocaust Postmemory* (Routledge Research in Cultural and Media Studies 29. New York: Routledge, 2011); P. Frosh & A. Pinchevski (eds), *Media Witnessing: Testimony in the Age of Mass Communication* (Basingstoke and New York: Palgrave Macmillan, 2009).

18. Steir-Livny, *Let the Memorial Hill Remember.*
19. A. Gan, *Korbanutam Omanutam* [*From Sovereignty to Victimhood: An Analysis of the Victimization Discourse in Israel*], (Jerusalem: The Israel Democracy Institute, 2014) [Hebrew]. See especially pp. 28-35.
19. A. Burg, *Lenatzeachet Hitler* [*To defeat Hitler*] (TelAviv: Yediot Aharonot, 2007); A. Ophir, *Avodat hahove: Masot al tarbut Israelit bazman haze* [*Working for the present: Essays on Contemporary Israeli culture*] (TelAviv: Hakibbutz Hameuhad, 2001), [Hebrew]. See especially pp. 29-51, 256-280.
20. D. Bar-Tal, *Lihyot im hasichsuch* [*Living with the Conflict*] (Jerusalem: Carmel, 2007) [Hebrew]; O. Meyers, M. Neiger & E. Zandberg, *Communicating Awe: Media Memory and Holocaust Commemoration* (New York: Palgrave Macmillan Memory Studies, 2014); I. Zertal, I. *Hauma vehamavet* [*The Nation and Death*] (Tel Aviv: Dvir, 1993) [Hebrew]; J. Feldman, *Above the Death Pits, Beneath the Flag, Youth Voyages to Poland and the Performance of Israeli National Identity* (New York and Oxford: Berghahn Press, 2008).
21. T. Segev, *Hamillion hashviyi* [*The Seventh Million*] (Jerusalem: Keter, 1991) [Hebrew]; J. Chaitin, J. 'Yeladim venechadim shel nizolim mitmodedim im hashoah' ['Children and grandchildren of Holocaust survivors deal with the Holocaust'], in Z. Solomon and Chaitin, J. (eds) *Yaldut bezel hashoah* (Tel Aviv: Hakibbutz Hameuhad, 2007) [Hebrew], pp.418-35.
22. Porat, *The Smoke-Scented Coffee*, pp.357-378; Steir-Livny, *Let the Memorial Hill Remember*, pp.17-36.
23. Solomon & Chaitin, *Childhood in the Shadow of the Holocaust.*
24. Bar-Tal, *Living with the Conflict.*
25. D. Bar-Tal, 'Lama atem lo rozim shalom' ['Why don't you want peace?'], Haaretz, Musaf, 2.9.2016, pp. 54-56.
26. To name only a few: Y. Hazan, 'Dor Sheni la Shoah' ['The second generation of the Holocaust: A questionable concept'] [Hebrew], *Sihot: Israel Journal of Psychotherapy*, 1 (1987), pp.104-108 [Hebrew]; D. Wardi, *Nosei hahotam* [*Memorial Candles*] (Jerusalem: Keter, 1990) [Hebrew]; Z. Solomon and J. Chaitin (eds), *Yaldut bezel hashoah* [*Childhood in the Shadow of the Holocaust: Child Survivors and Second Generation*] (Tel Aviv: Hakibbutz Hameuchad, 2007) [Hebrew]; A. Sagi-Schwartz Abraham, et al., 'Does Intergenerational Transference of Trauma Skip a Generation? No Meta-Analytic Evidence for Tertiary Traumatization with Third Generation Holocaust Survivors,' *Attachment & Human Development*, Vol. 10, No. 2, (June 2008), pp.105-121; Bar-On, D. *Bein pahad letikva* [*Between Fear and Hope: Life Stories of Five Families of Holocaust Survivors, Three Family Generations*] (Tel Aviv: Beit Lochamei Haghetaot and Kibbutz Hameuchad Press, 1994) [Hebrew]; Milner, *Torn Past*, pp. 19-35.
27. S. Freud, *Hatipul ha-psichoanaliti [Psychoanalysis Treatment], Tel Aviv: Am Oved* [Hebrew], pp. 138-171.
28. D. LaCapra, *Writing History, Writing Trauma* (Baltimore, MD: Johns Hopkins University Press, 2000), pp. 87-90.
29. A. Goldberg, 'Introduction,' in D. LaCapra, *Writing History, Writing Trauma* (Baltimore, MD: Johns Hopkins University Press, 2000), pp. 7-28.
30. C.R. Figley, 'Compassion fatigue as secondary traumatic stress disorder: An overview'. In: Figley CR, (ed). *Compassion fatigue: Coping with secondary traumatic stress disorder in those who treat the traumatized*, (Brunner-Routledge; New York, 1995), pp. 1–20.
31. A. Freud, *Haani vemaganonei haganah* [*The I and defense mechanisms*] (Tel Aviv: Dvir, 1977) [Hebrew].

32. A. Freud, *The I and defense mechanisms*, p.34.
33. P. Cramer, 'Defence mechanism in psychology today: further processes for adaptation', *American Psychologist* 55 (2000), pp.637-646.
34. Freud, *Beyond Pleasure*, pp. 106-142.
35. S. Freud, *Jokes and Their Relation to the Unconscious* (The Standard Edition), ed. James Strachey (New York: W. W. Norton & Company, 1990).
36. Levin, *Through the Tears*, pp 13-36; Ostrover, *Without Humor*, pp. 63-104.
37. Ziv, *Personality and Sense of Humor*.
38. Oring, *Engaging Humor*, pp.78-79.
39. On the importance of self-disparaging humour and black humour, see,for example: Ziv, *Personality and Sense of Humor*; Levin, *Through the Tears*; Ostrower, *Without Humor we would have killed ourselves*, especially pp. 63-104; Berger and Berger, *Second Generation Voices*.
40. L. J. Epstein, *The Haunted Smile: The Story of Jewish Comedians in America* (New York: Public Affairs, 2002); J. Boskin and J. Dorinson, 'Ethnic Humor Subversion and Survival,' *American Quarterly Special Issue: American Humor*, (37.1 1985), pp.81-97; Davies, 'Exploring the Thesis of the Self-Deprecating Jewish Sense of Humor'; P. Lewis, 'Three Jews and a Blindfold: The Politics of Gallows Humor,' in A. Ziv and A. Zajdman (eds) *Semites and Stereotypes* (Westport, CT: Greenwood Press, 1993), pp.47-57; L. G. Greenspoon (ed), *Jews and Humor* (West Lafayette, IN: Purdue University Press, 2011); H. Halkin, 'Why Jews Laugh at Themselves', *Commentary* (4, January 2006); S. Blacher Cohen (ed), *Jewish Wry: Essays on Jewish Humor*, (Bloomington: Indiana University Press, 1987); Ziv, *Jewish Humor*, pp. 47-76; V. Brook, *Something Ain't Kosher Here: The Rise of the 'Jewish' Sitcom* (New Brunswick, NJ: Rutgers University Press, 2003);J. Garrick, 'The Humor of Trauma Survivors', *Journal of Aggression, Maltreatment and Trauma* 12. 1-2 (2006), pp. 169-182; Wisse, *No Joke*, pp. 59-103; J. Sliwa, 'Jewish humor as a source of research on Polish-Jewish relations'. In Greenspoon, L. J. (ed), *Jews and Humor* (West Lafayette, IN: Purdue University Press, 2011), pp. 67-82; Sover, 'Jewish Humor'.
41. Ziv, *Personality and Sense of Humor.*
42. Ibid.
43. A.R. Florenthal, 'The Relationship between Death and Humor', *Humor Mekuvvan: Research Journal in Humor Studies*, 2 (January 2013), pp.69-87 [Hebrew].
44. Ziv, *Personality and Sense of Humor*.
45. K. Keidar Cohen, S. Ben-Ishay and S. Dimri, 'Humor, Mental Resilience and Post-Trauma in Gaza Envelope Residents Following 'Operation Protective Edge', *The 2nd Multidisciplinary Conference for the Research of Humor*, Seminar Hakibbutzim, 9 February 2016. Lecture. [Hebrew]
46. Ziv, *Personality and Sense of Humor.*
47. H. Milo, 'Gvura umavet: humor shahor beshirey folklore shel hayalim israelim' ['Heroism and Death: Black Humorin Folk Songs of Israeli Soldiers'], *Humor Mekuvvan: Research Journal in Humor Studies*, 4 (December 2014), pp.26-44 [Hebrew]. See also: H. Milo, *Shirim Nedabrim*, [*Talking Songs: Identity, Gender and Ideology in Folksongs of Male and FemaleIsraeli Soldiers*,] a thesis submitted for the degree Doctor of Philosophy, University of Haifa [Hebrew].

PART 2

HOLOCAUST HUMOUR, SATIRE AND PARODY IN ISRAELI CULTURE

4

Laughter through Pain: the Intergenerational Transmission of the Holocaust

There are more than 400 articles discussing the question of intergenerational transmission of the Holocaust trauma, from the survivors to their children. In the 1960s, when the issue began to be studied, it was clear that the second generation had common characteristics of unique mental health problems, unifying them as a group. In the last decades, however, the perception that they are a separate group is being questioned.[1]

The research studies examine whether the individuals belonging to the second generation are a distinct group in terms of their characteristics and whether this group has unique and more substantial psychological disorders compared to other groups in the population. The results of the studies can be divided into three main schools of thought. The first school of thought claims that second-generation Holocaust survivors have clear characteristics that are unique and distinguish them from other groups. Examples of typical attributes are: suspiciousness, fear, over-protectiveness, interpersonal problems, feelings of grief and guilt, anger, withdrawnness, a constant, haunting preoccupation with the Holocaust, and more.[2]

Research studies from the second school of thought argue that second-generation Holocaust survivors have no significant psychological disorders, and that the Holocaust has no long-term consequences on the offspring of the survivors. According to studies from this school of thought, the assumptions made by the first school are stereotypical and plagued by stigma.[3]

Scholars from the third school of thought speak of an interaction between parents and children which is unique to the relationship between the Holocaust survivors and their offspring, but it is expressed in many different ways and varies from family to family.[4]

The third-generation Holocaust survivors began to be studied in the 1980s, when psychologists in the United States who were treating a seven-year-old boy, the grandson of Holocaust survivors, claimed that the effects of the Holocaust strongly affected the child, and that the issue deserved comprehensive treatment in the psychiatric community.[5] Since then, psychologists and psychiatrists have been arguing about the term 'third-generation Holocaust survivors' and its characteristics. From the many studies dealing with the biological grandchildren of Holocaust survivors in Israel, three main schools of thought may be found: In the first school of thought, there are researchers who claim that it is possible to find 'intergenerational transference' in the third-generation. Researchers in the second school of thought claim that the third generation, as a group, do not have distinguishing trauma characteristics. In-between these two schools of thought is a third approach that discusses the impact of the Holocaust on grandchildren, but notes a wide spectrum of reactions to trauma.[6]

As noted, along with the many studies dealing with the questions of intergenerational transference of trauma to children and grandchildren of Holocaust survivors, other claim that the second generation and third generation are sociological and cultural terms, especially in Israel, where Holocaust awareness is intensive and comprehensive, much more than other places in the world.[7]

Humouring the Trauma in Road Trips to the Parents' Past

The television satire, *The Chamber Quintet* [*Hahamishia Hakamerit*] ('Matar' Productions, Channels 2-Tela'ad, Channel 1, 1993-1997) is one of the milestones of Israeli culture. It was the first TV satire to break the taboo and combine the memory of the Holocaust with a satiric perspective, while criticizing various aspects of Holocaust commemoration in Israel.

As of the 1980s, for example, second-generation Holocaust survivors joined the circles of art and creation in Israel. They brought to the forefront the stories of their parents and their own experiences as second-generation Holocaust survivors in a variety of cultural arenas: literature, cinema, poetry, theater, and other arts. The discussion of the Holocaust and its implications was so intensive at the time that it gave the feeling that all the second-generation Holocaust survivors were haunted by their parents' trauma and sought to use art as a way of coping with the open wound.[8]

In the skit 'Documentary', the creators ridicule the perception according to which second-generation Holocaust survivors had to deal with the consequences of transgenerational transmission of the Holocaust through art. In the skit, actor Menashe Noy recites a monologue. He is in his home, in his pajamas, describing how a BBC television crew knocked on his door one day, informing him that he was about to star in a show where he and his art would be showcased. He is surprised, complains at the intrusion and informs them that he is not an artist. Indeed, he has worked at the post office his entire life. According to him, the BBC crew refused to accept his explanation, claiming that given that he is a second-generation Holocaust survivor, it is clear that he dealt with his pain through art in order to produce a catharsis. Noy then suggests that they film him repressing. 'But repression does not photograph well', they reply. Eventually they agree that the BBC crew would wait in the front yard until Noy found his inner artist. But Noy insists 'the only thing I care about is mail'. He says he has tried to play the violin, paint, write poetry, but there is no hope, everything is repressed. 'No catharsis'.

This skit confronts the popular public perception of the second generation as if all of them have to relieve the burdens of transgenerational transmission through art. But, in fact, the mere writing of the skit is in itself a way of (humourously) dealing with the transgenerational transmission of the trauma through art. Therefore, the skit is both critical of the perception that second-generation Holocaust survivors use various forms of art in order to face their parents' trauma as well as itself affirming that second-generation Holocaust survivors (the writers) use art in order to deal with the trauma.

The fact that the Holocaust is deeply rooted in the identity of biological second- and third-generation Holocaust survivors seeking to deal with the trauma through black humour and self-deprecating humour appeared from the 1990s also in stand-up comedy and documentary cinema. Shmuel Vilozny was one of the first who dared address the Holocaust in his stand-up acts as early as the 1990s, recounting his experiences as a son of Holocaust survivors, citing the difficulties of growing up in a house of Holocaust survivors who, for example, have an obsession with food ('All my life I have been told "finish off your plate". To this day, before "finishing", I tell the girl – go get me a plate').

The documentary film *Daddy Come to the Fair* [*Abbaleh, bo l'luna park*] (Nitza Gonen, 1994), follows the Vilozny family's journey back to the realms of father Mordechai's childhood in Poland and the memories of his family murdered in the Holocaust. The film emphasizes that Shmuel, the son, uses humour as a defence mechanism against the transgenerational transfer of the horrors. Throughout the journey, Shmuel maintains a humourous façade that contradicts the serious and gloomy purpose of the journey. In the grim atmosphere of his father's search for the dead, Shmuel deliberately wears red flashy, funny-looking trousers, often putting on a red clown-nose and, in a vulgar and humourous manner, voices his aversion toward the Polish scenery which symbolizes the traumatic past. His way of dealing with the Polish space, in which his family was killed, mocks every aspect of it ('Ugly, shabby houses', he exclaims at the sight of the views seen from their car window on the way to the town of his father's youth), ridiculing the habits ('You brought the Polish customs to Israel: the need to hide and cover-up'), the food ('this is disgusting,' he tells his father. 'I'm going to settle something with you now, you piece of crap. Every Friday you forced me to eat that soup with those "lokshen" you need to fish out with a snorkel'), and the culture ('Perhaps you can still be saved,' he addresses a Polish baby sitting next to them at a restaurant). He is extroverted and loud. Throughout the journey, he rudely picks on the Polish people around him ('Where were you when they took my grandfather away? Probably as drunk as you are today') and tries to convince himself and the viewers that this journey has nothing to do with him, only with his father. As far as he is concerned, as he explicitly tells his father, the journey's role is to put the past behind. Leave the memories in Europe.

His sister plays a very important part in the journey. While her role in the film is relatively minor and her voice rarely heard, the few scenes where she talks to Shmuel about their experiences indicate that she, as opposed to him, has a positive, warm relationship with their father. These scenes are important because they dismantle the image of the second-generation Holocaust survivors as a homogenous group, and prove that even children brought up in the same house have different relationships, perceptions and coping mechanism with the trauma.

Eventually, reality strikes Shmuel in the face, and changes both him and his attitude. Upon their arrival in Auschwitz-Birkenau former concentration and extermination camp, where the family's grandfather perished, while Mordechai is shaken by the place, he does manage to restrain himself within the turmoil of grief. Unlike his father, Shmuel's encounter with Auschwitz causes him to break down - and his defence mechanism disintegrates. The encounter with Auschwitz causes him to sink into the horrors of the past. The person who went around Poland dressed like a clown, mocking his environment, is now hysterically crying. He lies down on the ground, wishing to die. The person who had previously requested from his father to disconnect from the past now takes rocks and grass from Auschwitz so he can 'plant them' in Tel Aviv.[9] The scenes showing his breakdown and his lack of ability to confront human evil further clarify that humour acted as an essential defence mechanism for him, which enabled him to try and rise above the mortifying memories of his father that haunt him.

Marianne Hirsch discusses the indirect affinity of second-generation Holocaust survivors to the trauma, structured on imagination and on memory that is inherited and is not an actual memory. Hirsch defines that affinity as 'postmemory,' and she maintains that it is a very strong form of memory. 'Postmemory' characterizes the experience of those controlled by events that happened before they were born, and who apply their imagination in places where they could not remember.[10]

Shmuel's 'postmemory' is very vividly represented in the scenes in Auschwitz. Researchers argue that in families in which a 'double wall of silence' was built (the parents did not tell and their children did not ask),[11] children often tended to fill in information gaps about the chronicles of their parents in the Holocaust using their imagination and fantasy. Talking to the camera, Shmuel recounts that as a child, he would imagine hearing the sound of boots crunching on the gravel, and that he would aimlessly wander along railroads for hours. He calls himself a 'coward', saying that had he been a prisoner at Auschwitz, he would not have rebelled.

Following his father's catharsis, who now feels as though he has symbolically paid final respects to his own father, Shmuel and Mordechai warm up to each other. Towards the end of the film, they are seen huddled together close on a park bench. Shmuel admits that while he has always wished to become the opposite of his father, he is, in fact, a lot like him and has even imitated him in many aspects. Mordechai realizes that his reticence created difficulties in his relationship with his son. The two agree that the Holocaust was and still is a central aspect of their lives as a family, but having openly dealt with it makes it possible for them to become closer. The film ends with a mutual understanding. Shmuel states that the journey has changed his outlook on life. He says that what is left to do now is to walk 'into the sunset', like they do in every Hollywood film with a happy ending, and they laugh together. Yet, like many Holocaust documentary films in Israel in the last decades,[12] the film does not end with full closure.

While Mordechai's entry into the realm of the past does help him break free of his silence, and while the journey indeed brings reconciliation and closeness between father and son, the film's message is that the memories of the past cannot be erased from the soul of the second-generation. Evidence of this assertion can be found in the ending scenes. Shmuel is filmed in his comedy club, ending his stand-up routine about the transgenerational transmission of the Holocaust, claiming that he has found the light and encouraging the audience to travel to Poland. He then joyously invites the photographer to come with him outside, to the beach. On the way to the beach, he is cheerfully humming a tune from Federico Fellini's *Eight and a Half* (1963), which was played in Fellini's film during a scene in which the artist reconciles with his troubled soul. Shmuel seems happy and joyful, again acting like a clown. It seems, therefore, that the cinematic homage attests to the massive change Shmuel himself experienced. He too was a troubled artist at the beginning of the film, and now, after the journey, he feels at peace with himself. In the final scene, Shmuel attempts to sing the children's song, *Daddy*

Come to the Fair [*Abbaleh, bo l'luna park*], which he dedicates to his father, but finds himself choking with tears. His tears illustrate how, in spite of the journey, in spite of his humouristic defence mechanism, the disturbing memories of the past and the former years of silence cannot be undone, there is no compensation for them. The childlike need for his father to come and be with him will probably remain with him forever.

The film *Pizza in Auschwitz* [*Pizza beauschwitz*] (Moshe Zimerman, 2008) shows the use of black humour as a cross-generational defence mechanism, which is used both by the first generation of survivors and the second-generation Holocaust survivors. The film follows Holocaust survivor Danny Chanoch and his two children, Shraga (Sagi) and Miri, during a six-day journey to Lithuania and Poland. The film reveals how Danny and Miri use black humour in order to cope with the horrors of the past. Danny, who states that he stopped crying as a child in Birkenau, describes himself as having a BA (Bachelor of Auschwitz) degree, tells everyone he had a private doctor (Mengele) and refers to the days surrounding the Holocaust and Heroism Remembrance Day as the 'High Season'. During the long drives, Danny explains to the camera, chuckling, the family's version of the alphabet game: 'A is Auschwitz, B is Birkenau, C is for (gas) chambers, D for Dachau'. 'I've spoken to Birkenau,' he tells Zimerman, the director, at the airport, 'the bunks are orthopedic. We can sleep there'.

Miri, his daughter, who narrates the film with her voice-over, deals with the trauma in the same way. She does not hesitate to voice her discontent with the journey and the manner in which it is proceeding. She complains: 'I'm trapped in a week-long reality show about the Holocaust' and declares that the family has decided to open a new baguette café which is to be called 'BaGhetto' [a phonetic play on words in Hebrew which means 'in the ghetto']. The past is mixed with the present also in the way she describes the journey and the way the director edits the scenes: 'We are leaving the hotel and moving onwards, like father and his family left for the ghetto', Miri begins to narrate the chronicles of the third day. When they leave a wreath at the place where the family was deported to the camps by train, a train comes along and cuts the frame. When they are eating bread, they joke by saying that they have now finished their two-day allowance. The traffic jam at the border crossing is referred to by Miri as a 'station along the transfer on the way to the *Lager*'.[13] In this way, both she and her father act out the past and use black humour in order to work through the trauma. The film suggests that Miri's intensive use of black humour is her way of avoiding wallowing in the trauma.

Miri describes how the experiences of her father, who has been telling her brother and her stories about the Holocaust since infancy, affected their childhood in a bad way. His stories about walking barefoot in the snow were for them a realistic substitute for *Hansel and Gretel*, and apparently caused Miri and her brother to have horrible nightmares. Miri explicitly criticizes the telling of stories like these to such young children, burdening them with details of the Holocaust. She says that having that knowledge made her feel fear with every knock on the door, thinking it might be the SS. This confession can explain that, as an adult, she tries to create a mental wall between her soul and the trauma, by using black humour.

Danny, on the one hand, recounts his memories with emotional remoteness, using much black humour and displaying mental resilience by not shedding a tear. On the other hand, he is living the past in the present. His past as a child who managed to escape the *Kinder Aktion* in Kovno[14] and survive Auschwitz influenced the manner in which he brought up his children. He taught them to trust no one, to keep running away, to always do the opposite of what they are told. Miri explicitly criticizes teaching this mindset to children, but Danny refuses to accept the criticism. He feels as though he has successfully brought up strong children.

Pizza in Auschwitz as well as *Daddy Come to the Fair* reveals just how fragile this defence mechanism is; while in Auschwitz-Birkenau museum, visiting the barracks in which Danny stayed as a prisoner, and after having heard difficult stories about his life there, Miri breaks into a harsh, piercing monologue, in which she demands, screaming, that they leave the place, as she can no longer handle the amounts of horrors 'injected straight into the vein', throughout the journey and throughout their lifetime in general.[15]

Along the journey Danny seems to be rejuvenated by the encounter with the realms of his childhood. This behavior reaches its surreal pinnacle when, on arriving at Auschwitz, Danny expresses his desire to spend the night on the bunk in the same barracks in which he slept in the past as a prisoner. His children try to dissuade him and in their heated exchange, Danny exclaims that he feels good there. His children refuse to accept his arguments and convince him to leave. On the way to the hotel Danny is infuriated, withdrawn and angry at the 'injustice' caused him by his children, who refused to stay with him and let him stay in the barracks.

Hagai Dagan and Gidi Dishon[16] argue that *Pizza in Auschwitz* features a unique model of 'nostalgia', contradicting how it is commonly perceived. They claim that nostalgia is a way of viewing the past in a positive light, therefore trauma and nostalgia are habitually thought of as contradictory. However, as they see it, *Pizza in Auschwitz* reveals that nostalgia can be applied to a traumatic past. Danny's nostalgic gaze is ostensibly directed at his pre-Holocaust childhood, which would be reasonable, yet his behavior in the Auschwitz barracks and the manner in which he explains the daily routine and sleeping arrangements there uncover nostalgic feelings toward his time in Auschwitz. He seems happy in the barracks, even referring to them as 'home' several times, thus combining nostalgia and trauma. In their opinion, the black humour, sarcasm and irony create a buffer between the trauma-struck person and the trauma itself, thus allowing nostalgia to exist. This form of nostalgia is not sweet and romantic, but rather sarcastic and combative, yet it still allows for reminiscence of the past, helping Danny cope with the trauma.

In *Daddy Come to the Fair*, the relationship between the father and the son at the beginning of the journey is illustrated as analogous to the relationship between the weak and old 'Diaspora Jew' and the active and fearless 'New Jew'.[17] However, during the journey, the tables turn: the father competes with his son in fencing, exudes confidence in the foreign environment, and holds himself together during the visit to Auschwitz as opposed to his son who broke down there. In *Pizza in Auschwitz*, the initial situation is quite the contrary. Danny is confident, easygoing, walks around proudly. His children and the camera crew barely succeed in keeping up with him (though he is in his seventies). He interferes in conversations of local strangers and forces them to listen to stories about how Jewish bodies were plundered, yells at the receptionist in the office of the Auschwitz concentration camp and demands that she and the manager allow him to do as he pleases and spend the night in the barracks. When the camera crew stumbles upon a group of German teens at the camp, he makes them listen to his stories, eventually declaring that all Germans are the same, 'something deep inside them is rotten'. In comparison, his daughter Miri is reserved, at times scared of her surroundings. Danny sees no problem with his orthodox son Shraga walking from the synagogue to the hotel by foot on Shabbat. Miri reproaches him and expresses her fear of having Shraga walk alone through these anti-Semitic grounds. Quite like Shmuel in *Daddy Come to the Fair*, she treats the surroundings through which they somberly wander with disgust whereas Danny is enchanted and treats Miri's fears with contempt.

As opposed to most Israeli documentaries about the Holocaust characterized by sheer realism, *Pizza in Auschwitz* successfully combines realism with surrealism, particularly prominent in the scenes capturing the visit to the Auschwitz-Birkenau museum. The contrast between the triviality of everyday life in the west, symbolized by the pizza and Coca-Cola given to the crew by Miri, and the setting in which it is happening, along with Danny's descriptions of the months of his imprisonment there, give the sense of a hallucinatory tragic-funny journey in which 'laughter through tears', one of the most prominent Jewish humour characteristics, is one of the main components.

Like most documentaries of that time, *Pizza in Auschwitz* does not portray a process of redemption. At the end of the film, the relationship between Danny and his children is fairly similar to its first state: black humour mixed with a great deal of sarcasm and pain. 'We really don't get you and we will never get you', states Miri. The goal of the journey, as Miri presented it in the beginning, was 'to put it [the Holocaust] back where it came from', that is, to break free of the memories of the past. This goal is not achieved, only slightly changed. Miri concludes: 'When I got off the airplane in Israel, I felt like somebody was following me. It was the Holocaust. It looked tired and a bit worn out. Maybe Zimmerman [the director] was right, when he said that there was no such thing as Holocaust survivors.'

The memories of the Holocaust will not fade and will continue to haunt the family. The relationship among its members will not be fundamentally changed, but even the realization that they will never be able to fully comprehend Danny, their father, is sufficient insight for them. Like other documentaries from that era, having a family is depicted as a partial form of redemption, providing support. At the end of the film, Danny speaks of the importance of family, being the element which links the past and the future: 'This is what [my] mother and father would have wanted, for us to live, start families… I've been living with your mother for 40 years and we have a wonderful life, we started a family together'. His children join in on this insight when Shraga refers to starting a family as a 'rescue' and when Miri expresses, throughout the journey, how deeply she misses her own family (her husband and children) who stayed in Israel. The film conveys the message that the Hanoch family is bound to learn how to continue living with the consequences of the Holocaust, with the hope that their love for each other will bridge the gaps between Danny and his children, though they will never be fully closed. Humour as a defence mechanism will continue to help Danny and his family try and work through the traumatic past that shaped their lives.

Acting Out and Reenactments in Literature, Graphic Novels and Poetry

Humour as a defence mechanism in order to cope with the second- and third-generation Holocaust survivors' acting out of their secondary traumatic stress is represented in literature, graphic novels, and poetry. The novel *Our Holocaust* [*Shoah shelnu*] (Amir Gutfreund, 2000) follows the story of two young Israelis in different periods of their lives: Amir (the writer) and his female friend Effi have become familiar with the chronicles of the Holocaust survivors living in their neighbourhood. Through the difficult stories they encounter, they gradually become exposed to the trauma which has been vague to them for many years. The binary divisions created by Israeli society between Germans and Jews (bad and good, respectively) become blurrier in the book through stories of Jews who were abusive toward other Jews in the Holocaust and honest, kind Germans and, in parallel, descriptions of sadistic, murderous Germans and good-hearted Jews.

The idea for the book came from a documentation process undertaken by writer Amir Gutfreund, a second-generation Holocaust survivor, of his family's history. Some of the stories in the fiction book greatly resemble his family's biography. For instance, the stories of the protagonist's mother and father in the book are based on the real experiences of the author's parents. The protagonist's name is Amir, like the author, and he is also the same age. His real-life family, as the family of his character in the book 'adopted' grandparents, uncles and cousins who were not biologically related to the family. Like the narrator, as a child, Gutfreund was curious about the half-told stories of the Holocaust with unclear allusions, hints and general vagueness kept secret from him, and later, in his adult years, came to delve into these stories and explore them. Some of the Nazi characters in the book are based on real-life persons while others were invented by the author, and their stories are a mosaic of stories he read while doing research in the *Yad Vashem* archives.[18]

Having been exposed to the horrific stories, the two main characters - living their neighbours' and parents' trauma in an Israeli neighbourhood in which the Holocaust is an integral part of the present - often use black humour, which clearly is used as a defence mechanism and a form of coping with the atrocities. 'I hadn't planned initially to write about the Holocaust with humor', says Gutfreund. 'But in retrospect the humor has a role. It allows the most horrible things to be heard'.[19]

The black humour is evident throughout the book, in several ways: first, it is a part of the way the narrator describes the characters' incredible biographies. For instance, the narrator refers to the tendency to 'collect relatives' with no blood relation in order to compensate for the relatives who perished in the Holocaust and will never return. It is described humorously as the 'Law of Compression':

> We called him Grandpa – Grandpa Lolek – due to our family's Law of Compression, a wonderful invention of our parents, the first generation of the Holocaust. Lacking brothers, uncles, fathers and mothers, they had done away with the requirement for precision. Anyone belonging to our parents' generation was simply called "Uncle". Their offspring were our cousins. [...] Our greatest need was

> for grandparents, and so we ploughed our way through the restrictions and gathered as many of them as we could.[20]

The narrator describes sarcastically the typical hierarchy among the survivors: 'Tragedy was commonplace, a daily occurrence, like drinking. [...] Those who had not lost their entire families in the camps got no respect'.[21] Elsewhere, he describes the peculiar ways of commemoration:

> Not much further, at 10-A Katznelson Street, lived Linow Community. Her real name was Hinda Goldberg, but since it was said that she alone remained out of all the Jews in her town of Linow, Effi came up with her nickname, Linow Community. Right below her lived Sarkow Community, a similar case. They had lost husbands, parents, families. And every morning at precisely nine o'clock, their two green front doors opened. Linow Community and Sarkow Community went down to buy vegetables at Sammy's. One tomato, one onion, a cucumber or a carrot. [...] We used to follow the Communities. We suspected there were still a few remaining Jews from Linow and Sarkow and that they were hiding them; they had reason to.[22]

Second, Amir and Effi use black humour as they observe their daily lives and encounters through the perspective of the Holocaust. For example, when a dignified professor from Frankfurt University arrives in contemporary Israel, decades after the Holocaust, Amir intentionally lets him carry his luggage by himself ('I hoped the three suitcases would make him look slightly hunched, [...]Why shouldn't *they* carry suitcases for once'?). Effi takes one look at the Professor and exclaims, 'You've really brought a Nazi', and promises, 'Adolf and I will get along just fine'.[23]

The manner in which Amir, the protagonist, perceives the space around him clarifies why black humour is so vital for him. When he travels throughout Haifa with the professor, he starts by describing the road through some sites most identified with Haifa ('We drove down the Carmel hillside through Neveh Sha'anan'.) Then, as a natural continuity, the Israeli domain begins blending with Europe's Holocaust domains: 'We passed by traffic lights, junctions, and the colorful commercial area. Heavy industry sprawled on both sides. Fences, chimneys, guard towers. [...] I drove among barbed wire and guard huts with a Nazi poster child sitting beside me'.[24]

In this Israeli world that acts out the memories of the trauma, the narrator reveals that black humour is not only a tool used by the second-generation Holocaust survivors but also frequently used by the first-generation survivors. For instance, the narrator describes Lolek, his stingy 'adopted' grandfather, as follows:

> Grandpa used to say, 'People have to die of something', and refused to donate to the war against cancer, the war against traffic accidents, or any other war. [...] But his most wonderful ruse involved a magical power over tea bags. Each bag, even upon its tenth descent into boiling water, yielded something of itself — the merest vapor of tea, just verging on physically tangible material. The hoisting of the bag out of the water was accompanied by an expertly suspicious look at the bag hanging off the teaspoon by its string. Based on signs perceptible only to himself, he would estimate the bag's vitality and decree its fate. *Selection,*[25] he called this ceremony when he wanted to be cruel to Grandpa Yosef.[26]

In the last decade, second- and third-generation artists have started dealing with the Holocaust and its impact on the younger generations also through graphic novels. Some of these graphic novels use Holocaust humour in the text and the drawings thus highlighting humour's role as a defence mechanism in dealing with the intergenerational transmission of the trauma. In his graphic novel, *Second Generation: Things I Never Told My Father* [*Hador hasheni: dvarim shelo siparty leaba*] (2013), Michel Kichka, an illustrator and cartoonist, describes growing up in the shadow of the Holocaust. He unfolds the life of his father Henri who survived Auschwitz and the family's life and problems. For many years, Henri did not speak about his past, and Michel tried to understand what actually happened through the bits and pieces he heard. Only years later did Henri became what Michel calls 'a Holocaust hero': Henri wrote a book about his life, and became a well-known guide in educational trips to the former concentration camps. The graphic novel is told through Michel's eyes, first as a child and then as a grown up and, through this perspective, Michel shows two perspectives of Holocaust humour: The Holocaust humour his father used and the Holocaust humour which helps Michel to deal with his father's past and tell the difficult family story.

Michel describes and shows how his father, who was an artist, ridiculed Hitler in his drawings (drew him as a buffoon with hairy legs, ragged clothes and a broom instead of a gun). Holocaust humour is also present in the Holocaust jokes Henri and his sons tell each other in his old age ('each one of us wrote his own phone number on his arm...ha ha ha').

Michel describes his own complex life and his attempts to unravel what really happened to his father by using Holocaust humour, which leaves the reader between laughter and tears. Through Holocaust humour, he explains how the Holocaust acted out in his father's life and in his own life as a child and as an adult. For example, he describes his parents' clothing store, 'I think that all the monsters from the past went with him to the back room. They went with him everywhere,' he states from a child's point of view, while the visual (drawn by the adult Michel) shows the back room, but instead of clothes it is packed with striped prisoners' uniform. Michel draws the 'industrial, filthy city' in which they lived in Belguim, as resembling Auschwitz ('Can you invent better scenery than that after Auschwitz?'). He also tells about his funny childhood attempts to figure out how his father looked in the Holocaust, what happened there, and the way as an adult he became aware of the second-generation syndrome. It seems that black humour enables Michel to openly write about the family's problems, his brother's suicide and the complex relationships of the children with their parents. Like in *Pizza in Auschwitz*, the graphic novel reveals that Michel inherited not only the trauma but also the use of Holocaust humour as an important defence mechanism.

In the graphic novel, *The Property* [*Haneches*] (2013)[27] comics artist Rutu Modan unfolds a week-long journey the protagonist Mica takes with her grandmother Regina back to Warsaw, Poland in an attempt to trace a prewar family property. The plot thickens as the real estate search is revealed as an excuse for Regina to trace her old gentile lover, while Mica gets involved with a gentile tour guide of Jewish historical tours. Modan uses the geographic journey from Israel to Poland as the foundation for an emotional journey of both the grandmother and her granddaughter to the memories of the past and its echoes in the present. Modan does not illustrate scenes from the Holocaust, but concentrates on its effect on the present. Thus, the drawings describe only the present, but the past is what leads the narrative and the way of the different characters. This combination of past and present is often represented through Holocaust humour which does not only function as Modan's way of dealing with the echoes of the past, but also as her way of critiquing Holocaust memory in Israel and Poland. For example, in one scene, Mica, accidentally enters a reenactment of the Warsaw ghetto uprising. Modan draws the ridiculous gestures of the actors, and the organizers, which believe that it possible to reenact that historic event, thus criticizing the commercialization and trivialization of the memory.[28]

The poetry book *A Visitor's Guide to Birkenau* [*Madrich lamevaker bebirkenau*][29] was written by Shmuel Refael, a second-generation Holocaust survivor. His parents were deported from Saloniki, Greece to Auschwitz and survived. Refael is a Ladino researcher and has written books about the

Holocaust in Greece. His poetry book is the outcome of his journeys to Poland with his students and colleagues.

In this book, Refael undermines social norms and hegemonic messages regarding the commemoration of the Holocaust. The graveness, pathos and national tone which are integral markers of the canonical remembrance and of many poetry books regarding the Holocaust are replaced with cynicism and black humour, providing a different outlook on the traumatic issues.

The first theme which runs through the book is the manner in which second-generation survivors are living their parents' trauma. The manner in which he describes how his parents dealt with the memories reveals 'repetition compulsion' in which the post-traumatic individual re-experiences the trauma while blurring the boundaries between past and present.

Refael illustrates, in several poems, that this repetition compulsion was transferred to the second-generation who, with their parents, live the echoes of the trauma also in the Israeli present (*Simple* [*Pashut*]; *Horse* [*Soos*]; *Happiness* [Osher]). In one of the segments in the poem *Simple*, he writes: 'One day father ceased his work as a sorter of the dead's belongings on the train ramp/ on the way to the gates of Birkenau/ and took me by the hand, to search for an appropriate teacher for my Bar Mitzvah/ on the cracked pavements of the south/ of Tel Aviv…'. The blend created by his father between past and present is transferred to him, and in his postmemory, the two timelines combine. This blur is also portrayed, for example, in the poem *Horse*, where 'on the stairs to the house of a Tel Aviv scholar/ father unstitched the striped prisoners' uniform from Birkenau'. He also describes how his father ate a non-kosher salami 'there', from 'seasoned Hungarian horse'. According to the father, the salami is what gave him the strength to rock his son on the wooden horse he bought in Israel using the reparation payments from Germany that Holocaust survivors receive. In this manner, the past and the present, the life of the father and the life of the son, the dead and the living are all intertwined into one unit.

The second recurring theme throughout the book is the cynical outlook on the commemoration of the Holocaust, especially the trips to Poland's former concentration camps which are very common in Israeli culture. His critique is written in the poems with sarcasm and black humour. Through his cynical outlook, Refael sheds light on the manifold problems involved in the remembrance, the commemoration and the tours in the concentrations camps. He displays the dissonance between the blossoming land and the camp itself through a discussion of the real estate options en route to Birkenau: 'Real bargains/ affordable to all […] Red loam or Jewish-blood-coloured plaster/ as much of that as one wants' (*Real Estate* [*Nadlan*]). He engages in the problematic aspects of turning the death camp into an ordinary tourist site: 'In Birkenau, electrical barbed wire is replaced every day, the old ones rust, crumble, are not worth the efforts of coming from afar/ the overpriced flight ticket and hotel/ and tourists demand, and rightfully so, a return' (*Barbed Wire* [*Hutei Tail*]). Refael reveals how Birkenau became a tourist attraction like any other, where the tourists are completely detached from the meaning of the site and are preoccupied with trivialities. For instance, in *Industrialized Memory* [*Zikaron metoas*], he describes things going through the mind of a 15-year-old overweight German high school student who was sent as an outstanding student to Auschwitz 'to visit relatives from the near past'. Throughout her visit there, she constantly deliberates on what she ought to buy: 'a Twix bar, for three and a half zloty?/ Orange Mirinda/ in a can? Or/ in a bottle?/ Perhaps a diet coke…'. Moreover, the 'souvenirs' sold at the museum are devoid of any emotional meaning to her. They are no more than commodities and her process of choosing resembles the manner in which one decides what blouse to buy in a boutique: 'the thoughts would not rest, would not rest/ Anne Frank in Swedish, Turkish or Japanese? A poster of leg amputees/ or a Jewish dwarf seated on a wicker chair'? The poems illuminate the superficiality of the remembrance of the Holocaust in Birkenau which has become a 'tourist site'. Refael also courageously handles matters which have previously been considered taboo and were excluded from the remembrance, due to the conception that referring to them would be a disparagement of the Holocaust, such as the collision between everyday needs and the sacredness of the site which seemingly requires rules of conduct rising above human needs. For instance, in *When the Stomach Growls* [*Keshehabeten mekarkeret*], he wonders 'What do you do in Birkenau when the stomach growls?/ Do you take out the sandwich you made at the hotel under the Polish waitress's projector gaze? Do you sneak a bite from a juicy apple? And if you do sneak one, should it be with an agonized look?' The poems, loaded with pain, uncover the open wound of the second-generation Holocaust survivors and demonstrate that the cynicism or the discussion of the tragedy which is soaked in black humour is not a form of disparagement or disrespect. It is simply the way in which a second-generation survivor, living his parents' trauma, chooses to cope with the postmemory of the Holocaust which overwhelms him.

Ridiculing the Cultural Intergenerational Transmission

In Israeli popular culture, Holocaust humour does not deal with the transgenerational transfer of the trauma only in the cases of biological offspring of Holocaust survivors. Skits often reflect how in a society so engaged with Holocaust memory, the trauma transfers to all Jewish-Israelis who were born after 1945, regardless of whether they have a biological connection to Holocaust survivors.

The Chamber Quintet satirists hold a fundamental belief that one of Israel's biggest problems is that the Holocaust is completely integrated into the present of all Jewish-Israelis: this is expressed in the skit 'Ghetto 2', which focuses on the efforts of a young man from Tel Aviv (Rami Heuberger) driving and trying to find his way to a party. When Heuberger asks a friend he meets on the street (Shai Avivi) for directions to the party, Avivi's responses reveal that all the street names are either redolent of death ('Hanged Men Street'), commemorating the names of heroes who sacrificed their lives for the State ('Eli Cohen[30] Street'), or are in some way tied to the Holocaust: 'Take Warsaw Ghetto Street, make a U-turn onto Concentration Camp Avenue, then park in Dachau Square', directs Avivi. 'Is it nearby'? Heuberger asks. 'Dachau? Dachau is right here, just around the corner', answers Avivi.

The skit criticizes the role of collective memory agents in the process of preserving the Holocaust as part of the individual and collective present. Collective memory is not constructed solely by historians (who write society's 'official texts') but also by artists, intellectuals, filmmakers and urban planners. Individual memory is not detached from society, family, symbols and its collective memory; it also includes events from the past that the individual did not experience directly, and these events are part of the collective memory of the group to which the individual belongs. In other words, the individuals remember and relate to them because they are a part of that group.[31] Every individual is always and of necessity connected to a community/group, and it is that attribution which shapes it and renders it deep and full of content.[32]

The skit with the driving directions does not directly engage with the Holocaust but focuses on its aftermath: the trauma of the Holocaust is integrated within the Israeli present day reality. In the skit, Avivi concludes his directions with a quick phrase that makes it clear how the memory agents have introduced trauma into the mundane, and transformed traumatic memories of horror and fear into integral parts of the present. The skit presents the Jewish-Israeli sphere as post-traumatic and in a state of acting out. It reflects how collective memory agents relive the trauma of the Holocaust through street names, and conduct a symbolic sphere in which the past and the present combine. This skit, as satire does, asks to acknowledge it, so it can be changed.

Other skits confirm the message of the skit 'Ghetto 2', and reveal that young generations act out Holocaust memories obsessively in the present and can look at the world only through a Holocaust perspective. The skit 'Dan Shilon', for example, is a parody on a TV host show with that name who was very popular in Israel in the 1990s. The host, Dan Shilon, a cultural second-generation, assembled a group of guests that usually had a politician or a military figure, a model or a singer, a common person who went through a personal tragedy, and a number of times – a transsexual. The skit 'Dan Shilon' takes place in Kiryat Shmona, a city in the far north of Israel which has often suffered from missile attacks from Lebanon. In the skit, the serious and solemn Dan Shilon (Menashe Noy) assembles his guests in a bomb-proof shelter and talks to them about their personal stories and the political context of the bombing. His guests are a military figure, a model, a man who lost his entire fortune in a Turkish casino and a transsexual. Shilon mentions the Holocaust in every question, every time he refers to one of his guests, regardless of whether the Holocaust is really a part of the biography of the interviewee. The multiple and consistent mentions of the Holocaust in every sentence are immoderate and ridiculous, yet his guests take them seriously: 'Colonel Yaakov Shemtov', he approaches the first interviewee, 'you have lived in Kiryat Shmona for eight years. You've probably known loss from every aspect. When the Germans entered Poland, your family lost traces of your grandfather, yesterday you lost your brand new car because a missile hit it. Do you feel now that you survived one Holocaust just to come here and go through another Holocaust in Eretz Israel?' Shilon doesn't wait for an answer and turns to the other interviewee Benni Birenbaum, who lost his fortune in a casino. Shilon asks him, as a second-generation Holocaust survivor whose parents survived Theresienstadt, if what he went through in the casino reminds him of his parents' stories regarding the death camps. Birenbaum listens carefully and even opens his mouth to answer but Shilon, who listens only to himself, jumps to the next interviewee. He approaches the model who he thinks is the transsexual. Shilon mentions that this model (the transsexual) was in Rabin Square 'on that terrible night' [referring to the night that Prime Minister Yitzhak Rabin was murdered] as well as was in Dizengoff Center 'on that terrible afternoon' [referring to a terror attack in the Center]. 'You were in bed when missiles were launched at Kiryat Shmona, do you feel, as a transsexual, as if you were in the Holocaust'? 'I'm not the transsexual, I'm the model', answers the interviewee. Shilon doesn't blink, as if nothing happened and continues in the same laconic tone: 'so as a model, when you model and you have a run in your stockings [In Hebrew, a run in a stocking is called a 'train'.], does it remind you of the trains to Auschwitz'? 'All the time', answers the model, 'I think this is why I decided to become a model'. The audience and the other interviewees clap their hands agreeably.

The ludicrous questions emphasize how the media, as scholars assert, treat the Holocaust as an ongoing trauma that affects everybody in present day Israel.[33] The answer of the model and the audience's reaction illustrates that the media succeeded – the transgenerational transfer of the trauma affected the young generations, regardless of their personal family history.

Wim Wender's well-known and reputed film, *Wings of Desire* [*Der Himmel über Berlin*] (1987), deals with two angels, Damiel and Cassiel, who roam the streets of Berlin in the late 1980s and listen to people's thoughts. They are invisible, and they collect and document bits and pieces of reality. The film is lyrical and poetic. It is shot in black and white, the manner in which the angels see the world, and it has scenes in colour when it represents the perspective of human beings. When Damiel falls in love with a human trapeze artist, he starts to see the world in colour.

The Chamber Quintet in the skit, 'Wings of Desire' ['Melachim bishmei Berlin'], offered homage to the film and turned it into a satire about the way Israeli society is unable to let go of the traumatic past and look at Germans as other than Nazis. In the skit, the two angels Damiel (Rami Hueberger) and Cassiel (Dov Navon) sit together on a rooftop in Berlin looking down, as in a famous scene in the film. Damiel talks softly in high language, poetic Hebrew with a German accent about the people in the streets of Berlin. The scene is shot just as the scenes in *Der Himmel über Berlin:* the two are shot in black and white looking down at the street from above (a bird's eye view). The scenes of the Berlin street are taken from the film and integrated within the skit. As opposed to the film, the gloomy poetic discussion in the people's lives is interrupted by Cassiel who, unlike Damiel does not have a German accent and speaks Hebrew combined with a lot of slang, representing the 'common Israeli'. Cassiel refuses to keep listening to the little misfortunes of the people in Berlin and to feel sorry for them 'because they are all Nazis'. Damiel protests and points at several people on the street but Cassiel claims reputedly that they are all anti-Semitic Nazis. 'They are all either neo-Nazis or alte-Nazis'. 'The poor guard lost his glasses', Damiel tries to change his perspective. Cassiel mocks him, 'These are the glasses through which he looked Anne Frank in the face! They are all Nazi sons of bitches. How can you pity them??' Damiel tries to show him people who were not even born in the Second World War, but Cassiel finds anti-Semitic characters in all of them, calling, for example football players who played against the Israeli team and won, or Judo artists who defeated the Israeli contestant, anti-Semites. Damiel talks longingly about his beloved trapeze artist but Cassiel summarizes in contempt: 'You want to fuck a Nazi'. The depth of the transgenerational trauma and its accuracy are intensified in the last scene in which Damiel goes to visit his love. He whispers soft words of love in her ears and she indeed seems naïve and pure, but as the scene ends and he promises to wait for her in the dressing room, all of a sudden she changes and screams at him aggressively 'come here you dog', a shout that echoes Nazi barking at Jews in Holocaust films. The skit portrays how Jewish-Israelis are all second and third generation. They are unable to look at Germans in another way since the trauma is so integrated within them. It criticizes these perceptions but agrees with them at the same time.

Another way of satirizing the acting out of the Holocaust in second- and third-generation Holocaust survivors is found in the fringe show, *A One-Time Satire Show Number Four: A Birthday for Simcha Babayof and a Funeral for the State of Israel* [*Erev chadpeami*], featuring Ayelet Robinson and Nadav Bossem (2006). The creators criticize the manner in which the Holocaust has been appropriated by collective memory agents and has become a tool to justify militarism and racism. In a monologue teeming with cynicism and black humour, given by a pregnant woman completely unaware of her extremely racist right-wing opinions, Robinson reveals how the memory of the Holocaust in Israel is the sole prism through which everyday occurrences are judged, and how the Zionist-Jewish lessons learnt from the Holocaust are used in the present to justify a narrow, racist and nationalist perception of reality. According to the pregnant woman, she and her husband were thrilled and excited when he was called for reserve duty because they are no longer willing to be 'led like lambs to the slaughter', as was the case in the Holocaust. Israeli militarism is portrayed as rejuvenating, arousing. She recounts that on the night before he left, they had the best sex they had had in a long time, resulting in her pregnancy. She recites mantras of the Israeli right-wing in an overtly cynical manner, linking the Holocaust with the Jewish-Israeli-Arab conflict and stating that we must attack in order to defend ourselves: 'Every bomb which is dropped on their citizens protects our life here – the lives of the first-, second- and third- generation Holocaust survivors'. She is overjoyed by bringing into the world 'the next generation, the fourth generation of Holocaust survivors, the child who came from love'. She cannot understand why people are upset when 'a few Palestinian children die', since, in the Holocaust, 'do you know how many children died? A lot more!' She wishes to minimize the media coverage of all sorts of 'minor' affairs, such as former Israeli president Moshe Katsav's sexual conduct, because her grandmother 'survived Auschwitz and Bergen-Belsen without crying so much, and believe me she had things to cry about'; she finds all those noble souls 'who don't want to deport the foreign workers, the Chinese and Thais' unacceptable: 'I beg your pardon! I don't recall China or Thailand fighting to save anyone during the Holocaust'. She also disapproves of the Jerusalem gay pride parade, Jerusalem being the holy city toward which the Jewish people prayed, 'especially during the Holocaust'. Through this monologue, Robinson and Bosem expose the absurdity of the twisted manner in which the Holocaust has been inserted into the minds of the second- and third-generation Holocaust survivors, a memory that, according to the creators, justifies cruelty and rejection of all 'others'.

A decade later, a different skit called 'The Berlin Museum' [Museon Berlin] (2008) by the comedy group the *Tross Brothers*, tells the same story in a different way, and shows that the Israeli perspective has stayed the same. The skit focuses on a young Israeli woman visiting a museum in Berlin. The explanations are given by the German museum guide Franz, who is very kind to her, but she understands his innocent explanations as being submerged in Nazism. So, when he says 'Hi', the woman hears, 'Heil'; when he points to a painting which is hung up high on the wall, she sees his hand gesture as the Nazi salute; when he explains abstract paintings, he briefly blurts out, as if barking, expressions such as 'the supreme race'; he requests her to leave her camera at the entrance, 'next to the pile of glasses and shoes'. The Israeli woman feels very uncomfortable around him. 'I have a problem', she says. 'Every problem has a solution. A final solution', he replies. In order to calm her down, he promises to tell her a knock knock joke: 'Knock knock', he starts, 'who's there'? she replies. 'The Gestapo'! he shrieks. She turns out to be a Mossad agent and conducts a search on him ('What are you searching for?' 'Antisemitism!'). She eventually finds a mobile phone, 'Third generation', he exclaims. This softens her, 'I'm third generation too', and the two reconcile on these grounds.

Through this skit, third-generation survivors deal with the way in which the Holocaust has been engraved into their identity and, with self-deprecating humour, criticize themselves for being unable to adopt a different outlook on Germany, due to the memory of the Holocaust. The Holocaust dominates their perspective in every aspect, making them still apprehensive toward German figures of authority and preventing them from normalizing their relationship with Germany. The skit criticizes the manner in which the memory of the Holocaust has been forced into the consciousness of young generations, not allowing for a new, different outlook on Germans and Germany. The past blends in with the present and the results of this are acted out in every aspect of daily life. Black humour and self-deprecating humour are used in order to expose this blend and fight it by creating a mental wall between the past and present.

The Israeli-German play *Post-trauma* (Deddy Baron, 2009) suggests a similar look but this time, from a double perspective: the Israeli and the

German. It is a collaboration between the *Habimah* Theatre and the *Düsseldorf Schauspielhaus* dealing with Holocaust memory and the third generation in Germany and Israel. A group of playwrights, four Israelis and two Germans, discuss how both peoples cannot release themselves from the echoes of the Holocaust. In skits and songs, they present a provocative black-comedy approach to Holocaust memory. They deal with sex between a Jew and a German woman as a ridiculous act of revenge, and explain in a song the differences between third-generation Israelis and young Germans in their age, with the lovers singing a duet that hints to familiar words from the Holocaust era ('Your *Arbeit* isn't my *Arbeit*'). Through surrealistic scenes, it is demonstrated that the transgenerational transfer of the trauma keeps the memory alive and kicking, in the third generation too, dictating relationships between the two peoples.

Ran Sarig's *Chaim Shtaim*[34] is a collection of short stories focusing on simple people living in the gap between contemporary Israel and the traumatic memories of the Holocaust past. The story, 'The Metamorphoses of the S-Word' ['Gilgulia shel milat hashin'], meaning the Hebrew word for Holocaust: Shoah, demonstrates how the essence of being Israeli is integrally interwoven with the Holocaust. The bulk of the story revolves around how Israeli society has made the Holocaust into an Israeli religion, obsessively reliving its memory and passing the trauma on to the next generation. Black humour and fantasy is Sarig's choice to deal with the dominance of the trauma over the Israeli present. He uses it to describe the character of Itai Corneliu, a baby who was born in Israel but speaks German from childhood, uses Nazi expressions and behaves as though he was living in 1930s and 1940s Germany. He comes to develop a highly charismatic personality and grows a little moustache. The writer calls him 'the Führer of Holon' (a small town in Israel). According to the story, all Israeli Jews are different versions of Itai: living the Holocaust in the present time, after having breathed it in, ever since childhood. Sarig uses black humour in order to discuss how all Jewish-Israelis are second- and third-generation Holocaust survivors. As he claims, 'Auschwitz is the Jews' Euro Disney',[35] and he argues that the consciousness of the Holocaust is so intensive that it is not unlikely that in the near future, little children will be taught the alphabet through the use of concepts from the Holocaust. He suggests that kindergarten children might sing the following alphabet song, with reference to the famous Hebrew alphabet song written by Naomi Shemer: 'A is Auschwitz/B is Birkenau/C for Camp, be it big or small/And what is D? It stands for Dachau, which was opened first of all'.[36]

In 2013, comedian Tal Menkes uploaded his song, 'Stop' [Tafsiku] to YouTube. The song is a satire on the way young Jewish-Israelis refer to every bad thing that happens to them as a 'Holocaust', and call everyone who is not nice to them or hurts them 'a Nazi'. With a ridiculous little guitar, deliberate sad music that contradicts the lyrics and his funny high voice, he exposed a simple truth: the Holocaust is not a far-away trauma but is an integral part of the Jewish-Israeli everyday vocabulary and association. Menkes, in his song, tries to show how ridiculous it is when we use the word 'Nazi' to describe a parking inspector who gives a parking ticket, a teacher who gives a bad grade in an exam, a guard who will not let someone into a party and so on, or to refer to a bad day in the office, or the inability to find a parking space as a 'Holocaust'. 'It is not a Holocaust. This is Holocaust', he sings while using footage that was shot when the allies liberated the camps. 'This is not a Nazi. This is a Nazi', he sings while moving from shots of everyday Israel to scenes of Hitler. While trying to fight this phenomenon, and showing how it cheapens the historical event, this song strengthens the understanding that the trauma is an integral part of the young generations' identity.

Black humour which indicates how alive the Holocaust is in the Israeli present also has various examples in Israeli social media. Facebook posts and Tweets based on Holocaust black humour and self-deprecating humour are a daily routine. The multiple, daily examples reveal how many Jewish-Israelis, who grew up in a society soaked in Holocaust awareness, relate to their present through Holocaust glasses: how a passing train in Israel is a reminder of the trains transporting Jews in the past, how a knock on the door can be the Gestapo, how choosing a date in a dating app is a reminder of a 'selection', and how strange sounds from the second floor of a house might be Anne Frank moving around. There are numerous examples of these references in the social media. For example: ordering pizza ('The most frightening knock on the door on a scale from one to two: 1. The pizza delivery boy who came to our house tonight. 2. The Nazis; marital life ('My wife invited a friend over. I hide in the bedroom like Anne Frank'); Family relations ('I'm at a family gathering. The levels of anxiety I experience resemble the moment Anne Frank was captured'); public transportation ('I would like to say that riding that bus is as bad as the Holocaust, but the transportation in the Holocaust was much more efficient') [37]

These posts and tweets are a part of the conscious and subconscious attempts to subvert Holocaust canonic memory agents that create constant victimization by dismantling the frightening elements through humour. But at the same time, they strengthen elements of acting out of the trauma by completely blending past and present, turning the Holocaust and the Israeli present into one unit.

These various texts which tackle the transgenerational transfer of Holocaust memory directly reveal that for many Jewish-Israelis who were born after 1945 and grew up in a society drenched in Holocaust awareness, the trauma became an integral part of their identity, even if their parents or grandparents were not Holocaust survivors.

Other texts address the transgenerational transfer of the trauma to the second- and third- generation Holocaust survivors in an indirect humouristic manner that proves that every Jewish- Israeli is in a situation of postmemory. These texts do not mention the Holocaust, but the trauma is present in the visual aspects or the symbolic aspects.

Tobias Ebbrecht claims that the many cultural representations of the Holocaust in western popular culture have turned the Holocaust into a 'master paradigm': a series of well-known, repetitive Holocaust narratives and visuals that have appeared so often in western popular culture that they have almost become clichés. These familiar historic images from the Holocaust and its immediate aftermath are continuously dissociated from their original historical background and sources. They migrate into popular culture as emblematic signs to convey contemporary themes.[38] This master paradigm is especially strong in Israeli culture.

For instance, Adir Miller and Ran Sarig, the creators of the sitcom *Traffic Light* [*Ramzor*] (Keshet Broadcasting, Channel 2, 2008-2014), integrated Holocaust black humour associations into many episodes and emphasized through them how Holocaust recollection is an integral part of the young generations' lives. The series revolves around the lives of three thirty-something-year-old men in contemporary Israel. Amir, one of the three male characters of the sitcom, uses the 'Jewish Partisans'[39] anthem' as the personal ringtone for when his mother calls, alerting him that it is her on the phone. In one episode, when one of the men takes his wife to a B&B, they learn that the place has strict vegetarian rules, including a prohibition on mobile phones. They decide to escape, in a scene reminiscent of escape scenes from concentration camps in Holocaust films (with barbed wire, dogs barking in the background and watchtowers). In another episode, while Amir and his wife, Tali, explore the genetic tests they need to undergo before getting pregnant, they find out that the Israeli obsession with reproduction and the desire to create the perfect baby has infiltrated Israeli society from Aryan ideology in the form of a company named *Highgene*, where you can choose all the ingredients to form the perfect child as well as abort embryos which are suspected of minor 'faults', such as having red or curly hair.

In his new sitcom, *Miller's Junction* [Tzomet Miller] (Keshet Broadcasting, Channel 2, 2016] Miller plays an extreme comic version of himself: a well-known stand-up comedian who tries to stay popular. In one scene, his PR guy persuades him to go to a children's hospital to let the sick children take a picture with him. Miller says that this is a problem: in these events, the sick children always bring along their families, and all the healthy children run to have their picture taken with him, bypass their sick relatives and eventually, because lack of time, the sick children do not manage to take a photograph with him. His PR guy promises he will help him. When they arrive at the hospital, the PR guy gets on a chair and starts screaming, 'All those who are healthy go to the right. All those who are sick, go to the left'!! Miller looks at him shocked. 'Why are you so alarmed'? asks the PR guy, 'it is [meaning the clear association] just in your head'! and continues the 'selection'. But, of course, it is not just in Miller's head. It is 'in the head' of the spectators, who can immediately understand the association.

In conclusion, these texts demonstrate through black humour and self-deprecating humour that all Jewish-Israelis are subject to the postmemory of the Holocaust which locks them in a constant subconscious and conscious state of anxiety, victimhood and fear. The trauma haunts everybody and humour is a basic defence mechanism. Humour is used to expose this abnormality and acknowledge it, with the hope that this awareness will, perhaps, tone down the acting out of the trauma in the Israeli present. However, at the same time, paradoxically, these texts increase the dominance of the Holocaust in Israeli popular culture, social media and everyday life, and thus strengthen the acting out of the trauma.

Notes

1. N. Kellermann, 'Transmission of the Holocaust Trauma', in Z. Solomon and J. Chaitin (eds), *Yaldut bezel hashoah* [*Childhood in the Shadow of the Holocaust: Child Survivors and Second Generation*](Tel Aviv: Hakibbutz hameuchad, 2007), pp.286-303 [Hebrew].
2. For example, see Wardi, *Memorial Candles;* C. Kidron, 'Hahavnaya hahevratit shel dor sheni lashoah' ['The Social Construction of Second Generation Survivors: Support Group Narratives of Wounded Carriers of Memory'], in Z. Solomon and J. Chaitin (eds.), *Yaldut bezel hashoah* [*Childhood in the Shadow of the Holocaust: Child Survivors and Second Generation*] (Tel Aviv: Hakibbutz Hameuchad, 2007), pp.261-285 [Hebrew]; Z. Solomon, 'Ha'avara bein dorot shel hashoah' ['Transgenerational Effects of the Holocaust: The Israeli Research Perspective'], in Z. Solomon and J. Chaitin (eds.), *Yaldut bezel hashoah*[*Childhood in the Shadow of the Holocaust:Child Survivors and Second Generation*](Tel Aviv: Hakibbutz Hameuchad, 2007), pp.304-336 [Hebrew].
3. To name a few: Hazan, 'The second generation of the Holocaust'; H. Klein, 'Hipus nizolei hashoah ahar mashmaut vezehut' ['The survivors' search for meaning and identity'], in: I. Gutman and R. Manber (eds), *Nazi Concentration Camps, Lectures and Discussions in the 4th Yad Vashem International historical conference* of Holocaust Researchers (Jerusalem: Yad Vashem, 1980), pp. 543-553 [Hebrew]; A. Sagi-Schwartz Abraham, et al. 'Does Intergenerational Transference of Trauma Skip a Generation? No Meta-Analytic Evidence for Tertiary Traumatization with Third Generation Holocaust Survivors,' *Attachment & Human Development*, Vol. 10, No. 2, (June 2008),

pp.105-121.

4. For a complete discussion of the various schools of thought, see Solomon and Chaitin, *Childhood in the Shadow of the Holocaust.*
5. P. Rosenthal & S. Rosenthal, 'Holocaust Effect in the Third Generation: Child of Another Time,' American Journal of Psychotherapy, October 34:4, 1980, pp. 572-580.
6. For examples of the first school, see M. Scharf & O. Mayseless, 'Disorganizing Experiences in Second- and Third-Generation Holocaust Survivors,' *Qualitative Health Research*, November vol. 21 no. 11, (2011), pp. 1539-1553; M. Scharf, 'The Trace of Trauma: Third-Generation Holocaust Survivors,' *Development and Psychopathology*, Volume 19, Issue 02, April (2007), pp. 603-622. For examples of the Second school, see: A. Sagi-Schwartz, M. van IJzendoorn Marinus & M. J. Bakermans-Kranenburg, 'Does Intergenerational Transference of Trauma Skip a Generation? No Meta-Analytic Evidence for Tertiary Traumatization with Third Generation Holocaust Survivors,' *Attachment & Human Development*, Vol. 10, No. 2, June (2008), pp. 105-121. For examples of the Third school, see D. Bar-On, *Bein pahad letikva* [*Between Fear and Silence: Life Stories of Five Families of Holocaust Survivors, Three Family Generations*] (Tel Aviv: Beit Lochamei Haghetaot and Hakibbutz Hameuchad Press, 1994) [Hebrew]; T. Litvak-Hirsch & D. Bar-On, 'Livnot et hahaim mehadash' ['Rebuild Your Life: A Follow-up Study on Intergenerational Transference of Trauma of the Holocaust'] Megamot, *Journal of Behavioral Sciences*, Vol. 45, No. 2, December (2007), pp. 243-271.
7. Milner, *Torn Past*, pp. 19-35.
8. Steir-Livny, *Two Faces in the Mirror*, pp. 96-127.
9. See N. Gertz, N. *Nizoley shoa zarim ve-aherim* [*A Different Choir: Holocaust Survivors, Aliens and others in Israeli Cinema and Literature*] (Tel Aviv: Am Oved/The Open University, 2004) [Hebrew]. See pp. 99-100; Steir-Livny, *Two Faces in the Mirror*, pp. 121-123.
10. M. Hirsch, 'Past Lives, First Memories in Exile', *Poetics Today, Winter 17* (1996), pp. 659-67.
11. Bar-On, *Between Fear and Hope.*
12. Gertz, *A Different Choir*, pp. 99-100; Steir-Livny, *Two Faces in the Mirror*, pp. 121-123.
13. German word for camp.
14. Kinder Aktion in Kovno – On 27–28 March 1944, almost all of the children in the ghetto (approximately 2,500) were killed or deported to Auschwitz.
15. Steir-Livny, *Two Faces in the Mirror*, pp. 160-164.
16. H. Dagan and G. Dishon, 'Holocaust-Nostalgia: Rethinking Trauma and Nostalgia in Light of Pizza in Auschwitz', *Theory and Criticism*, 38-39 (Winter 2001), pp.185-209 [Hebrew].
17. The 'Diaspora Jew' and the 'New Jew' are complex terms that have been simplified many times in Eretz Israeli and Israeli culture in order to emphasize the transformation Jews underwent in the Zionist *Yishuv* (pre-state Israel) and Israel. The Diaspora Jews were often portrayed as old, passive and malignant, while the new Jews were represented as young, vital, active and heroic. See, for example: O. Almog, *Hatzabar: dyukan* [*The Sabre: A Portrait*] (Tel Aviv: Am Oved, 1997) [Hebrew]; A. Shapira, *Yehudim yeshanim, yehudim hadashim* [*New Jews, old Jews*], (Tel Aviv: Am Oved, 1997) [Hebrew].
18. Roccas, R. 'Some of the Secrets Are Revealed', *Haaretz*, 9.4.2002 http://www.haaretz.com/israel-news/culture/leisure/some-of-the-secrets-are-revealed-1.48264 Accessed 10 May 2010.

19. Ibid.
20. A. Gutfreund, *Shoah Shelanu [Our Holocaust]* (Tel-Aviv: Zmora-Bitan, 2000), p.4.
21. Ibid., p.56.
22. Ibid., p.60.
23. Ibid., pp.174-175.
24. Ibid., p.172.
25. *Selection* – a term that is used to describe the way the Nazis selectedthe Jews that would survive or would be exterminated. (italics in the original)
26. Ibid., p.4.
27. R. Modan, *The Property* [*Haneches*] (Tel-Aviv: Am Oved, 2013).
28. Rosenberg, 'Holocaust Graphic Novels'; R. Cooke, 'The Property by Rutu Modan – review', *The Guardian*, 15 July 2013 https://www.theguardian.com/books/2013/jul/15/the-property-rutu-modan-review Accessed 16 July 2013.
29. S. Refael, *Madrich lamevaker bebirkenau* [A Visitor's Guide to Birkenau] (Tel Aviv: Sifreir Iton 77, 2015) [Hebrew].
30. Eli Cohen was an Israeli spy in Syria in the 1960s. He was captured and sentenced to death in 1965.
31. M. Halbwachs, *On Collective Memory* (Chicago: The University of Chicago Press, 1992).
32. S. Hall, 'The Question of Cultural Identity' In: S. Hall, D. Held, A. McGrew (eds), *Modernity and Its Futures* (Cambridge: Polity Press, 1992), pp.274–316; M. Sandel, *Liberalism and the Limits of Justice* (Cambridge University Press, 1982, 1998); M. Walzer, *On Toleration* (Yale: Yale University Press, 1997).
33. See in Chapter 3.
34. R. Sarig, *Chaim Shtaim* (Jerusalem: Keter, 2005).
35. Ibid., p.63.
36. Ibid., p.49.
37. L. Steir-Livny, 'Anne Frank as a Comic Figure', *I'm Allowed. I'm Jewish* (Wayne State University Press, forthcoming); L. Friesem, *Mi 0 le 180 kamash* (*kilometer shoah*) [*From 0 to 180 Mph**(**Mile per Holocaust*): *Holocaust Tweets as an Act of Resistance*], a seminar in the course Jews, Hebrews, Israelis: Cultural Aspects of Jewish Identity (Ra'anana: The Open University, 2017) [Hebrew].
38. T. Ebbrecht, 'Migrating Images: Iconic Images of the Holocaust and the Representation of War in Popular Film', *Shofar – An Interdisciplinary Journal of Jewish Studies* 28, No. 4 (Summer, 2010), pp. 86-103.
39. *Partisan* – A member of an underground military force that fights the ruling regime. In Israel, the term and specifically, the 'Partisan anthem' describe Jews and non-Jews who escaped to the forests in Europe during the Second World War, hid there and fought the Nazis.

5

Black Humour in Alternative Holocaust Remembrance Day Ceremonies in Israel

Memorial ceremonies are important 'memory sites' in the process of the construction of a national identity. Through them, the main socio-political-ideological perceptions of a group are endorsed.[1] The ceremonies, with their repetitive narrative, are used as an effective tool for structuring society's worldview, and convincing people of the correctness of that worldview. They structure the national memory of events, people, and processes, with the aim of uniting the group around collective content. For that purpose, they propose a subjective interpretation of history, emphasizing certain content and themes while sidelining others to accord with the society's ideology and the guiding models with which it seeks to shape and define itself.[2]

Official ceremonies marking *Holocaust and Heroism Remembrance Day* [*Yom hazikaron lashoa velagvura*] are part of this memory. They are held in Israel every year on the Jewish date of 23 Nissan, and take place on the eve before Holocaust and Heroism Remembrance Day as well as on the following morning and evening. The central ceremony is held in *Yad Vashem*, the main commemoration institute of the Holocaust in Israel as well as in other institutions and places throughout Israel.

As mentioned in previous chapters, Israeli culture has recoiled from dealing with the Holocaust from a humourous or satirical perspective for many years. The canonical ceremonies reflect these notions as their content is solemn, serious, and full of sorrow and grief. The canonical ceremonies marking Holocaust and Heroism Remembrance Day have a similar narrative structure: they begin with the lighting of six memorial candles, commemorating the six million Jews murdered in the Holocaust, and the lowering of the national flag to half-mast, to symbolize mourning. The *Yizkor* prayer[3] is recited in the first part of the ceremony, followed by spoken texts and passages of melancholic poetry or music. Generally, the texts are taken from survivors' testimonies or documents written during the Holocaust, relating the impossible struggle against the Nazi machine. Other texts often highlight the importance of the Jewish State as the antithesis of the past. Towards the end, *El Malei Rahamim*[4] is recited and some also say *Kaddish*[5]. The ceremony always ends with singing of *Hatikvah,* Israel's national anthem.

Alternative ceremonies are an integral part of the changes that have developed in the commemoration of the Holocaust in Israel since the 1990s. After the constitutive stage of nation-building through State symbols, Israel is transitioning to an era of multiple narratives, some of which are alternative and subversive. In tandem with the State-Zionist-Jewish memory, the detailed consciousness of Israeliness structures other memories. The changes are mirrored in the struggle over Holocaust memory in public, cultural, and academic discourses,[6] and also in the new ceremonies held on Holocaust and Heroism Remembrance Day which, in recent decades, display a mosaic of memories and counter-memories that extend the boundaries of the canonical memory of the Holocaust.[7]

The first alternative ceremonies were held in 1999 in the *Tmuna* Theatre in Tel Aviv, and in *Beit Lihiot* in Holon. In recent years, many alternative ceremonies can be found in additional places in Tel Aviv and other cities in Israel.[8] The most successful alternative ceremony in the past few years is *Remembrance in the Living Room* [*Zicaron basalon*]: a platform that invites Israelis to gather on the eve of Holocaust and Heroism Remembrance Day in the intimacy of living rooms and discuss the Holocaust. These ceremonies reject the National-Zionist aspect of the canonical ceremonies and instead, spotlight individual voices, stories, and perceptions that are not represented in the canonical ceremonies. In a very informal, unorthodox manner, they present ways in which the Holocaust shapes Israeli identity in the present. In so doing, they extend the borders of the Holocaust Remembrance Day ceremonies and of Holocaust remembrance in Israel. The ceremonies in *Tmuna* and the *Remembrance in the Living Room* gatherings still take place every year; the ceremony in *Beit Lihiot* ended in 2012 when Zipi Kichler, the guiding spirit behind this unusual ceremony, retired. This chapter deals with the various characteristics of Holocaust humour in *Tmuna, Remembrance in the Living Room* and *Beit Lihiot* alternative ceremonies.

The *Tmuna* Ceremonies

The pioneer of the alternative ceremonies at the *Tmuna* Theatre is Sahara Blau, a second-generation Holocaust survivor, an author, journalist and an artist. Blau relates that when she relocated to Tel Aviv in the late 1990s, she was appalled to see that her new friends' plan for Holocaust and Heroism

Remembrance Day included the renting of movies from a vending machine to get them through the evening. She decided to create an alternative ceremony, an event with which even people sated by the canonical ceremonies could identify. Blau called the first ceremony, held in 1999, 'Preservation and Memory'. She distributed leaflets and pinned them to trees in Tel Aviv but the response was negligible. The following year, she renamed the ceremony 'An Alternative Holocaust Remembrance Day Ceremony' and held it at *Logos* – then, a popular Tel Aviv pub. The new, trendy setting, coupled with the different name, made clear the difference between her ceremony and the official ceremonies. It projected youth and innovation regarding the Holocaust, piqued curiosity, and people turned up. Since then, the ceremony's new home is the *Tmuna* Theater, a fringe theater that offers an appropriate setting for the ceremony and its classification as 'alternative'. *Tmuna* is small, crowded, and unofficial, with a neighborhood ambiance and no need to show invitations.

The alternative ceremonies at the *Tmuna* Theater were condemned in the beginning of the 2000s by prominent public figures, among them Holocaust survivors, who maintained that they cheapened the Holocaust, and that the event was nothing more than a stand-up comedy and jokes at the victims' expense. Over time, though, criticism of the ceremonies has lessened. The audiences attending the ceremonies became more heterogeneous. From an esoteric phenomenon that threatened one of Israeli society's founding myths, the alternative ceremony model has now entered the mainstream, and its success has led to its emulation in other places in Israel.[9] Despite the original intention to produce a small-scale, intimate ceremony, each year more people attended.[10] In 2011, the *Tmuna* theatre opened another auditorium and the events in the main hall were shown on large screens, but in 2016, the ceremony returned to the small auditorium because fewer people attended.[11] Until 2011, Blau produced the ceremony with Avi Gibson-Barel, an actor and theatre director, but then announced that she was leaving the role due to the emotional stress that the ceremony causes her. Gibson-Barel continues to produce it with Sarit Sabo, one of producers of this ceremony from its beginnings, while Blau has the significant role of giving the ceremony's opening and closing addresses.

Blau and Gibson-Barel hold that the ceremonies are not intended to replace the canonical ceremonies, but rather to coexist with and modify them, as requested by the younger generation's retreat from the whole subject. 'Memory's second floor', as Blau calls it. The *Tmuna* ceremonies intentionally start at 22:00 on the eve of Holocaust and Heroism Remembrance Day, when the broadcasted ceremony at Yad Vashem has ended. Alongside her respect for the canonical ceremony, Blau believes it is vital to update the memory of the Holocaust in changing times. She claims that, 'We're in an era when the Holocaust must be "sold" to a new generation in a language they understand. Invoking the six million and reciting *Yizkor* are no longer enough'.[12]

Gibson-Barel and Blau explain that the need to establish an alternative ceremony was caused by the emotional need of the young generations to talk about how the Holocaust influences their lives. The canonical ceremonies deal with the trauma itself and with the past. If these ceremonies do relate to the present, they reflect only the Zionist lesson of the Holocaust.[13] Therefore, the *Tmuna* ceremonies intentionally do not deal with the Holocaust itself, but rather with its influence on the present – socially, politically and emotionally.[14] Their focus is on the different current perspectives of Holocaust recollection and not on the historical events.

The central monologues delivered at the *Tmuna* ceremonies over the past ten years express recurring central themes that together constitute the narrative of the alternative ceremony, such as the Impact of the Holocaust on the Young Generation; the Perspective of the 'Other' on the Holocaust; ethnicity and the Holocaust and the political aspects of the Holocaust.[15] In their monologues at the *Tmuna* ceremonies, the speakers try to change the collective memory of the Holocaust, to explain that the borders of the memory of the trauma must be extended, and to highlight that these new perceptions do not ridicule the Holocaust or condemn it. On the contrary, the speakers explain how Holocaust memory is an integral part of their identity.

The narrative of the *Tmuna*'s ceremonies is thoroughly planned and anchored in a clear conceptual framework. Following the organizer's opening address, there are ten speakers who represent contemporary Israeli culture: artists, musicians, journalists and others. Each presents an original, personal perspective about how they perceive the Holocaust, and its impact on their lives and those of other Israelis. One after the other, the speakers take the stage, and between each monologue, the sound of a train rattling on rail tracks is heard. The organizer also gives the closing address, and the whole ceremony lasts about fifty minutes.

Unlike the narratives of the canonical ceremonies that are filled with sorrow and agony, the monologues at *Tmuna* are generally 'lighter' because they intentionally refrain from introducing the survivors' stories and descriptions of the horrors of the Holocaust. Occasionally, there are monologues with humourous aspects.

Sarit Sabo was the first who combined Holocaust jokes in her monologue in the 1999 ceremony. She claims that for her, it was a tribute to her grandmother, a Hungarian Holocaust survivor who loved life and herself used Holocaust black humour.[16] In the 2004 ceremony in *Tmuna*, the journalist Guy

Meroz, a second-generation survivor, bemoaned the public's inability to deal with the combination of humour and the Holocaust. He recalled that when a German football team came to play against Israel, he asked the match organizers, during his radio broadcast, if they would be bringing the supporters to the stadium by train. On another occasion, on his TV show, he screened a scene from Claude Lanzmann's documentary film *Shoah*(1985) which, against the backdrop of survivors' testimonies, was dubbed with a provocative humourous Hebrew text with sexual connotations. Meroz stated in his monologue his mixed emotions regarding the harsh comments to that scene:

> I'm terribly sorry about that scene, even though I don't believe in light satire, rather in using whatever means are available. I'm sorry because of the six million eyes of regulators and media people who 'judged' this scene. Somebody also tracked down a survivor who appears in *Shoah*, and screened our parody to him. I've never seen such an abuse of a human being since the film *A Clockwork Orange*. But this time I'm guilty. I admit it.

Meroz claimed that as a second-generation Holocaust survivor, he believes humour to be a vital aspect of coping with the trauma.[17] Sabo's and Meroz' actions and explanations echo the role of black humour as a defence mechanism for the second- and third-generation Holocaust survivors. Meroz asserted in interviews that as a second-generation Holocaust survivor, this is his way of coping with the atrocities.[18] Black humour, in the way he used it, reduces the emotional burden.

In the 2009 *Tmuna* alternative ceremony, media person and satirist Kobi Arieli, an ultra-Orthodox Jew who lives and works in Israel's secular media realm, defined humour as a language that empowers Holocaust memory, and ended his monologue with a Holocaust joke. In his monologue, he asked to remind the audience that there are many ways to remember and these ways are not wrong, but simply different from the canonical memory. His aim was to show that connecting the Holocaust and humour does not cheapen the Holocaust, but is simply another way of dealing with the memories.

Another humouristic perspective was offered by the writer Yoram Kaniuk. In the 2011 ceremony, Kaniuk talked about Jewish self-deprecating black humour during the Holocaust, and criticized what he believed to be a false notion in Israel: that on Holocaust Remembrance Day, one must be sad and mourn. He claimed that the day should be a happy celebration for Jews because they are the heroes who survived. It should be a holiday that celebrates the revival of a people who overcame a traumatic disaster and so, Israelis must celebrate instead of being serious and wallowing in grief.

But the fact that the humouristic monologues are a small part of the ceremonies reveals that even though there is a change towards Holocaust humour, this subject is still very sensitive, especially on that specific date (Holocaust and Heroism Remembrance Day), and even the 'alternative' at the *Tmuna* ceremonies, as in many other alternative ceremonies, touches it very carefully.

As noted, in 2016 fewer people attended the *Tmuna* ceremony. Sarit Sabo claims that the decline in participants is due to two reasons: the first is that the ceremony became more and more radical in its left-wing perspectives over the years and it alienated many people. The second is the huge success of *Remembrance in the Living Room* [*Zikaron basalon*].[19]

Remembrance in the Living Room

Remembrance in the Living Room (also known as *Memories@Home*) is a social initiative to mark Holocaust and Heroism Remembrance Day in the privacy of the home amongst friends and guests. The initiative began in 2011 in one living room in which dozens of friends, gathered together to try and find a meaningful, relevant way to deal with the trauma.

Adi Altschuler is the initiator of the project. She is the manager of Google for Education, Israel and a social entrepreneur. In 2002, she founded *Krembo Wings* [*Cnafaim shel krembo*], Israel's first and only youth movement for children with special needs.[20] In 2014, when she was 27, she was named a 'Next Generation Leader' by TIME magazine for her role in building communities of kindness.[21]

Altschuler says that *Remembrance in the Living Room* started in 2011 because on Holocaust and Heroism Remembrance Day 2010, she was working hard and completely forgot what day it was. She remembered only when she drove home and there were sad songs on the radio. She started looking for a ceremony to go to. Her mother invited her to come to the ceremony in the Cameri theatre. She came and noticed that she was the only one below the age of fifty. There she began to realize that her generation was detaching from that day, that young people who are not a part of an organized institution, such as a school, the IDF, the academe or a youth movement that organize ceremonies, cannot find a suitable place where they can gather and 'remember'. Altschuler relates that sitting in the Cameri theatre ceremony, she looked around and wondered:

> How did we get to such a problematic state? Is it because canonical ceremonies are too bombastic? Maybe these ceremonies don't speak

> our language? Maybe it is not the ceremonies but us [her generation], maybe we are indifferent? Or are we simply scared to let the sadness interfere with our daily life? And if I'm so detached from that day, how will my children experience it?[22]

That was the reason that in the next year, Altshuler and her partner Nadav Ambon decided to organize a social encounter/alternative ceremony which would take place in their living room: an intimate evening in a different atmosphere than that of the official ceremonies. An evening where people could gather and discuss the Holocaust in a free and lighter atmosphere, including beer and snacks. They sent the invitation to twenty of their friends and had no idea how many would show up. To their surprise, sixty people arrived. They listened to the testimony of Holocaust survivor Hana Gofrit, friends played instruments and sang and afterwards, they had conducted a meaningful discussion regarding the trauma, asked how future generations would remember the Holocaust and addressed other topics that concerned the memory of the Holocaust. The evening was very moving for everyone and, when it ended, it was obvious to them that they had to share this experience with others.[23]

Altschuler connected with known young public figures in Israel, told them about the new gathering and asked them to host a gathering in their living room, and many agreed. The word spread regarding this new and unique way to remember. In 2012, *Remembrance in the Living Room* took place in twenty living rooms in Israel.[24] In 2015, 150,000 people took part in this project in 1500 gatherings, and in 2016, half a million Israelis took part in it[25], in Israel and abroad, and not only in private houses. In 2016, *Remembrance in the Living Room* was conducted also in boarding schools, social clubs, prisons, communities of asylum seekers from Africa, Women's shelters, centres for people with addictions, and more. The Department of Education recommended that high school students take part in these evenings and the Israeli president, Reuven Rivlin held a *Remembrance in the Living Room* evening in the presidential residence.[26] 'This was the most moving event we've hosted here', he said afterwards.[27]

While the initiators were a group in their twenties and thirties who were worried that their generations' connection to that day was weakening, it became clear, very quickly, that this will become a project which will combine people of various ages and groups, men and women, leftists and right-wingers, secular and religious. It seems that in the conflictual and divided Israeli society, *Remembrance in the Living Room* is a project that succeeds in connecting the various groups and is a consensus among many different parts of the Jewish-Israeli population.

The project suggests either hosting or joining a neighbourhood group. The hosts and participants sign up via a Facebook page or on the project's website.[28] Altshuler and her colleagues do not impose a unified format on the gathering: 'there is no one way to host this gathering; on the contrary, the end justifies the means and the means are diverse. We are here to assist with the content, give ideas, suggest which people should be invited and think outside the box', Altshuler says.[29] She and her colleagues refer to *Remembrance in the Living Room* as an 'open code', meaning that they supply a platform which different people can use in various ways. Nevertheless, in their site and Facebook page, they suggest a format in which they think the evening should be conducted. 'We believe that in order to remember the Holocaust, first and foremost, we should listen to the Holocaust survivors', says Shani Broslivsky, one of the initiators. 'We also believe that in order to deal with the Holocaust in ways that fit contemporary Israel, we should free the Holocaust from its canonization, that for years alienated many people', she adds.[30]

That is the reason the initiators suggest that the evening will be combined from three parts: the first is a testimony of a Holocaust survivor, the second part is artistic and can include singing, playing instruments, reading meaningful texts and more, and the third part is an open discussion. On their website, the initiators offer free kits for the hosts and the guests that describe in a thorough way how these three parts can be conducted: how to contact Holocaust survivors who will come to tell their stories, what can be integrated in the artistic part and which subjects can be brought up for the open discussion. In this third part, Holocaust humour is an integral part of the suggestions for discussion.

Remembrance in the Living Room's YouTube channel contains skits, stand-up comedians who discuss the Holocaust and the project's website suggests that the hosts screen them during the evening in order to enrich the discussion. The website also supplies suggestions for questions that the hosts can ask in order to create a discussion regarding Holocaust humour, such as: what are the borders for Holocaust humour? Does Holocaust humour cheapen the Holocaust? Can one define what is right and what is wrong regarding Holocaust humour? Can we laugh about the Holocaust? Can only Jewish comedians deal with Holocaust humour or maybe Jewish comedians should sustain from dealing with it? Can Holocaust humour help Jewish-Israelis to learn more about the Holocaust and its lessons?[31]

The initiators of the project hold seminars for those who volunteer to host such an evening. Holocaust humour, the various attitudes towards it, its importance and, on the other hand, the perceptions that it might cheapen the Holocaust, are an integral part of these seminars; for example, in the 2015 seminars, the writer, a Holocaust humour researcher was invited to give a talk and, in another seminar that year, the film *Pizza in Auschwitz* was screened and Miri Chanoch[32] came to speak with the volunteers.

A Vigil at *Beit Lihiot*

Every year, from 1999 to 2012, Tzippi Kichler conducted an alternative ceremony at *Beit Lihiot* on the evening of Holocaust and Heroism Remembrance Day that was termed a 'vigil'.[33] These ceremonies did not comply with the inflexible regulations governing Holocaust commemoration. They disregarded the unwritten rule barring the inclusion of humour in Holocaust Remembrance Day events, and Kichler's chaotic ceremonies drew on humour, laughter, spontaneity, and unscripted, unconventional dialogues.

Kichler is a second-generation Holocaust survivor. She was born in 1946 in Bergen-Belsen, Germany (a concentration camp which, after the liberation, was converted to a displaced persons camp). Her parents – Basha née Tannenbaum and Leon Kichler – both survived the Krakow ghetto and the camps of Plaszow, Auschwitz, Birkenau, Mauthausen, and Bergen-Belsen. For 32 years, Kichler was an outstanding and highly esteemed teacher in the city of Holon, strongly involved in fostering awareness of the Holocaust and its lessons among youngsters across Israel. In the late 1990s, at her own initiative, she approached Hannah Hartzman, the general director of Holon's city hall, and proposed that the city's teenagers present local Holocaust survivors with certificates of esteem whose message is 'all of us salute you', for their ability to survive, for establishing their own families, and for believing in humanity despite everything. Over the following years, 300 Holocaust survivors received these certificates. Out of the successes of the project came the idea of setting up a place where local Holocaust survivors could go, simply 'to be there' (the translation of '*lihiot*' in Hebrew as in *Beit Lihiot*). Following approval from Mayor Motti Hasson, in 1998, Kichler was allocated a private home with surrounding gardens, where Holocaust survivors could come to spend time together, to have coffee, exchange memories, and discuss their fate. The photographs Kichler collected from them over the years are displayed on the walls and their testimonies, recorded by Kichler, are kept in the library, which is overflowing with books about the Holocaust. Many Holocaust survivors in the city consider *Beit Lihiot* their second home. The facility also functions as an educational institution for schoolchildren, teachers, and soldiers who come to hear the survivors' testimonies. Over the years, four volumes of the book *Lihiot* have been published, containing the names, photographs, and some details about local residents who are Holocaust survivors as well as the names of six 'Righteous Among the Nations'[34] living in the city.

Kichler believes that humour is a remedy for the soul that helps in deconstructing the horror. For her, humour as a defence mechanism is not an unconscious mechanism, and she is very aware of the importance of humour to her. She relates that, as a second-generation Holocaust survivor who, from infancy heard her mother cry and scream in the middle of the night because of nightmares, always had a heavy feeling of a mental burden. One day she accidently told a Holocaust joke. She expected that everyone around her would pounce on her, but that did not happen. On the contrary, it was the first time in her life she felt relieved, unburdened from the pain, from death. From that day onward, she turned the incorporation of humour into a way of life and it helped her to live life in a freer way.[35]

The survivors who spent time in *Beit Lihiot* every day with her enjoyed a warm, empathic and serious welcome; their stories were heard and documented, and the attitude to the tragedy that befell them was sensitive and cautious. Yet Kichler also used black humour in her approach to them and their offspring. Familiar with Kichler's methods and approach, the Holocaust survivors attending *Beit Lihiot* did not feel hurt or cheapened, evidenced by the many letters of thanks she has received over the years. They accepted with understanding her way of coping – a way that allied the tragic with the comic.

The double perspective of her approach (the serious and the humouristic) in dealing with Holocaust memory is clearly reflected in the ceremonies she conducted on Holocaust Memorial and Heroism Evening. Every year until she left the position in 2012, Kichler held a 'Generations Evening' at the *Yad Labanim Center* in Holon, on the day before Holocaust Memorial and Heroism evening. Holocaust survivors and their offspring addressed the audience, speaking about the intergenerational transmission of the trauma. Conducted with great gravity, the ceremony provided another aspect of the process for which Kichler collected testimonies. The following day, on the evening of Holocaust and Heroism Remembrance Day, she took part in the city's official ceremony, which begins at eight in the evening and is conducted simultaneously with the State ceremony at Yad Vashem. The city ceremony is run by second-generation survivors who live in Holon, and it features speeches by representatives of young people, city dignitaries, and politicians. Matching the narrative of the canonical ceremonies, the program includes candle-lighting, the *Yizkor* prayer, recitations of excerpts from testimonies, melancholy music, and the national anthem. Every year, until 2012, Kichler gave a talk and highlighted the links between the national and her personal tragedy, without a spark of humour. She often spoke of her parents, her birth in the Bergen-Belsen DP camp, and about her aunt Lena Kichler who was involved in saving many children after the Second World War ended.

At the end of the ceremony, the audience was invited to nearby *Beit Lihiot*, where memorial candles were lit commemorating victims from families, and they could share with others their family's stories via an open microphone to everyone present in the gardens. Displayed in a tent were works of art created by pupils from the local Kugel High School, each reflecting in its own way the narratives that the pupils had heard from survivors living in Holon.

The second part of the evening that began when the survivors went home was totally different. In the 'living-room' of *Beit Lihiot*, Kichler conducted a vigil, an alternative wild ceremony based on black humour.[36]

Around 22:00, Kichler would urge the crowd to come inside with cries of 'Happy Holiday' and 'Welcome to the party', and would exhort that 'This is a party and if you don't feel like it, you can leave'. She would then launch into a string of jokes on the subject (for example, calling the survivors 'schnitzolim' (a Hebrew play on words with 'nizolim' – the term for 'survivors' and 'shnitzel', a dish which is very popular in Israel). The vigil attracted dozens of people, and the 'party' began once it was completely packed with second- and third-generation Holocaust survivors.

Whereas the speakers at *Tmuna* and *Remembrance in the Living Room* engage with the connection between humour and the Holocaust in an interpretive way, discussing the option of linking humour and trauma and society's attitude to the matter, at the vigil in *Beit Lihiot*, the humouristic theme is not discussed: it is the given starting-point. People attended the vigil in order to laugh and celebrate life. During the evening, participants would tend to ridicule each other ('We regret that his parents survived. It can't be helped, you don't choose who to save') and to connect every profession to the Holocaust ('So you're a teacher! Did you shout *schnell schnell*[37] at your pupils'?). Every item in the room received an associative interpretation with the Holocaust. At the 2004 ceremony, for instance, when a participant entered the living room holding a bowl of potato crisps, another participant apologized for 'running out of potato peels' (Jews sometimes ate potato peels during the Holocaust due to the lack of food) and urged them to eat, using the Yiddish expression, '*Ess, ess mein Kind*' ('Eat, eat, my child'), which also sounded like the Nazi SS. When the waves of laughter subsided, the participant remarked that this was not his own joke; his Holocaust survivor parents had passed it down to him and his family. He told the people who were present that when his mother took a roots journey and visited the Mauthausen concentration camp, a clerk asked if she had paid at the entrance, and she replied 'Last time I was here, Jews entered free'.

The 2011 ceremony was attended by teenagers who had just returned from their high school journey to Poland. Kichler asked them 'Were you cold there? Did you step into the ovens to warm up'? Among her anecdotes, she described an interview that she had given that afternoon to Israeli TV, in which she discussed the importance of humour. She complained 'I wanted to appear naked for the interview, but they refused'. When someone spoke tearfully about his Holocaust survivor father, and the impact of the Eichmann trial on him, Kichler first listened, then patted his back ('I don't remember your name, but can I give you a back rub'?), cheerfully noting that even during the Holocaust, Jews made love, and suggested that they go on a date and 'start a new generation'. When he didn't react to the proposal, she roared, 'What's wrong?! Got cold feet, like my mother in Auschwitz'?

The canonical ceremonies marginalize the way the Holocaust affected North African Jews.[38] The *Tmuna* ceremonies address this marginalization and fight it with monologues by Mizrahim who describe their attitude towards the memory of the trauma, its effect on them and the feeling that they have been left out of this national memory.[39] In the *Remembrance in the Living Room* ceremonies, the third part of the evening is open to discussion regarding how the trauma affects the young generations, the remembrance of the trauma amongst different groups in Israel, and the way the ethnical conflict in Israel integrated within the memory of the trauma arises in discussions. In *Beit Lihiot*, the subject is addressed, but jokingly. Anyone entering the *Beit Lihiot* ceremony leaves the politically correct world outside, and the intimacy and dominance of the Ashkenazi world are also reflected in ethnic jokes. 'Mizrahim getting reparations now? What next'?! a woman grumbled in front of the handful of Mizrahim at the 2010 ceremony. 'Our entire lives were a mess, we lived with small families while they had huge families, aunts and uncles, and now reparations on top of that'? Unanimously, everyone warbled '*kulululu*' (the ululating sound made by North African Jews).[40]

Kichler tried to disassociate her ceremony from the music associated with the Holocaust canonical ceremonies. In the vigil, she would hand out song sheets at the start of the ceremony, with the heading 'Love Songs', and they included the songs of 'Good old Israel' (such as, Naomi Shemer's songs 'Let it be' and 'If birds could speak') together with Yiddish songs. Most of the Hebrew songs differed from one year to the next and some years, the sing-along was accompanied by an accordionist while in other years, participants sang unaccompanied. The sing-along would be stopped sporadically, when Kichler or someone in the audience wanted to tell a joke, share a story, relate an anecdote, or discuss how the Holocaust had influenced their lives, their childhood settings, and formed their characters.

In contrast to the ceremonies at *Tmuna* and the suggestions on how to conduct the evening of the *Remembrance in the Living Room's* initiators, there was no fixed structure to the *Beit Lihiot* ceremonies. Kichler tried to set a theme for discussion when the evening opened, but frequently the discussion leaped associatively from story to story, and what was meant to be the central theme was forgotten and sidelined. The participants could speak and stop the discussion when they felt like it. The conduct of the discussion changed every year because it depended largely on the reactions of the audience, which were unpredictable, as well as Kichler's intentions - which were equally as unpredictable. Inevitably, the stories ranged between tragic and comic, from sobbing to jokes, from moving testimonies to black humour. Kichler orchestrated everything, intervened in each story, hugging, mocking, crying, but most of all encouraging the audience to celebrate and enjoy.

At the 2011 ceremony, for example, the theme was the second generation's gastronomic upbringing. The second-generation Holocaust survivors who attended the ceremony described the daily menu of former Poles in Israel, laughing and weeping as they recalled the jellied calf's foot, the carp swimming in the bathtub, and the 'laundered chicken' (a boiled chicken that has no taste), describing to the youngsters how their mothers would burn off the chicken's feathers over a gas flame (Kichler accompanied the narrative with gestures of vomiting). Their whole generation, they maintained, believed that carp swam with a slice of carrot stuck in their mouth and that *liftan* (cooked fruit) was the proof that some kind of fruit should really be somewhere else than on your plate.

But then, a participant decided to tell a different story. He told about a German officer forcing a Polish woman who had concealed Jews to become his sex slave. The audience listened silently to the story and sadness spread across the room. 'How come that never happened to me'? Kichler pondered aloud, instantly shifting the register of emotions from grief to gales of laughter. Each year, Nathan Dattner, a prominent actor, a second-generation Holocaust survivor, attended the ceremony, and would respond to every story or statement with a sarcastic response that would set off roars of laughter. In the 2012 ceremony, the actor looked admiringly at the audience: 'What young people', he enthused, 'apparently our Holocaust is a huge success'. To the fact that the loud singing and laughter could be heard outside the building, he responded cynically, 'That's not very nice'. 'Never mind', someone replied, 'Next year we'll do it outside with a barbecue, my parents' barbecue'. The informal atmosphere in the room allowed participants to interfere, nod in agreement, or argue among themselves. Kichler made no attempt to quiet the hullabaloo; indeed, that was the heart of the matter.

Unlike the *Tmuna* ceremonies, but like the *Remembrance in the Living Room* gathering, at the *Beit Lihiot* ceremony, the second- and third-generation Holocaust survivors did not deal only with the present and the impact of the Holocaust on them, but also with the trauma sustained by the survivors themselves. Unlike the *Remembrance in the Living Room* gathering, Holocaust survivors did not attend the vigil, their offspring brought to the ceremony their written testimonies and diaries as well as memories they had heard. Some of the stories that the second-generation related dealt with their parents' tragedy, others focused on how their parents coped with memories, and others highlighted the theme of transgenerational transfer. At the 2010 ceremony, for example, a second-generation comic actress tearfully shared with the audience memories of her dying mother. Another woman revealed a family secret she had just discovered: in the late 1940s her mother and her two girlfriends had made a secret vow never to disclose that she had become pregnant by a married British soldier, and had his child in one of the Displaced Persons Camps in Europe after the Holocaust. In 2010, a woman participant described the silence that enveloped the home every time the radio program *Seeking Relatives* [*Hamador lehipus krovim*] was broadcast. The intimate atmosphere helped the audience to share and cry. To that end, the ceremonies functioned also as a support group for the second- and third-generation Holocaust survivors.

As mentioned in previous chapters, there are disputes among psychologists and psychoanalysts regarding the question whether offspring of Holocaust survivors are separate groups that have special characteristics. The vigil showed that while the Holocaust is an integral part of the identity of every Jewish-Israeli, there are biological offspring of Holocaust survivors, especially second-generation, who share special dynamics. The people who attended the ceremonies in *Beit Lihiot* shared similar memories, experiences, understood each others' pain, related to one another as if they were familiar with each others' problems, were able to complete each others' stories and functioned as a community with specific terminology, pain and experiences.

The political connections between the Holocaust and the Arab-Israeli conflict is often cited at the canonical ceremonies, focusing on the Zionist lesson of the Holocaust and the current security threats in Israel. The *Tmuna* ceremonies address this issue mainly from a left-wing and radical left-wing perspective. Many left-wing speakers claimed in their monologues that the IDF's acts in the Occupied Territories are reminiscent of Nazi acts.[41] This is the type of issue that could be part of the discussions in the third part of the

Remembrance in the Living Room evening. This politicization of the Holocaust had no place in *Beit Lihiot*. The message that Kichler aimed to transmit through the 'party' was universal: love of humanity everywhere, and acceptance of the other. Her belief was that when hate assumes control of people, disaster soon follows. Every nation can deteriorate to Nazism, if its people let hatred overcome them. That is why, she maintained, we must always love. Yearly, she and other participants told the younger audiences that life must be celebrated, that humour is a legitimate and desirable form of coping, that Holocaust survivors themselves used humour to survive, and members of the second generation do so to deal with their pain. Beyond that, the party celebrated victory over the Nazis, and this changed the way in which Holocaust survivors are perceived. 'We are the children of transparent people, invisible to other citizens', commented a participant at the 2009 ceremony, 'they built the State but nobody noticed their efforts...we don't want them to remain transparent, so they wouldn't stop us from being seen. We returned the pigments to our transparent parents so people can grasp their contribution – and that's why it's a celebration'.

These gatherings, which broke every taboo of Holocaust and Heroism Remembrance Day ceremonies and which were based on black humour did not constitute any cheapening mechanisms. On the contrary, the way the participants talked, shared, laughed and cried together highlighted the open wound of the second- and third-generation Holocaust survivors. The manner in which the people who attended the vigil subverted the burden of death by using black humour resembles other situations in Israeli society where black humour, as noted, is being used not only by traumatized people, but also by those who surround them.[42]

In conclusion, in line with the theories of intergenerational transmission of the trauma, secondary traumatic stress, black humour, and self-deprecating humour as defence mechanisms,[43] the humouristic monologues at the *Tmuna* alternative ceremonies as well as the topics for discussion in the third part of the evening in the *Remembrance in the Living Room* gatherings reflect the need of the younger generations to break the taboo over Holocaust humour in Holocaust and Heroism Remembrance Day ceremonies, and to explain that for some, this is an important mental tool that helps deal with the trauma. This need was strongly represented in the ceremonies in *Beit Lihiot*, which were, in fact, defence mechanisms created by the second- and third-generation Holocaust survivors who tried to unburden themselves a bit from the trauma and the constant anxiety they felt, even for short periods.

As such, these ceremonies do not constitute cheapening mechanisms. People address humoristic aspects, or take part in humouristic discussions in the alternative ceremonies, not because they have detached themselves from the trauma, but because they cannot detach themselves from it. Thus, far from denigrating the memory of the Holocaust, these humouristic expressions prove the great extent to which the Holocaust is a living part of the Jewish-Israeli identity.

Notes

1. P. Nora, 'Bein zicaron vehistoria' ['Between Memory and History'] *Zmanim* 43 (1993), pp.5-13 [Hebrew]; M. Azaryahu, *Tiksei medina* [*State Rituals*] (Beer Sheva: Bialik Institute, 1995) [Hebrew]; D. Ohana & R. Wistrich (eds), *Mitus vezikaron[Myth and Remembrance*] (Jerusalem: Van Leer, 1996) [Hebrew].
2. S. Mor, 'Izuv moadei hazikaron shel medinat yisrael' ['Israel's Memorial Days: An Arena for Cultural Wrestling'], *Alei Moed* 27 (2009), pp.25-29 [Hebrew]; Halbwachs, *On Collective Memory*; J. E. Young, *The Texture of Memory: Holocaust Memorials and Meaning* (New Haven, CT: Yale University Press, 1993); Alexander, *Toward a Theory*.
3. The *Yizkor* prayer is a Jewish memorial prayer for the deceased.
4. *El Malei Rahamim* is a Jewish prayer for the souls of the dead.
5. *Kaddish* is a Jewish mourners' prayer.
6. Steir-Livny, *Let the Memorial Hill Remember*; D. Ofer, 'The Past That Does Not Pass: Israelis and Holocaust Memory', *Israel Studies* 14.1 (2009): 1-35; Ofer, 'We Israelis Remember'.
7. Azaryahu, *Tiksei medina;* Meyers, Zandberg & Neiger, *Communicating Awe;* L. Steir-Livny, 'Alternative Memory: Alternative ceremonies on Holocaust and Heroism Remembrance Day,' *Dapim Leheker Hasoah*, 28, pp.131-150 [Hebrew].
8. For examples, see: S. Raav Meir, 'Yesh gvul' ['There is a limit'], *Yediot Aharonot, Hamusaf Leshabat*, 20 April 2012, pp. 18 [Hebrew]; T. Imagor, 'Yom hazicaron lashoah velagvurah 2012' ['Holocaust Memorial Day 2012'], *City Mouse online*, April 18, 2012 [Hebrew].
9. See examples in: Steir-Livny, 'Alternative Memory'.
10. G. Cohen, *Beit lihiot: bein zicaron ishy lezicaron leumy [Beit Lihiot: between personal and collective memory]*, Seminar (Sapir Academic College: Department of Culture, Creation and Production Department, 2011) [Hebrew].
11. S. Sabo, 'Alternative Ceremonies', *International Experts Seminar on Holocaust Education*, Massuah, 19 May 2016.
12. D. Hakim, 'Hayey saharah', ['The Life of Sarah'], *Haaretz*, 18 February 2003 [Hebrew] http://www.haaretz.co.il/hasite/pages/ShArtPE.jhtml?itemNo=264761&contrassID=2&subContrassID=13&sbSubContrassID=0 Accessed 12 October 2014 [Hebrew]; M. Yudelevitz, 'A makeover for the Holocaust', *YNET*, 29 April 2003 http://www.ynet.co.il/articles/0,7340,L-2594315,00.html Accessed 10.5.2012 [Hebrew].
13. Y. Esterkin, 'Az veachsahiv – al elo zrachim onim hatkasim haalternativim' ['Then and now –What needs does the alternative ceremony answer?'], *NRG*, 18 April 2012, http://www.nrg.co.il/online/47/ART2/358/706.html?hp=47&cat=306&loc=68 Accessed on 14 April 2012 [Hebrew].

14. Esterkin, *Then and now*.
15. Steir-Livny, 'Alternative Memory'.
16. Sabo, 'Alternative Ceremonies'.
17. Yudelevitz, 'A Makeover'.
18. Ibid.
19. Sabo, 'Alternative Ceremonies'.
20. A. Altschuler- A Biography, *TEDx*, http://www.tedxjerusalem.com/speaker/adi-altschuler/ Accessed 1 July 2016.
21. V. S. Press,' Young Israeli social entrepreneur named 'leader of tomorrow' by TIME magazine', *Israel 21c*, 29.9.2014 http://www.israel21c.org/young-israeli-social-entrepreneur-named-leader-of-tomorrow-by-time-magazine/ Accessed 1 July 2016.
22. Altshuler, a suggestion.
23. A. Altschuler, 'Hazaa lemifgashim slternativim lezichron hashoah' ['A suggestion for alternative encounters to commemorate the Holocaust'], *YNET*, 7.4.2012 http://www.ynet.co.il/articles/0,7340,L-4216611,00.html Accessed 1 July 2016 [Hebrew].
24. K. Shalhevet, 'Zicaron basalon' ['*Remembrance in the Living Room*], *Local*, 19.4.2012 http://www.local.co.il/hod-hasharon/94415/article/Accessed 1 July 2016 [Hebrew].
25. Channel 7, 'Zikaron basalon – basalon shel hanasi' ['*Remembrance in the Living Room* – In the president's living room'] *Channel 7*, 3.5.2016 http://www.inn.co.il/News/News.aspx/321257 [Hebrew] Accessed 1 July 2016.
26. Channel 7, '*Remembrance in the Living Room*'.
27. A. Azulay, 'Lehangish et hazicaron lecol ehad' ['Making the memory accessible for everyone'], *Israel Today*, 1.5.2016 http://www.israelhayom.co.il/opinion/377587 Accessed 10 July 2016 [Hebrew]; J. L. Balint, ' Remembering the Holocaust in Israel's National Living Room', *IsraelForever*, 7.4.2016 http://israelforever.org/interact/blog/remembering_the_holocaust_in_israels_national_living_room/ Accessed 10 April 2016.
28. Balint, ' Remembering the Holocaust'.
29. Altshuler, a suggestion.
30. M. Nofa, 'Zikaron basalon: letzayen et hashoah bezura kzat aheret ['*Remembrance in the Living Room*: Remembering in a different way'], *City Mouse*, 12.4.2015 http://www.mouse.co.il/CM.articles_item,720,209,78320,.aspx Accessed 1.5.2016 [Hebrew].
31. 'Shoah bechol makom' ['Holocaust everywhere'], *Remembrance in the Living Room website*: http://www.zikaronbasalon.com/#!blank-6/frbrq Accessed 1 July 2016.
32. See Chapter 4.
33. *A vigil* refers to a Hebrew term that describes the custom of reading the Psalms until dawn during the night of the Shavuot holiday.
34. *Righteous Among the Nations* are non-Jews who acted against Nazi tyranny and helped Jews during the Holocaust.
35. Z. Kichler, 'Hahumor shel bnei hador hasheni lashoah' ['Second-generation Holocaust humour'] *The New Memory of the Holocaust Conference*, The Open University, February 2015 [Hebrew].
36. With Kichler's retirement ('I've divorced Hitler', she says), her successor did not continue the yearly vigil, and since 2012, there are no other ceremonies in Israel that 'celebrate' the Holocaust and Heroism evening like she did.
37. A well-known phrase, meaning 'quickly, quickly' from German Holocaust films.
38. H. Yablonka, *Harhek mehamesila: Hamizrahim vehashoah [Off the Beaten Track: The Mizrahim and the Holocaust*] (Tel Aviv: Misskal-Yedioth Aharonot Books, 2008) [Hebrew]; Steir-Livny, *Let the memorial hill remember*, pp. 113-148.

39. Steir-Livny, 'Alternative Memory'.
40. Regarding the use of *Mizrahim* in Holocaust humour, see Chapter 8.
41. Steir-Livny, 'Alternative Memory'.
42. See Chapter 3.

6

Satirizing the Instrumentalization and the Commercialization of the Holocaust

In his book *Laughter: An Essay on the Meaning of the Comic* (1900), Jewish-French philosopher Henri Bergson laid the foundations of what would later be known as the social theory of humour and laughter. He saw laughter and the comic as sociological phenomena, a tool with which society punishes individuals who deviate from the norms it dictates. Bergson also emphasizes the educational role of humour. Laughter is meant to humiliate the person who is its object, thus driving him/her to amend their shortcomings.[1]

Freud's perception is that aggressive humour is a conversion of what previously was physical aggressiveness. Since society criticizes physical aggressiveness, people invented another way to release their aggressions through humour. This conversion is a result of education, cultural developments and cultural prohibitions. These prohibitions are notable in social norms of behaviour or rules, and when breaking them, results in punishments.[2] However, this kind of humour allows individuals to express hostility and respond to many frustrations while enjoying the possibility of a punishment-free offence. It takes on various different forms, from direct, blunt insults to sophisticated and nuanced wordplays.[3]

Later research asserts that laughter can have the power to change not merely the personal behaviour of one individual, but also the behaviour of institutions and even whole societies. Humour ridicules ugly human phenomena in the hope that by doing so, it will be able to eradicate and improve them. Laughter evoked by presentation of the absurd is meant to rectify the world, to increase attention to the injustice that exists in the society. Moreover, many times with the help of humour, a message is more easily conveyed than when using didactic methods.[4] Humour makes the spectators laugh, that is, it gives them emotional pleasure by throwing the absurd into prominence. Their laughter focuses on the phenomenon that the writer of the text considers in need of improvement.[5]

The arts and the various means of mass communication are the way by which humour can fulfill this role. For example, Sayed Kashua, an Arab-Israeli[6], and one of the most prominent writers in Israel, succeeded in putting

Arab-Israelis on prime time TV in his satire *Arab Work*, a successful series that tells the story of Arab-Israeli families and their relations with Jewish-Israelis. In contrast to the marginalization of Arab-Israelis on Israeli television and their problematic images,[7] *Arab Labor* heralded a change. It was written and acted by members from the Arab-Israeli minority; it focused on their lives, and Arabic was its dominant language (80% of the dialogues were in Arabic). Kashua notes that 'padding the screen'[8] was necessary, in order to expose Jewish-Israelis to their problematic attitudes towards Arab-Israelis. He claims:

> I use a lot of humor, and I follow the saying that if you want to tell people the truth, you better make them laugh first, otherwise, they will shoot you. So I can tell you a joke and maybe you will laugh at the beginning. But it's not about telling jokes. I tell you a joke to make you listen to me, and then maybe I will tell you another joke that we can laugh at together and feel equal. And then I will tell you a story hopefully that will make you cry.[9]

Comic and satire have the same function - to 'reform society' - but there are several important qualitative differences between them. Comedy's criticism of life emphasizes the human side of events and behaviour, the good aspects as well as the bad ones. Satire, on the other hand, scourges certain events, sometimes with brutality, and emphasizes their negative aspects almost entirely. As to preferred topics, comedy focuses on general human characteristics, such as miserliness, hypocrisy, and snobbery. These are to be found in every society, and a humourous presentation of them speaks to everybody. Comedies, therefore, can readily be translated and put on stage in different countries without losing their relevance. Satire, in general, focuses on situations specific to a given society and period. To understand the nuances of the satire, the spectator must know the society in question. Hence, satire can only rarely be transferred from one society to another. In addition, since comedy criticizes general phenomena that are fundamentally human and 'eternal', the writer of comedy does not expect that the subjects to which they give comic treatment will disappear as a consequence of this treatment. Satire desires to change actualities, and the element of aggression in satire is certainly far more prominent and embittered than in comedy.[10]

Satiric discourse usually combines three major functions of humour and carries them out simultaneously: the aggressive function, the intellectual function that give the satirists a feeling of superiority, and a social function that helps reinforce intra- and inter-group bounds, strengthening the cohesiveness of interpersonal relationships, and is very important especially for opposition groups.[11]

Aggression is one of the instinctive impulses of humankind, but every society knows that allowing the expression of aggression might lead to destruction; therefore, each society employs a set of rules prohibiting manifestations of aggression. At the same time, society knows that it is advisable to find methods to express that impulse. Thus, every society designs its own mechanisms to unleash aggression, so-called 'pressure relief valves'.[12] Humour is a tool for venting aggression in a way that does not threaten the structure of social relations.[13]

Aggressive humour motivated by the need to feel superior allows the expression of hostility toward those of equal status and even higher status. In this manner, humour fulfills its aggressive function, and helps its creators obtain a momentary yet enjoyable feeling of superiority. It is the laughter of the helpless, releasing the feelings of vengeance and contempt. This kind of humour allows the helpless to rise above their oppressors, even if for a moment.[14] By directing the darts of humour toward persons of stature, one can remove their superiority and avenge them for the frustrations they have caused.[15] For a short while, humour can make feelings of anger, depression and anxiety disappear and can strengthen social cohesion amongst those who experience these feelings.

The Battle over Holocaust Memory on Israeli TV

Israel, among other countries, has transitioned in the past two decades from a 'melting-pot' policy and ideology to multicultural awareness. This change raises a range of questions about the identity, rights, and representation of different groups and sectors.[16] Television, alongside other forms of mass media, is a major player in the field of culture, having an important role in the politics of recognition and in shaping the identity of individuals and groups. Television is a dominant arena in the battle over Holocaust memory that has been waged between different groups in Israel over recent decades.[17] Yet if we accept the Bourdieuian picture in which actors in the cultural field struggle for recognition, legitimacy, dominance, and prestige, and where possessors of prestige will strive to boost and preserve their legitimacy and dominance, we can assume that, since television is owned and managed by power groups in society, it will try to bulwark its hegemony and immobilize the margins.[18] Indeed, such a tendency can be seen in the Israeli context, where television (and particularly the three main channels - 1, 10, and 22) attempts to conserve, even in this multicultural era, a kind of tribal campfire that helps shore up the sense of national pride, and endorses Jewish and

Zionist values. This is particularly noticeable in televised broadcasts at times of crisis, and during Jewish and national holidays.[19]

Bearing all this in mind, and despite the power-driven hegemonic discourse, others believe that television also provides opportunities for change. John Fiske maintains that it would be a mistake to assume that television is an agent for preserving the status quo, and that it is not involved in social or cultural changes. Popular television narratives are not flat or one-dimensional, and in most cases are open and polysemic, with multiple interpretations. Fiske holds that one can construe television texts through three pivotal readings: the dominant-hegemonic reading, which fully adopts the dominant ideology's codes; an oppositionary reading, which undermines the hegemonic codes and positions alternatives from the perspective of minorities and weakened groups; and a polysemic reading, typified by a combination of hegemonic and subversive positions. Since commercial television aims to attract broad and different groups, it must create texts that enable various subcultures to elicit varied meanings from them. Popular television texts are therefore open and possess multiple meanings,[20] and different readers can imbue the same text with a range of meanings.[21] Contemporary cultures examine themselves through their art, maintain Horace Newcomb and Paul Hirsch, who address television as a 'cultural forum': a spectrum in which controversial, diverse issues and points of view can be openly discussed almost without punishment, and it presents a multiplicity of meanings rather than a monolithic point of view.[22]

Television's status as a guardian of the hegemony, on the one hand, and as a presenter of certain subversive content, on the other, becomes more complex where humourous skits are concerned, due to humour's polysemic nature.[23] With the help of humour, the hegemony can preserve the narrative it seeks to promote, yet it has the subversive potential to present positions contradicting the hegemonic ones, and to deconstruct those positions.[24] On the one hand, humourous skits are generally perceived as a tool for representing superficial, reproduced stereotypes,[25] and to strengthen hegemonic control.[26] Yet, on the other hand, the comic dimension may leave room for criticism by creating a carnivalesque situation enabling a temporary release from inflexible hierarchies;[27] by building antithetical frameworks of context between the possible and the unfeasible;[28] by generating conflict between different meanings;[29] or by exaggerating and vulgarizing stereotypes to the point where they are diminished or shattered.[30]

Satirical skits that have been broadcast on major Israeli television channels since the 1990s and address the Holocaust, among other issues, protest against the way collective memory agents exploit the Holocaust by instrumentalizing it and commercializing it. These skits vent the frustration of groups who feel that Holocaust memory is being manipulated and used in order to achieve personal and collective profits. They also strengthen social cohesion amongst these groups by creating their own 'forbidden language': Holocaust humour in a society in which the canonical memory rejects it.

The most successful TV satire shows in Israel that address these issues were and are *The Chamber Quintet, It's a Wonderful Country* [*Eretz nehederet*] (Keshet Productions, Channel 2-Keshet, 2003- present), and *The Nation's Back* [*Gav hauma*] (Channel 10, 2014-present, formerly, *The State of the Nation* [*Mazav hauma*], Keshet Productions, Channel 2, 2010-201)]. Diverging from arguments that these satirical skits addressing the Holocaust disrespect the Holocaust and its survivors, or trivialize the Holocaust and Nazism, this chapter maintains that, instead, they articulate the powerful position the Holocaust holds as a constituting event in the consciousness and identity of younger generations in Israel. The satirists do not diminish the Holocaust but rather critique the instrumentalization and commercialization of Holocaust memory in Israel. They use satire as a rhetorical strategy for venting frustration and improving society. Many times they use intellectual humour in order to ridicule the carriers of these phenomena and feel superior even for a few minutes. By doing so, they reveal a new intellectual, ideological, and an aesthetic point of view of the collective memory of the cataclysm. The chapter will also show how sometimes, in their need to critique, the satirists who protest against the use of the Holocaust instrumentalize the Holocaust themselves.

Criticizing the Commercialization of the Holocaust

Some skits criticize the way Israeli society has turned the Holocaust into a commodity. The aggressive black humour does not deal with the historical trauma or the Holocaust survivors, but with the people who use the Holocaust in contemporary Israel in the name of the victims to gain profit - be it financial, national or personal.

The skit, 'The railway agents' ['Sochnei hamesilot'] by *The Chamber Quintet*, represents an Israeli (Shai Avivi) entering a tourist agency who overhears the tourist agent's phone conversation. She is trying to sell a tourism package. She begins with a touring deal to a resort in Turkey, then continues in the same tone and very naturally tries to sell a different tour deal to the concentration camps museums in Poland. In a didactic voice she recommends:

> I have a weekend in Poland that includes a visit to three concentration camps [...] I have a whole week in Poland that includes seven concentration camps and a shopping day in Warsaw, and I have a tour in all of Poland that includes visits to all the concentration camps, including Auschwitz, but it doesn't include a day for shopping in Warsaw.

She recommends taking the tour to see all of the concentration camps museums in Poland and mentions in the same didactic tone that her nephew cried in Auschwitz. As the phone conversation develops and continues, the camera focuses on the waiting Israeli fidgeting uncomfortably in his chair. When he wants to protest ('I don't want to offend you but it sounds horrible'), the tourist agent doesn't understand the problem ('Well, what happened there was pretty terrible, wasn't it'?). The skit claims that the commercialization of the Holocaust has made Israelis numb. It deals with the superficiality of Holocaust memory and the way the historical trauma is turned into a tourist attraction.

Another critique on the commercialization of the Holocaust in Israel was reflected in a skit broadcast in *It's a Wonderful Country* in 2004. The skit was broadcast after a terror attack in the Sinai desert (Israelis used to take many vacations in the Sinai) and at a time when warnings regarding travel were published in Israeli media. In the skit, a travel agent (Tal Friedman) suggests that a couple (Orna Banai and Dov Navon) worried about flying to dangerous places consider flying to a concentration camp memorial site. When they arrive at the site, the woman remarks that she feels really safe because of the watchtowers and the electrified fence. The skit sparked numerous complaints to the Israeli Second Television and Radio Authority as well as to Yad Vashem. Keshet, the show's production company, responded that there had been no intention to ridicule the Holocaust or use its memory as entertainment. Its spokesperson pointed out that *It's a Wonderful Country* is a humourous and satirical program whose skits are intended not solely to provoke laughter but also to warn – even to shock. He claimed that the skit was an allegory for the state of fear that Israelis lived in after the recent terror attack in Sinai and warnings regarding overseas travel, which added to the sense of siege.[31]

The skit criticizes the 'industry of fear' in Israel[32] which feeds off recurrent warnings about the likelihood of terrorist attacks. Criticism is directed not only to the threats but toward their reflection in the media, and the way it combines well with the transformation of the death camps to a regular sightseeing attraction as in any other vacation. According to the skits, the commercialization of the Holocaust eliminates the former death camps' historical value by turning them into a simple tourist attraction.

The critique regarding the commercialization of the Holocaust is not targeted only towards Israelis, but also towards film makers who have affected Holocaust remembrance worldwide. The skit, 'Schindler's List' ['Reshimat schindler'], created by *The Chamber Quintet*, combines a parody of Claude Lanzmann's *Shoah* (1984) and a parody of Steven Spielberg's *Schindler's List*: an interviewer with a French accent is walking through a field interviewing a man (Rami Heuberger, who was also an actor in *Schindler's List*) who tells him about an impressive-looking man stepping out of a car one night. He describes hardships, fear, anxiety. The skit is structured like a documentary interview with a Holocaust survivor, resembling many interviews in Lanzmann's *Shoah*. 'And was it Schindler'? asks the interviewer at the end of the conversation. The interviewee fails to understand: 'It was Spielberg yelling at everybody, saying that it was all bad and that we need to redo everything. It was awful [...] afterwards they paid us and we went home [...] they paid little, very little [...] he received an Oscar for it'.

Jean Baudrillard saw post-modern culture, as of the 1970s, as a new organization of the relationship between the reality that is represented and the symbols which represent it, a culture constantly shining away from its origins, leading to the loss of the connection between perception and reality. At the basis of the new semiotic structure he believed was taking over western culture is simulacrum, which is defined as a copy with no original – a representation of a former representation. Culture, according to Baudrillard, is turning into a simulacrum – a series of imitations disconnected from reality which do not refer to the historic origin but to a compilation of representations. The difference between reference and referent is erased, making it impossible to differentiate between reality and its representation. This leads to a cultural discourse moving from one empty representation to the next, their origins long forgotten.[33]

The skit criticizes the commercialization of the Holocaust in cinema, the way the Holocaust has turned into a blockbuster, a springboard for directors, who use the historic story and its real characters. In this skit, the historical discussion of the Holocaust dissolves, and what is left of it is simulacrum - a copy with no original, concealing the Holocaust and rendering it fiction rather than reality. The Holocaust turns into a representation narrative in all senses. The inside joke (using Heuberger who acted in *Schindler's List* as the interviewee) strengthens this simulacrum.

The problem, however, is that by criticizing this phenomena, the satirists remove themselves and their audiences even more from the historical event. This skit turns the Holocaust from an historical event to a representation of the representation, a situation in which the creators do not refer to actual historical events from the Holocaust, but rather respond to other texts representing the Holocaust as acts of homage to them. In this manner, the creators try to fight the commercialization but the outcome is also estrangement from the historical trauma.

Made in Israel (Ari Folman, 2001) is a post-modern feature film which demonstrates the way the commercialization of the Holocaust and its instrumentalization by politicians and public figures permeates to the common people, and turns the memory of the Holocaust in Israel into a commodity or a way to achieve personal profit.

Made in Israel is a black humour cynical film that describes a time in the future of Israel in which the last Nazi is caught and is brought to trial in Israel. The character of the last Nazi in the film was inspired by Alois Brunner, a Nazi war criminal who had been hiding in Syria. The surrealistic film follows a series of hallucinatory characters that pursue the Nazi in order to achieve financial profit. The only one who wants to capture and kill the Nazi because of his former actions is Hoffman, a second-generation Holocaust survivor who seeks revenge in the name of his deceased father. In order to ensure success, he sends two teams of assassins: the first team is made up of Dodo and Vitali, a male-female pair of lovers from Russia. The second team are Perach and Tiktak, two small ridiculous criminals. None of the assassins care about the Holocaust or Nazism; for them it is just another 'job'.

The time is unclear (sometime in the future), and the film's depiction of Israel is defamiliarized and disintegrated. The landscape of the Golan Heights, photographed in winter, looks as though it belongs to some frozen European country, not balmy, mediterranean Israel. The restaurant-bus in which the Nazi and his capturers eat is American territory, where English is spoken. The underground bunker where Perach and Tiktak find shelter is Israeli military territory, and the Russians' vehicle is Russian territory, where Hebrew is a foreign language. In addition, the dichotomy between the 'good' and the 'bad' is blurred. The Nazi shows some signs of humanity. He is an elderly man, exposing a feeble physique, looking defeated, saying that 'he is just the same as everyone else', and even expressing a desire to be baptized in the Jordan River in order to be purified.[34] In contrast, the Israelis appearing in the film elicit some Nazi associations: the officer guarding the Nazi describes the technique of kosher slaughtering at length, as if he relished every part, leaving the viewer feeling disgusted and creating an analogy between different types of killing, whereupon the Nazi states that Hitler was a vegetarian. Perach, the Israeli dog trainer, describes the harsh and strict measures he uses to train his dogs, in a way which associates Tiktak's dogs with the dogs the Nazis used in the concentration camps. Tiktak blurts out the numbers of deported Jews in the Holocaust like an automated machine, creating an associative analogy to Eichmann – a man of numbers, viewing the Jews of Europe as lists instead of people. All of these characters are portrayed in a very sarcastic manner. The film also creates an associative analogy between the 'death marches' of the Jews through the snow and the road through which the Nazi is taken to his place of execution, through the snowy scenery of the Golan Heights.[35]

The film challenges the manner in which the Holocaust is treated in Israel. According to the film, the Holocaust has become a business in Israel, in the full sense of the word. In the scene where second-generation Holocaust survivor Hoffman recruits Vitali, Hoffman's daughter is busy killing Nazis in her computer game. The argument surrounding the payment in exchange for the last Nazi emphasizes how commercial the Holocaust had become. This commercialization is also evident in a scene where Perach and Tiktak drive to the Golan Heights in order to search for the Nazi. Perach recites numbers and facts about the deportation of Jews from various locations. He does so laconically and with no emotional involvement, as if it were computer output. Tiktak struggles to understand how Perach who is of Iraqi origin is connected to the Holocaust, and Perach explains to him that the Holocaust is a 'niche' in which he can advance. Also, the Holocaust is not viewed as an actual historical event but rather as Baudrillard's simulacrum - a collection of images and symbols which deviates from the original occurrence. Vitali tells Dodo that they are using the Holocaust to make money, just like Schindler. 'Who is Schindler'? she asks, 'You know, the guy from *Schindler's List*', Vitali replies.

According to the film, the cheapening of the Holocaust memory in Israel can also be found in the politicization of the Holocaust which stresses the eternal state of victimhood of the Jewish-Israelis. In one scene, the camera focuses on a tour guide incoherently recounting and completely twisting the story of the 'Zvika Force', one of the mythical stories of bravery from the Yom Kippur War. She replaces the name of the hero (Zvika) with 'Marco' ('Super Marco', as she calls him). She often uses preposterous hand gestures while explaining that he 'went up the hill and down the hill, up the hill and down the hill'. In broken English, she proceeds to argue that his heroism was also reflected by the fact that being a second-generation Holocaust survivor, he decided that 'second Holocaust no be'. Even the bullets beginning to fly over her head do not cut off her absurdly enthusiastic story-telling.

Folman, the director, himself a second-generation Holocaust survivor, strongly criticizing the memory of the Holocaust in Israel and its commercialization, was careful not to involve the survivors themselves. The reason for this might be his anger at their negative image in Israeli society:

> I have always been upset by this image associated with Holocaust survivors in Israel. My mother would always show me pieces she'd find in the paper such as 'Holocaust survivors attacked by a robber' and then you see this image of a small, shrunken, pitiable person and that's the image they try to sell you. You tell yourself 'Oh, here's the pathetic survivor from the Holocaust, the poor fugitive.' My mother herself would find it funny, because my parents are the exact opposite of that image – strong and proud. I think that the Israeli image of the survivors is that they ought to be this pitiable, but as a matter of fact the people who survived the camps are the exact opposite. They are people who have extraordinary strength. Otherwise how could they have gone through what they went through and survive it?[36]

According to Folman, Israelis cannot keep on living the memory of the Holocaust as part of their present. It is an unhealthy situation that is maintained by problematic collective memory agents.[37] This assertion is pronounced at the end of the film. Hoffman awaits the forces which are to bring the Last Nazi to the Mountain of Mars with his daughter. His ill daughter is coughing and Hoffman, upon realizing that the team he recruited is not going to come anytime soon, leaves everything and takes his daughter home. The entire chase ends in a subdued tone. The Last Nazi is left alone on the snowy mountain with a gun so that he can take his own life. This ending emphasizes the message that Jewish-Israelis should stop reliving the trauma in the present and, instead, should relate to the Holocaust as an historical event from the past that has ended.

Lampooning the Instrumentalization of the Holocaust

Other satirical texts expand the debate on the misuse of Holocaust memory, while addressing the instrumentalization of the Holocaust by public figures. A renowned skit by *The Chamber Quintet*, 'Feldermaus at the Olympics' ['Feldermaus baolimpyada'] is set in Stuttgart, Germany, during the Olympic Games. Two Jewish-Israeli wheeler-dealers (Menashe Noy and Shai Avivi) have managed to enter the area alongside the running track. In broken English spiked with Hebrew and Yiddish, they demand that the starter, who is poised with his starting pistol, give the Israeli runner an advantage over the other athletes to reduce the 'historic injustice' and 'to reduce the humiliation'. The athlete, Zion Cohen is the antithesis of the Zionist model of 'muscular Judaism': short and scrawny, he has 'legs like ice-cream sticks'. Since the Israeli runner seems incapable of competing with the other participants (non-Jews) through physical strength, the wheeler-dealers summon up a stereotypic Jewish tactic

- bargaining - which is here accompanied by the quintessentially Israeli quality of chutzpah. The latter is expressed as the two men burst onto the running track to demand benefits for the Jewish-Israeli runner, not as a favour but because of the rights accruing to the Israeli as a result of the historic injustice of the Holocaust. The two Israeli wheeler-dealers operate in the tradition of the Jewish *schnorrer* (freeloader), combining their dealing with Israeli aggressiveness that soon devolves into curses and threats, yet ultimately manages to convince the starter to do their bidding.

The skit emphasizes Jewish-Israeli manipulation of Holocaust memory, and critiques the exploitation of Jewish suffering to achieve gains in the international sphere. Uzi Weil, a screenwriter for *The Chamber Quintet*, asserts that such manipulations of the Holocaust have intensified and swollen into unpleasant and disproportional dimensions: 'Someone says "Holocaust" and everyone shuts up.' He believes the Holocaust has become a mechanism for forcing people's consciousness to stand at attention whenever the word is spoken; he links this phenomenon to that of the 'Holocaust industry', which includes the *de rigueur* school trips to Poland, the selling of right-wing politics in the guise of sensitivity to the Holocaust, and so on. Weil says that using humour to highlight the Holocaust's instrumentalization is a way to counter hypocrisy, and to close the gap between people's words and their genuine emotions.[38] Confronting the pathos-ridden, political exploitation of the Holocaust, the satirists of the 'Feldermaus at the Olympics' skit hold up a mirror to emphasize, through humour, how ridiculous and wrong it is.

Another example is the skit, 'This Terrible Place' ['Hamakom hanora haze'] by *The Chamber Quintet:* the Israeli Prime Minister (Menashe Noy) and his entourage are shown touring Poland with a crew of security guards and photographers, when they use the site of a mass murder as a photo opportunity. The Prime Minister demands to be photographed next to a specific tree 'in this terrible place'. He is not really sad or touched once he realizes the camera is not working. He is all smiles, cracking jokes, entirely detached from the significance of the site. When the photographers start filming, he puts on a serious face. All he can do is repeat the mantra, 'In this terrible place, in this horrible place, Jews were slaughtered'. In broken English, he mumbles a series of clichés along the lines of, 'Look at this tree. This holy tree was watered with blood'. His movements are ludicrous: he pushes his wife (Keren Mor) aside, tries to find a place in the center frame, above the heads of the still photographers crowding around him. As he is swept away by the metaphor of a tree symbolizing the Jewish people, its roots emblematic of the roots of the Jews whose ancestors were killed next to that tree, a security guard steps away and discovers that they are standing at the wrong tree. The actual correct tree is a few yards away. The prime minister's embarrassed advisors ask the delegation and photographers to move to the right tree and start again; the politician's wife smiles her hypocritical smile. When they arrive at the right tree, the politician resumes the exact same speech, cliché-ridden and detached. With the very same pathos, he repeats his speech about what happened 'in this terrible place'. The skit shows the cynical manipulation of the Holocaust by politicians who are emotionally detached from the trauma and use it only as a political tool.

The skit does not address a particular prime minister. It does not name names or use impressions to implicate a certain individual; instead, the pathetic prime minister in the skit is a synecdoche for politicians who have no real feeling about the trauma and use it as a political instrument. Ami Meir, producer *of The Chamber Quintet*, maintains that skits citing the Holocaust are intended to show how it has been enlisted for a manipulative need to justify actions in the present. For him, the goal of the satire, in this case, is to make the audience understand the pathetic exploitation of the Holocaust.[39] 'When it comes to jokes, the question is always who is being laughed at', says Uzi Weil. 'Humour may be a weapon, so who is it we're actually fighting against? In my skits, I attack the contrast between the bland language we use and the way we exploit the emotion surrounding the Holocaust for reasons that are far from being high-minded'.[40] The satirists attempt, through humour, to pull back the curtain of hypocrisy from the memory of the Holocaust in Israel, unveil the instrumentalizationof the Holocaust, and thus try to demarcate the past from the present.

Self-instrumentalization of the Holocaust in Israeli Satire

Israeli Holocaust satire does not only fight the instrumentalization of the Holocaust, but at times, satirists instrumentalize the Holocaust themselves in order to vent frustration and protest against general issues in Israeli culture that bother them and have nothing to do with the Holocaust. They do it when they want to criticize socio-cultural phenomena which demonstrate, in their view, society's bestiality and cultural deterioration. For instance, in 2000, what satirists Yoni Lahav and Guy Meroz saw as a preposterous number of musicals being produced in Israel, resulted in a skit on their show, *The Cleavage* [*Hamachsof*], where they ostensibly want to put up *Anne Frank – The Musical*. The skit was disqualified for broadcasting and Meroz, himself a second-generation Holocaust survivor, responded by claiming that 'it is simply impossible to refer to the Holocaust on the main television channels [...] masses were killed in the war of the Maccabees and that's a legitimate laughing matter, but that is, after all, a matter of the past, while the Holocaust is still too recent, still present'.[41] He argues that artistic freedom cannot end with the Holocaust and that with time, people in Israel will have an easier time accepting that kind of humour as well.

But the phenomenon did not stop. In a skit called 'The Festigal[42] Holocaust' ['Shoat hafestigal'], comedian Nadav Bossem appears dressed in women's clothing and embarks on a monologue full of sentences such as 'they gathered us all together and put us on buses, it was crowded and children were shouting'; he describes chaos, shrieking speakers, calls for help. Only at the end of the skit does it become clear to the viewer that Bossem portrays a grandmother talking about her experiences from the Festigal. Through this monologue, Bossem uncovers how the memory of the Holocaust has become a series of structured, well-known paradigms – a series of fixed verbal images which have become an integral part of the collective memory. He also demonstrates that in a society which lives the trauma in the present the best way to portray a disaster is by returning to Holocaust associations. But by doing so, he himself instrumentalizes the Holocaust.

One recurring theme is the use of the Holocaust as a form of protest against the culture of reality shows. In one of his comic strips, Zeev Engelmayer, Israeli illustrator and comic artist who often deals in his art with the combination of Holocaust, humour and vulgarity[43], criticized the reality TV show *Survivor*[44], in which contenders are sent to a deserted island where their abilities to survive without the luxuries of the twenty-first century are tested. This creates an analogy between the 'survivors' on the island in the reality show and Holocaust survivors. The comic strip includes sentences, such as 'the images of the miserable survivors are broadcast throughout the country, dumbfounding the Jewish population [...]', as well as 'after the selection, survivors return to their lands of origin'. One participant is portrayed reading Hitler's book *Mein Kampf* and asking about the whereabouts of the showers in the camp.

The TV satire show *1.70 Meters* features a skit called 'Promo for a Holocaust Reality Show – 2010'. 'It was the most dreadful event of all', announces the broadcaster, while an animation of barbed-wire fences, yellow badges and grey frames is seen in the background, and then he changes his tragic, dramatic tone and joyfully declares, 'Starting again soon – in your own living room'!!!. He presents the new Holocaust reality show entitled *Holocaust 2010 – Israel's next top survivor* – where twenty contenders are to live in one barracks, with no water or food, competing for the love of the audience, in this Holocaust-simulating programme. The skit which simulates a TV promo includes segments from the contenders' testimonials, as do most actual promos for reality TV shows, except in this case, the contenders are dressed in striped clothing and talk of their hardships self-indulgently, revealing their stupidity, inarticulateness and lack of understanding of the

Holocaust. 'I thought grandma was just exaggerating', says Tali the model, who explains that as far as she is concerned, eating a slice of bread a day means getting fat. 'I gained 4 kg, oh my god, like, how many carbs can you eat… they don't say it for nothing – the Holocaust really was awful'. She bursts into tears, crying about how the production divided them into two groups, sending her to the left side without considering the fact that her left side does not photograph well. 'This Holocaust is one you'll never forget', assures the broadcaster. Since this skit was censored, the show's creators uploaded it to YouTube.

A year later, a skit in *It's aWonderful Country* used the Holocaust in a different way in order to criticize the dumbness of reality TV contestants in Israel. In a skit called 'The Camp' ['Hamahane'], actor Yuval Semo portrays a cruel casting director for reality TV, supposedly holding auditions for a new show. The candidates (who were unaware that they were being shot for a satire programme) were presented with the German reality TV format under the name, *The Camp – Only One Can Win*. The format resembles that of *Survival*, and the big prize awaiting the winner is, symbolically, six million NIS [New Israeli Shekel]. Rather than having two tribes living on two exotic islands, competing against each other for immunity, two groups were presented – the Germans and the Jews. The candidates, oblivious of the true objective of the filming, were asked if they would be willing to participate and what they would agree to do whilst filming. Their answers indicated that people are willing to do anything to achieve their 15 minutes of fame. They said they were willing to fight until the end and that they would agree to do anything the production asks them – get married, have children, beat up an elderly woman, hurt their mothers. The casting director showed the potential participants a model of the camp and explained that the Germans would be lodged in a hotel while the Jews would stay in 'shabby' barracks. When asked which group they would prefer joining, most potential participants replied 'the Germans'. Even when the interviewer challenged them with questions which left no doubt regarding the analogy between the 'new TV show' and Holocaust-related events, candidates remained steady in declaring they would do everything in order to gain the right of appearing on reality TV: agree to serve as cruel Kapos, abuse their barrack-mates, etc.

These texts allow their writers to use the Holocaust in order to express their disgust toward the world of reality TV, blurring the boundaries between fact and fiction for both participants and viewers. They criticize the shallowness of thought and the hollowness of current popular culture, which diminishes the tragedy of the Holocaust. On the other hand, however, one might argue that the creators of such texts instrumentalize the Holocaust for their own needs.

All the examples offered above reveal the deep frustration of satirists regarding the face of Israeli society, the commercialization and the instrumentalization of the Holocaust. Venting frustration, however, as noted, also has its problems. Paul Lewis emphasizes these problems by claiming that sometimes this type of humour can distort reality and gloss over painful and important truths. It can lead to a situation in which, instead of fighting, people laugh and therefore do not change the harsh reality but give up.[45] Ziv claims that totalitarian regimes possibly do themselves a disservice in preventing manifestations of humour against themselves, for laughter is an excellent way to release tension and frustration. Feelings of hostility and frustration may well be increased among the oppressed by the restraint enforced on humourous expression. When such feelings build up and must be held in, a kind of 'pressure cooker' is created which can explode in violent ways. It is to be supposed that in democratic societies, in which freedom of expression is given, satire indirectly serves the interests of the government. The possibility of venting feelings against the State by means of laughter offers release; otherwise, hostility might be demonstrated in far more violent forms, even outright rebellion[46]. Wisse claims that laughter is not a way to solve problems in the real world and there is a possibility it will hold back political action and turn to passivity.[47]

In conclusion, satirists use black humour and self-deprecating humour in order to pour out their frustration regarding the cynical commercialization and instrumentalization of Holocaust commemoration. Satirists also instrumentalize the Holocaust themselves in an attempt to critique the vulgarity, brutality, and stupidity in Israeli culture. But this fight is complex and problematic because, as noted, it can lead to passivity and neutralize the will to change society. Moreover, the texts that mock the instrumentalization and the texts that themselves instrumentalize the Holocaust in order to protest against general issues, strengthen the place of the trauma as an integral part of Jewish-Israeli popular culture. In this sense, they add new layers of acting out to the post-traumatized sphere.

Notes

1. H. Bergson, *Laughter: An Essay on the Meaning of the Comic*, (London: Macmillan, 1911).
2. Freud, *Jokes and Their Relation to the Unconscious.*
3. Ibid.
4. Ziv, *Personality.*
5. Ziv, A. 'Humor as a Social Corrective.' In: Laurence Behrens and Leonard J. Rosen (eds) *Writing and Reading Across the Curriculum* 3rd ed. (Glenview, IL: Scott, Foresman and Company, 1988), pp.356-360.
6. The Arab minority in Israel is also referred to as Palestinian Arabs/ Palestinian Israelis or Palestinians.

7. A. Mendelson-Maoz and L. Steir-Livny, 'Hibridiyut batelevizia haisraelit' ['Hybridity in Israeli television – the first Israeli-Arab sitcom'], *Media Frames* [*Misgarot media*] 6, pp.31-59. [Hebrew].
8. R. Zoabi, 'Haaravim neged avoda aravit' ['The Arabs versus 'Arab Labor"], *City Mouse*, 2 November 2007, http://www.mouse.co.il/CM.articles_item,789,209,18223,.aspx Accessed 11 April 2016 [Hebrew]
9. K. McEvers, "It's A Surviving Tool': 'Native' Tells Satirical Stories Of Life In Israel', *NPR*, 12 February 2016 http://www.npr.org/2016/02/12/464920474/its-a-surviving-tool-native-tells-satirical-stories-of-life-in-israel Accessed: 11 April 2016.
10. Ziv, 'Humor as a Social Corrective.'
11. P. Simpson, *On the Discourse of Satire: Towards a Stylistic Model of Satirical Humor*, (Amsterdam/Philadelphia: John Benjamin's Publishing Company, 2003).
12. Ziv, *Personality and Sense of Humor.*
13. Oring, *Engaging Humor.*
14. Ostrower, *Without Humor we would have killed ourselves.* Especially pp. 105-120.
15. Ziv, *Personalityand Sense of Humor.*
16. Steir-Livny, *Let the Memorial Hill Remember*, pp. 17-36.
17. Ofer, 'We Israelis Remember'.
18. P. Bourdieu, 'The Field of Cultural Production, or: The Economic World Reversed,' *Poetics* 12 (1984a), pp.311-356; P. Bourdieu, *Distinction: A Social Critique of the Judgment of Taste* (London: Routledge, 1984b).
19. N. Yuran, *Arutz shtayim: hamamlachtiyut hahadasha* [*Channel 2: The New Statehood*] (Tel Aviv: Resling, 2001) [Hebrew].
20. J. Fiske, *Television Culture* (London: Routledge, 1987).
21. S. Hall, 'Encoding/Decoding,' in S. Hall et al (eds), *Culture, Media, Language*, (London: Hutchinson, 1980): pp.128-138; Shifman, *Televised Humor*, pp. 1-9.
22. H. Newcomb & P. Hirsch, 'Television as a Cultural Forum: Implications for Research,' in H. Newcomb (ed), *Television: The Critical View*, (New York: Oxford University Press, 1994).
23. J.Meyer, 'Humor as a Double-Edged Sword: Four Functions of Humor in Communication,' *Communication Theory* 10. 3 (2000), pp. 310-333; O. H. Lynch, 'Humorous Communication: Finding a Place for Humor in Communication Research,' *Communication Theory*, 12.4 (2002), pp.423-445; Shifman, *Televised Humor*, pp. 1-9.
24. Shifman, *Televised Humor*, pp. 1-9.
25. Brook, 'Virtual Ethnicity'.
26. H. K. Bhabha, 'The Other Question: Stereotype, Discrimination, and the Discourse of Colonialism,' in H. K. Bhabha (ed) *The Location of Culture*, (London: Routledge, 1994), pp.66-84; Hall, 'Encoding/Decoding'; O. Lubin, *Isha koret isha[Woman Reading Woman*] (Haifa: Haifa University/Zmora Bitan, 2006) [Hebrew].
27. M. Bakhtin, *Rabelais and His World* (Bloomington: Indiana University Press, 1993).
28. J. Palmer, *The Logic of the Absurd: On Television Comedy* (London: BFI, 2003).
29. Shifman, *Televised Humor*, pp. 1-9.
30. Lubin, *Woman Reading woman.*
31. R. Heller, 'Eretz nehederet pagu berigshot nizolei ha-Shoa' ['Eretz Nehederet Hurt Holocaust Survivors'] *Ynet*, 10.11.2004, http://www.ynet.co.il/articles/0,7340,L-3002314,00.html Accessed November 10, 2004.
32. Zertal, *Hauma veha-mavet*;Ophir, *Israeli Culture*; Bar-Tal, *Living with the Conflict*; Feldman, *Above the Death Pits.*

33. J. Baudrillard, J. *Simulakrot vesimulatzia* [*Simulacrum and Simulations*] (Tel Aviv: Resling, 2007). [Hebrew].
34. The film received no funding from official film funds. The reason for this, according to Folman, is that the referees of the funds felt threatened by the 'nice Nazi'. See: D. Spector, 'hashoah ze passe', ['The Holocaust is Passe'] *YNET*, 12 November 2001 http://www.ynet.co.il/articles/0,7340,L-1302168,00.html Accessed 20 February 2006 [Hebrew].
35. A. Fruchtman, *Zichron hashoah ketzir merkazi bahevra haisraelit berei haseret 'Made in Israel'* [*Holocaust Memory as a central core of the Israeli culture, as reflected in the film Made in Israel*], A seminar paper in the course 'Holocaust Survivors in Israeli Cinema,' The Open University, 2006 [Hebrew].
36. Spector, 'The Holocaust is Passe'.
37. Ibid.
38. Shifman, *Televised Humor,* pp. 143-150; Gan, *From Sovereignty to Victimhood,* pp. 144-146.
39. S. Blau, 'Misheu amar shoa?' ['Somebody Said Holocaust?'], *Ha'aretz*, April 22, 2004, http://www.haaretz.co.il/news/health/1.961589 Accessed September 7, 2014 [Hebrew].
40. S. Blau, 'You Must be Joking!', *Index on Censorship*, Volume 34, Issue 2 (2005), pp.57-62.
41. Blau, 'Who said Holocaust'.
42. The Festigal is an annual Israeli song and dance show for children.
43. For examples, the group exhibitions *Hazar vehamucar* [The Strange and the Familiar] (Tel Aviv, 2015), and the exhibition *Haaretz hamuvtahat* [*The Promised Land*] (also in Hebrew, a play of words with the Hebrew word for 'ass'] (Tel Aviv, 2016).
44. Comedian Larry David addressed the same issue in his comedy series, *Curb Your Enthusiasm* (HBO, 2000-2011). See in Chapter 2.
45. P. Lewis, 'Three Jews and a blindfold: The Politics of Gallows Humor', in A. Ziv & A. Zajdman (eds) *Semites and Stereotypes: Characteristics of Jewish Humor* (London: Greenwood Press, 1993), pp.47-58.
46. Ziv, *Personality and Sense of Humour*; Ziv, 'Humor as a Social Corrective.'
47. Wisse, *No Joke*, pp. 143-181.

7

Holocaust Satire and Parody as Political and Social Protest

In Jewish-Israeli culture, the complex story of the Arab-Jewish dispute that accompanied the Zionist settlement in Israel as early as the late nineteenth century was often phrased simplistically after the Holocaust. From the late 1940s until the late 1970s, a distinct parallel between Arabs and Nazis was discernible in Israeli culture. Wars against Arab nations were termed wars to prevent a 'second Holocaust' that could strike Israel at any moment, and Arab leaders were described as Nazi successors. Demonizing the Arabs and forging links between past and present helped unite the ranks in Israel, and create immediate empathy for Zionism in the western world. If, in the past the Allied forces had fought the Nazis, today it became their duty to subjugate the Arabs.[1] Thus, in the Israeli collective memory, the Holocaust also became a tool in a political struggle.[2]

In the 1970s, the hold of Zionist ideology gradually began to weaken for several reasons: the 1973 Yom Kippur War and its harsh consequences; stagnation and corruption in the left-wing Labor party that had been in power since the days of pre-statehood; the consequent ascent of the right-wing Likud party to power (1977); and the growing legitimacy of multicultural trends that replaced the dominant ideas about a homogeneous Israeli society. The glorification of the Zionist ethos and the absorption process was replaced by a profound criticism of early Zionism and its treatment of marginal groups.[3]

With the exception of a few years, a right-wing government has been in power in Israel from 1977 until the present. Nurith Gertz[4] maintains that, as right-wing attitudes spread throughout the Israeli public and new militant groups have sprung up from the nationalist religious right, the left lost its ability to influence the political establishment. Instead, it rose to dominance in the country's intellectual life, art, literature, and academia. The Lebanon War in June 1982, the start of the first *intifada*[5] (1987), the second *intifada* (2000), The second Lebanon war (2006), the various military operations since then, and the new studies of the post-colonial and post-Zionist researchers from the 1980s onward who opposed the Zionist narrative regarding the Israeli-Arab conflict further entrenched this critical tendency. Culture became the mouthpiece of the disappointed left-wing and radical left-wing circles that used it to voice their sorrow over Israel's condition.

As part of a narrative that seeks to reevaluate the way in which the collective memory of the Holocaust was endowed to the Israeli public in the last decades, left-wing scholars and intellectuals claim that Holocaust memory was and is politically manipulated in order to present Israel as an eternal victim. This victimization causes constant fear and paranoia and, according to them, was and is used in order to justify violent policies against the Arabs in Israel and the Palestinians in the occupied territories as well as blocking any opportunity for a peace treaty with the Palestinians.[6]

Thus, from the 1970s onward, a huge gap between right-wing and left-wing narratives can be discerned. The right-wing continues, many times, to recycle the 'Arabs equals Nazis' equation in speeches, interviews, etc.[7] The left and extreme left-wing, however, many times turn this equation upside down and create a reverse equation in which both national traumas are equated (the Holocaust and the *Nakba*) and/or Israelis in general, particularly IDF soldiers, are equated with Nazis.[8] This division reflects the confusion and ambivalence in Israel's collective memory of the Holocaust and indicates the struggle between different memory agents[9] on the collective memory of the Holocaust.[10]

Israeli Satire and the Politicization of the Holocaust

As noted, as the right-wing strengthened its hold in Israel, the left-wing strengthened its critique in various cultural fields, often using humour to vent frustration. From the 1990s, Israeli satire has been a part of the left-wing struggle against the politicization of the Holocaust by the right-wing. Through satire, the creators criticize the right-wing, its attempts to relive the Holocaust in the present in order to create constant fear and anxiety that will never enable a dialogue between Jews and Palestinians. As the right-wing tries to widen the gaps between Jewish-Israelis and Palestinians, Arabs and Muslims, left-wingers use satire in order to protest against this dichotomy and unveil its manipulation. However, left-wing satirists also use Holocaust satire in order to portray right-wing politicians and public figures as Nazis. In other words, those who use satire in order to protest the politicization of the Holocaust sometimes use satire in which they politicize the Holocaust themselves, or use it in order to protest against what they see as social wrongs. In both cases, the skits are a way to vent frustration, create social cohesion among left-wingers and are a part of the left-wing's attempts to influence and change public opinion.

TV satire shows that criticize the connection made by right-wing politicians between the Holocaust and the Jewish-Israeli-Arab conflict address various figures from the right-wing, but the most vilified politician is Prime Minister Binyamin Netanyahu. This emphasis is the result of Netanyahu's constant use of the Holocaust when he discusses the Jewish-Israeli - Palestinian conflict or the Jewish Israeli - Arab conflict or the Jewish-Israeli - Muslim conflict. In the past decade, he has often stressed the parallels between Arabs and Nazis, Palestinians and Nazis, and the nuclear threats of Iran's former president, Mahmoud Ahmadinejad with Hitler's goal of exterminating the Jewish people. Netanyahu has repeatedly promoted the impression that Iran would be responsible for a second Holocaust. Left-wing Israelis often seriously critique these sorts of analogies by Netanyahu as well as ridicule his attempts to conjure up atavistic fears.

During the 2012 Purim holiday, for example, Netanyahu held a series of meetings with President Barack Obama in the United States to discuss, among other things, the nuclear threat from Iran, and whether Iran should be preemptively attacked. Netanyahu found it appropriate to bring Obama a gift: the *Book of Esther* [*Megilat Esther*][11] which relates how the ancient Persians set out to exterminate the Jews and how their plans were ultimately foiled. In his speech to Obama, he also produced an historical document, dating from the Second World War, in which Jewish-American representatives requested that the American government bomb Auschwitz. Netanyahu hinted that this time the Jews would not wait for the US to refuse such a request but would handle matters themselves.

In an episode screened on Purim 2012, the skit 'Remembrance Day for Shushan and Heroism' ['Yom hazicaron lashushan velagvuran'] in *It's a Wonderful Country* satirized the political links between the Holocaust, ancient Persia and modern-day Iran. The skit depicted employees (Mariano Edelman and Eli Finish) at a nuclear reactor in Iran, in the midst of marking 'Remembrance Day for Shushan[12] and Heroism.' In this skit, the ceremonial hallmarks of Israel's Holocaust and Heroism Remembrance Day are reproduced and turned upside down: in Israel's first decades, survivors were sometimes criticized for having gone to their death in the Holocaust 'like sheep to the slaughter'. In the skit, the master of ceremonies speaks of the downtrodden Persians who, under the rule of Ahasuerus (the ancient Persian ruler), went like 'sheep to the slaughter'. The phrase, 'and these are the names of the fallen', intoned during observances of Holocaust and Heroism Remembrance Day in Israel, is used in the skit in tribute to Haman's murdered sons.[13] The two-minute siren that is sounded throughout Israel on Holocaust and Heroism Remembrance Day is here replaced by shaking a rattle.[14]

On Holocaust Remembrance Day in Israel, the TV schedule is altered to broadcast programs dealing only with the Holocaust and its memory, and sad songs are played throughout the day on Israeli radio. In the skit, we learn that the TV program schedule in Iran has also been changed, and the radio plays songs of 'good old Iran' while the Israeli 'Zionists' who stuck to their usual schedules that day are slandered by the Iranian nuclear reactor' employees as 'Purim-deniers' (a satirical play on the term 'Holocaust deniers'). The skit also depicts a well-known phenomenon in Israel: when people find it difficult to stifle their laughter during the two-minute siren. Here, an Iranian reactor employee cannot keep himself from laughing during the ceremony. The hilarious role-switching in the skit ridicules Netanyahu's attempts to represent the Israelis as eternal victims. By deconstructing the behavioral patterns of Holocaust Remembrance Day, the writers showed the ease with which memory can be manipulated. The skit criticizes the way Holocaust Remembrance Day has become a political tool – yet another manner of the politicization of the Holocaust by the right-wing.

Other examples of the way left-wing satire criticizes Netanyahu's political use of the Holocaust was when on 20 October 2015 in his speech to the World Zionist Congress in Jerusalem, Netanyahu stated that Hitler did not want to murder the Jews, but only to expel them, and that it was the Arab Mufti Haj Amin El-Husseini who advised him to murder the Jews. At a very tense time in Israel (October-November 2015) that some refer to as *The Third Intifada*, Netanyahu's subtext was clear: every Arab – from the past to the present wants to obliterate the Jews. This comparison again turns the Jewish-Israelis into eternal victims, trapped in a repetitive Holocaust by the Nazis and the Palestinians combined.

The Israeli right-wing hurried to use this equation in order to prove their claim that Palestinian terror is not related to the Jewish settlements in the West Bank, but that Palestinian terror existed long before the 1967 war. Right-wing public figures claimed that the Arabs in Eretz Israel wanted to obliterate the Zionist entity and the Jews in Palestine, and the fact that Israel still controls the West Bank and Gaza, and that there are Jewish settlements in the West Bank, was and is not the reason for Arab terror.

From the other side of the political map, left-wingers responded in two ways: one, serious and one humorous. The narrative of the serious responses emphasized Netanyahu's historical mistake, reminded that the Mufti, who indeed was a Nazi sympathizer did not represent all the Arabs in Eretz Israel and claimed that this speech was another example of the attempts of the right-wing in Israel to increase hatred and racism and to dissolve any opportunity for a dialogue. The second way of criticizing and dismantling Netanyahu's statement was through satire and parody. On the internet, left-wing surfers released and shared in the Israeli social media many humouristic memes[15] mocking this statement.

An analysis of 'The Mufti made me do it' memes reveals that they can be divided into several main groups. The first is Political Memetic Photos. Meme-based political discourse often begins with a single 'memetic photo' that relates to political actors and controversies. In memetic responses to such photos, creators expose their use as inauthentic, flawed and manipulated.[16] The famous picture of the Mufti meeting Hitler is known and genuine. The surfers did not dispute the photo, but added a picture of Netanyahu as if he were there to listen to the conversation, or added ridiculous subtitles to the photo as if 'naïve' Hitler wants to hurt the Jews by denying them ice cream, and the Mufti replies 'No. Kill them'. By manipulating the picture, creators signal that they are aware of the political manipulation undertaken by Netanyahu.

The second group is made up of memes that draw on vast arenas of pop culture to create a comic effect: pop culture is used in memes as a common ground to discuss politics. As pop culture is part of people's everyday lives and cultural identities, using it to talk about politics makes the latter more comprehensible. Pop culture, then, serves as a platform through which individuals can communicate with each other about politics in a playful and engaging way.[17] There were many memes created which referred to popular culture characters blaming Haj Amin El Huseini for everything bad that happened on TV shows, sitcoms, etc. For example, on a famous episode of the sitcom *Friends*, Ross and Rachel have decided to separate for a while and Ross kisses someone else. This episode caused turmoil amongst *Friends* fans, and this kiss was discussed at length in other episodes. In the meme, under a picture of Ross and Rachel, the caption says that Ross did not really want to kiss that girl, the Mufti made him do it. In other memes, under a picture of Gargamel, the villain in the cartoons *The Smurfs,* the caption says that he actually liked the little blue creatures, but one day he met the Mufti who convinced him otherwise; under a picture of Jerry Seinfeld, the caption says that all the Israelis wanted to go to Seinfeld's stand-up performance in Israel, but the Mufti bought all the tickets. Under a picture of Biff Tannen, the villain in the famous film *Back to the Future* (Robert Zemeckis, 1985), the caption explains that the Mufti is the vicious power that turned innocent Biff into the bad guy.

Another humourous way that emphasized Netanyahu's statement as a ridiculous political manipulation, and thus protested against the Arab-Nazi equation was to plant the Mufti's head in pictures representing iconic pop culture heroes, suggesting that he was in charge of bad things that happened. For example, the Mufti's head was planted in a picture of *The Beatles*, thus 'explaining' who really caused their break up.

The third group were new versions of the *Hitler Rants* meme[18] that dealt with Netanyahu's declaration through the parodies on the famous scene from the film *Downfall*. For example, in one video, Hitler is presented as a great Jew lover who wants to help 'the poor Jews', but is pushed to killer behavior by the evil Mufti. In the second one, he gets angry because Netanyahu took from him the credit for killing the Jews.

'The Mufti made me do it' memes emphasize the need to vent frustration, dismantle the fear and anxiety caused by the intense Holocaust remembrance in Israel, not only through a critique on the Israeli present, but also by dismantling the Arab-Nazi equation. They are distinct from left-wing critiques in Israeli satire programs, such as *The Chamber Quintet, It's a Wonderful Country* and *The Nation's* Back because like other web-based responses, they enable surfers to express their protest immediately, without the need to wait for a specific broadcast each week. Netanyahu's statement was made on 20 October 2015. Surfers responded immediately and tens of memes were released only hours after Netanyahu's statement as well as on the morning of the 21 October, and shared in the social media. *The Nation's Back* addressed the absurdity of this declaration only in its program on 24 October, in a long set of skits that referred to the 'Arab Holocaust of the Jews'. By the time *The Nation's Back* ridiculed Netanyahu's speech, it was, in today's terms, old news.

There is much research regarding the complex and diverse effects of digital social media, participatory media and mass popular platforms for user-created video. The research engages in the transfer from a top-down distribution model to a horizontal model, in which the circulation of content is increasingly driven by audiences who share, comment, critique, reframe and remix the content. Memes offer a new way of civic participation, one where citizens are able to express political opinions and participate in important debates. This argument connects with other studies in the field of new media which discuss how online networks might inspire conventional political participation, and wonder how user-generated content may function as a mobilizer for citizens who are not usually able or willing to convey their political opinions in the traditional mass media.[19] 'The Mufti made me do it' memes are part of a technological change that transferred power to the individuals, the 'small citizens' who are directly involved in the circulation of political content. The surfers stop being passive observers of the political game. The social media platforms enable them not only to nod in agreement while watching left-wing critique in television satire, but also to take an active part in a bottom-up battle against the right-wing politicization of the Holocaust. They do not ridicule the Holocaust or condemn it. In fact, they do not engage with the Holocaust itself but with its memory in Israel and, to that end, they expand the range of participatory options in political struggles. They constitute a new arena of political discourse and, possibly, of bottom-up political influence.[20]

But satire regarding Netanyahu's political use of the Holocaust did not stop with the Mufti. In May 2016, the Deputy Chief of Staff, Yair Golan, gave a speech on Holocaust and Heroism Remembrance Day in which he said that the Jewish-Israeli must look reflexively at Jewish-Israeli society and recognize trends of racism and violence: 'What's frightening me in the memory of the Holocaust is to recognize disheartening processes that happened in Europe and especially in Germany then, and finding evidence of them here in 2016'. His speech caused turmoil. Netanyahu was one of the prominent politicians who criticized him and his speech. He said that Golan 'cheapens the Holocaust'.[21] This statement was very blunt, given the fact that Netanyahu himself, as noted, constantly politicizes the Holocaust.

Satirist Asaf Harel, for example, in his late night *Asaf Harel* (Channel 10, 2015-2016) created a skit called 'Mr Holocaust'. This skit is a paraphrase on Charles Roger Hargreaves's famous children's books series, *Mr. Men*. In the skit, Harel is holding a book that looks as if it is taken from that series but instead of *Mr. Happy, Mr. Tickle* or any of the other childish protagonists, Harel reads from a book entitled *Mr. Holocaust*. The protagonist resembles Hargreaves' images (monochromatic round image of a head with small body), but it is a cartoon of Netanyahu with purple hair (many comedians and satirists have ridiculed Netanyahu's hair color in the past years). Harel reads the story as if he is talking to children: 'Mr. Holocaust lived in a big house with a dog and many servants. He had purple hair and a lot of influence. From morning till dawn he kept on comparing, frightening and warning: '**it** might come back. This is the reason you should vote for me'. Turning the pages of the book, Netanyahu's cartoon is drawn with a yellow star coming out of his mouth, which looks like the yellow badge Jews were forced to wear on their clothes. Harel continues:

> And as Mr. Holocaust repeated these messages, he got reelected again and again. Nobody knew what would have happened to him if he hadn't repeated **that**. One evening he met Mr. Security, who stood on stage, compared and warned and even dared to alert. Mr. Holocaust became so upset 'the Holocaust is mine! You have

> no right!! If somebody else talks about the Holocaust, it is cheapening'![22]

While reading these lines, the camera shows a cartoon of Yair Golan looking sad and lying in his bed. Through the window near his bed, violence rages. Harel ends: 'Mr. Security went back to his home sad and upset and thought to himself that from now he wouldn't compare the Holocaust to socio-political phenomena in Israel. And since that day everybody understood that there is only one man that can warn, frighten, compare'. While reading this line, the camera shows a cartoon of Netanyahu embracing the yellow badge, as if he owns it. The 'lesson' of the story, as if taught to children, emphasizes the hypocrisy in Netanyahu's statements against Golan but also alerts the public to, as Harel and other left-wingers see it, Netanyahu's constant use of the Holocaust as a political tool as well as his intimidations which are not based on real facts, but on his will to create constant fear and anxiety in order to get reelected.

In recent decades, right-wing circles have broadened the purview of groups that can be compared to Nazis: those expressing left-wing positions and/or those who are ready to give up the occupied territories (or parts of them) for a peace treaty are sometimes represented as 'collaborators with the Arabs', and as Nazis. For example, a photograph of Yitzhak Rabin, doctored so that he appeared to be wearing a Gestapo uniform, was brandished at a right-wing demonstration in Jerusalem's Zion Square in 1995. The doctored photo became a major symbol of right-wing resistance to the Oslo Accords, and it ultimately played an integral part in the demonization process that ended with Rabin's assassination in November 1995. When Jewish settlements in the Gush Katif bloc were evacuated in August 2005, IDF soldiers and the government that sent them (a right-wing government, headed by Ariel Sharon) were sometimes referred to as Nazis. Holocaust survivors living in Gush Katif were dispatched to the media to relate how the evacuation reminded them of their expulsion during the Second World War. The settlers called the evacuation 'the expulsion', wore orange stars (reminiscent of the Nazi-era yellow star), and frequently compared the disengagement to the expulsion of European Jews from their homes. After the disengagement, they declared their intent to found their own *Yad Vashem* to commemorate their tragedy.

Left-wing satirists respond to these trends sometimes by ridiculing them and sometimes by creating the opposite equation and portraying right-wing politicians as Nazis. During the Gush Katif evacuation, after hearing how the resemblance to the Holocaust was used again and again, the satirists Sahi Goldstein and Dror Rephael wrote a short column that was published in the

Ma'ariv newspaper. It was titled 'As in the Holocaust' and they ridiculed the political manipulation of those who were evacuated from Gush Katif,:

> The settlers are right. What's happening now really resembles the Holocaust. And there are other things that resemble the Holocaust. In the Holocaust, it was hot. Now it's also hot. Now it is exactly like in the Holocaust. In the Holocaust, there were flies. In Tel Aviv there are also flies. Tel Aviv is like the Holocaust…In the Holocaust there were six million. In the Lottery there are also six millions. The lottery is like the Holocaust. The Holocaust happened in Europe. My neighbour was also in Europe. My neighbour is the Holocaust...In the Holocaust conditions were very hard. Writing a good column every day is also very hard. Writing a column is like the Holocaust.[23]

On another occasion, in the second season of their TV satire, *This is Our Country* [*Zua arzenu*] (Channel 2, Reshet, 2001), a skit was created in which the attempts of the right-wing to use the Holocaust in order to impart nationalistic ideas to Israelis was criticized. In the skit, the Likud minister Limor Livnat gives Rephael a lesson in Zionism which quickly turns into a lesson in racist nationalism and he, who follows her words, salutes her over and over again in a gesture that is reminiscent of the Nazi salute. In 2006, Knesset member Avigdor Lieberman, made intransigent statements about exchanging territory with the Palestinian Authority and transferring Arab citizens of Israel to the Palestinian Authority in return, and then compared members of *Yesh Gvul* (a human rights, anti-occupation movement) to *Kapos* in the Nazi extermination camps. He became the focus of a controversial *It's a Wonderful Country* skit in December 2006. Each time Lieberman's character appeared in the skit, he was greeted with 'Heil Lieberman!' and a right-arm salute.[24]

These skits reveal that the new satiric memory of the left-wing brings with it contradictory positions. On the one hand, these skits express the attempts of second- and third-generation Holocaust survivors to move from the 'acting out' of the Holocaust to the 'working-through'. On the other hand, they attest that Holocaust memory is still alive and being acted out in the young generations. The skits described here seek to expose the right-wing politicization of the Holocaust, to make clear that the Jewish-Zionist conclusions about the Holocaust can also become nationalistic and violent. But these skits also contain an inherent paradox: left-wing artists criticize the right-wing in Israel for using the Holocaust for political reasons, but then do the same when they want to emphasize the brutality and racism of the right-wing.

While the bulk of Israeli satire does not critique the left-wing political and social use of the Holocaust, *The Nation's Back* ridicules the politicization and the social use of the Holocaust in the present on both sides of the political map: the left and the right. Throughout its seasons, the satirists of the panel have addressed the Holocaust in almost every show; however, in the past few years, the amount of 'Holocaust jokes' has been intensified. Their number and the time dedicated to them have grown much larger. Often, the producers have received angry emails and complaints which have caused the lead panelist, Lior Shlain, to apologize while on air, and to explain that he and his colleagues are not making fun of the Holocaust, but condemn those who use the Holocaust in order to gain political profit. Most of the times, the panelists condemn the politicization of the Holocaust but, contrary to other satirists, remind the audience that this is not only a right-wing trend in present-day Israel: 'Nazi' is the most common accusation in the Hebrew vocabulary, especially in politicians' vocabulary. For example, in their show on 30 January 2016, more than 11 minutes in the 44-minute show were dedicated to Holocaust satire. The main subject was the way the left-wing uses Nazism in order to protest against TV anchor Ilana Dayan who, in her TV show *Fact* [*Uvda*] (Channel 2, Keshet Productions) on January 2016 focused on the misdeeds of left-wing activists in the West Bank. Left-wing activists were furious, and published on the satiric Facebook page *Statusim Smolanim* [*Left-Wing Statuses*] a photomontage of Hitler giving Dayan a bouquet of flowers. 'Did they get six million likes'? asked the *The Nation's Back* panelist Tom Ahron. As a retort, Lior Shlein asked 'Is that what you're doing now on Facebook? and we thought that only radical right-wingers call people who don't agree with them "Nazis"'. Then he broadcast a group of interviews with left-wing politicians, scholars and intellectuals who use the word 'Nazi' for right-wing people (for example, writer Amos Oz referred to the settler youth who committed terrorist acts in the West Bank as 'Neo-Nazis'; two professors from the Hebrew University called the right-wing Minister of Justice 'neo-Nazi scum'). While broadcasting these interviews, Shlein kept shouting 'but I've asked for right-wing people who use this term, where are all the right-wing people?' The contrast between the interviews and his shouting emphasized that the Israeli left-wing politicizes the Holocaust in the same way as the right-wing. Shlein explained that everyone in Israel, right or left, politicizes the Holocaust and uses the term 'Nazi' on a daily basis, be it in regard to the Occupation, Jewish terror, the Prime Minister, the President, or the Minister of Justice: 'Right-wing and left-wing don't talk anymore, they don't try to persuade each other, they just keep yelling at each other that they are Nazis 24/7. Enough with the incitement and the cynical use of the Holocaust. Let's explain once and for all why the right-wing and the left-wing are not Nazis'. That was the cue for a line of short monologues in which the comedians on the panel used Holocaust metaphors in order to 'explain' why nobody in Israel is a Nazi and in this manner exposed how preposterous the political use of the Holocaust is. For example, the panelists claimed that the Israeli Labour Party (which is infamous for its inner struggles) could not be a Nazi party because they weren't be able to march in a straight line and salute without stabbing each other in the back'.[25]

Holocaust Political Satire: Returning to the Past

Holocaust political satire often refers to the present. *The Jews are Coming* [*Hayehudim baim]* (Channel 1, Yoav Gross production, 2014-present) is a skit show that satirizes people and major events in Jewish and Israeli history. Their skit 'Hannah Szenes' is exceptional in the world of Holocaust political satire because it returns to the days of the Second World War in order to criticize an historical event that became an Israeli myth.

During the Second World War, in collaboration between the Jewish Yishuv (which was dominated then by *Mapai* – a social left-wing party)[26] and the British Mandate, the British military dropped several dozen Jewish Eretz-Israeli parachutists (including three women) behind enemy lines in Eastern Europe and the Balkans. According to Baumel-Schwartz, their British mission was to find Allied pilots who had fallen in enemy territory and assist them.Their Zionist mission was to contact Jewish communities, help their members escape from the Nazis, and assist them in rebuilding the local Zionist movement. Seven of the parachutists lost their lives in this mission; Szenes was one of them. From a military point of view, the operation failed. Szenes was caught by the Nazis, tortured and executed in Budapest, Hungary on 7 November 1944. Even though the operation failed, the parachutists and especially Szenes went through a sanctification process, and became a myth in Israeli culture for the next decades. They were represented and perceived as symbols of heroism and sacrifice. A song Szenes wrote, 'A Walk to Caesarea' ['Halicha lecaesaria'], became one of the songs that is always played on Holocaust and Heroism Remembrance Day on the radio and in ceremonies. From the 1950s, she became the protagonist in books, a play, and a film, and her story is known to every child who studies in the Israeli educational system. As of the 1990s, as part of the renewed examination of the past, the myth of Szenes and the parachutists began to show cracks. Scholars and artists began to question why and how these few people were supposed to achieve such complex goals.[27]

The skit, 'Hannah Szenes' is exceptional because it does not ridicule the politicization of the Holocaust in the Israeli present, but returns to the historical event itself while criticizing the misdeeds of the leaders of the *Yishuv*, which was dominated by the left-wing. It 'describes' the last briefing before parachuting. A commander stands in front of the camera, speaking to an unknown group and briefs the soldiers (using the plural)regarding their parachuting into occupied Europe and the way they should fight the Nazis.'O.K. guys. This is the moment of truth', says the commander in an extremely serious tone, while in the background there is the music of military marches. 'The Nazis rule Europe and this is exactly the time to show them that the Jews in Eretz Israel are not a bunch of fags, so come on'. In a pathos-driven speech, he orders, 'Show them! Defeat the Nazi enemy. Come on guys. There are hot drinks upstairs'. One female soldier raises her hand and in a heavy Hungarian accent says: 'I'm sorry Commander, but how can we defeat the Nazi army'?'What is your name', asks the Commander. 'Hannah Szenes', she replies. 'So, Hannah', he says condescendingly, as if explaining a simple plan to a dumb soldier, 'the plan is to parachute brave Jewish warriors into Nazi Europe and then defeat the Nazis. So, everybody I wish you good luck… '. Szenes interjects, raising her hand again to ask another question. 'Yes, Hungary', he says impatiently. 'I couldn't help noticing something', she says. 'What'? he asks. 'That the Nazi army has hundreds of thousands of soldiers in Hungary, and we, on the contrary are..' 'Yes?' the commander still doesn't understand. 'One', says Szenes. The camera zooms out to discover that Szenes is alone in the room with the Commander. But he continues as if everything is fine, with the same pathos: 'It is true. We are few but smart'. 'We'? continues Szenes. 'You', admits the Commander. 'It is true that I'm small but clever and very good in combat, but what can I do alone in front of an entire army'? asks Szenes. 'Oh, but we have a plan', says the Commander and presents in a childish manner a plan in which she flies to Europe (he demonstrates with a plastic airplane her route in a buffoon-like manner) and then she lands. 'This is the plan'. When Szenes says that she is bothered about what happens after the landing, completely unaware of the absurdity of the plan, the commander says that she will attack from three places simultaneously. 'This is the plan'? asks Szenes, confused. The Commander hurries to correct himself, 'You are right', he says. He doesn't change the absurd plan but changes the three locations from where she is supposed to attack simultaneously. 'Any questions'? Szenes raises her hand trying to ask but the Commander looks around as if there are other people there:'O.K, so there are no more questions. Good luck'. He helps Szenes get into the parachute jacket and escorts her out of the room as the narrator explains that she parachuted and never came back.[28]

The skit, at the beginning, is dependent on the lack of knowledge of the viewers regarding the number of people who actually attended the briefing and, later on, the blindness and stupidity of the Commander echoes a serious debate that is to be found in Israeli research in the last decades regarding the myth of the *Yishuv's* parachutists' operation in the Second World War. The debate addresses the myth in a critical manner, asks hard questions regarding the parachutists' failure, captivity, the motives of the *Yishuv's* leaders who sent such a small group to Nazi Europe, and addresses the reasons and different ways in which Israeli culture turned them into heroes in the service of national mythologizing and collective memory – issues which, until then, appeared in research as well as in a serious manner in other cultural fields, but not in satire.[29]

Holocaust Satire in the Battle Against Social Problems

Many artists who protest against the politicization of the Holocaust by the right-wing, themselves use the Holocaust in order to promote their social agenda. One of the main issues in this context is the debate regarding refugees and migrant workers from Africa.

In March 2010, right-wing Knesset member Yaakov Katz circulated a memorandum calling for African asylum seekers who had entered Israel through Egypt to be grouped together in a 'distant city' that they would build themselves through 'workfare'.[30] Paying homage to the opening sequence of *Inglourious Basterds* (Quentin Tarantino, USA, 2009), an *It's a Wonderful Country* skit (March 2010) addressed the theme of the right-wing's persecution of refugees and illegal migrant workers. It showed Katz, depicted by the actor Tal Friedman, as the Nazi officer, Col. Hans Landa who, in the film hunted down Jews in occupied France. In the skit, Katz is shown going from house to house pulling out asylum seekers and foreign workers. Several of Friedman's lines also repeated memorable quotations from the film. This skit thus used the Holocaust in order to claim that the historically victimized had become the present-day perpetrators.

In May of 2012, during a demonstration held in South Tel Aviv against allowing African refugees to live, work and stay in Israel, African bystanders were attacked by right-wingers, shop windows were shattered and some of the goods in the shops were stolen. As part of the left-wing protest against this event, in particular, as well as against the right-wing attitude toward the refugees from Africa, in general, left-wingers posted in the Israeli social-media many serious and black humour comparisons to *Kristallnacht* and caricatures comparing the protestors and their supporters to Nazis.

Miri Regev (at the time, a Knesset Member; today, Minister of Culture) who attended the demonstration referred to the African refugees and foreign workers as 'a cancer in our body'. Caricaturist and illustrator Mysh Rozanov, published a caricature in which Regev is approaching a group of Ku Klux Klan members. In the caricature entitled *Kristallnacht*, they turn to her saying: 'Thanks for coming to complete our *minyan*,[31] Miri'leh'. The leftist group *Mussolini Was Right* [*Mussolini Tzadak*] which uses black humour in order to protest against social and political injustice, uploaded a photograph of a yellow patch with the word 'Sudanese' written in the center, captioning it:

> I was asked how we could distinguish between regular Ethiopians and refugees from Sudan. We ought to keep our daughters from all of them so they will not soil our pure race, but the Sudanese are not even Jews, and are therefore far more inferior. From now on, whenever you encounter a Sudanese person, put this patch on them, inspired by the star which appears on South Sudan's flag. It is advisable to also print a large copy and glue it in their shops.

The Facebook group *Entrecotes from Holy Cows* [*Entrecote miparot kdoshot*] uploaded a photograph of a protester wearing a shirt with the words 'Death to the Sudanese', 'glued' next to a picture of Hitler talking on the phone, giving the illusion that Regev was calling him. They both seem happy with the conversation and the caption, 'No, you hang up' illustrates their loving relationship.

In December of 2013, following the refusal of African asylum seekers to be sent to the *Holot* detention facility, a formal document was published in which the asylum seekers were not mentioned by name, rather given numbers. Many respondents compared the numbers to those tattooed by the Nazis on the arms of Jewish prisoners in Auschwitz. A photograph uploaded to the Facebook page of the Israeli satirical TV program *It's a Wonderful Country* presented former Minister of Interior Gideon Sa'ar getting ready to tattoo an anonymous refugee.[32]

Humour, in a way, is a preservative of social interaction: it promotes social processes, such as increasing group cohesion and relieving stress within the group. It boosts the group's morale and strengthens the bonds between its members, helps obtain consensus within the group, and minimizes the distance between its members. Humour also contributes to social cohesion by creating a common language, a milieu which emphasizes the group's uniqueness. Private jokes also serve as a defence against strangers, to the extent of feeling superior to the 'stranger' who is not laughing because s/he does not get the joke. In addition, aggressive humour mocking other groups emphasizes the superiority of the group using it.[33]

In various social groups – family, neighbours, classmates, traveling partners and colleagues – there is a channel of humour in which each member of the group participates. Each member of the group creates humourous situations for the sake of the other members of the group. When the individual laughs along with the group, it means that s/he agrees with the group's state of mind and manner of thought. While laughing, the individual is reinforced by the laughter of the other members, and the individual's own laugh reinforces the other members of the group.[34] Humour as social cohesion helps people who belong to the political opposition feel encouraged aspart of a larger group. In the political and social Holocaust satire and parody of the left-wing, humour gives the defeated left-wing a sense of power, and is used not only to vent frustration but also to create social cohesion.

The satirical use of the Holocaust made by the left-wing in order to protest political and social injustice reveals that even those who want to avoid politicizing the Holocaust and its domination over Israel's everyday lives, find themselves recreating the exact same link, albeit with the contrary narrative.

Eyal Zandberg suggests a four-phase development of Holocaust humour in Israel: the first, a 'taboo' period until the 1990s in which Holocaust humour was not represented in Israeli culture. In the second phase, humour was used in order to explore and criticize Holocaust commemoration; in the third phase, humour about Holocaust memory was used to comment on other social fields; and in the fourth phase, in the last few years, Holocaust memory itself is used to create humour. Holocaust memory, once taboo, is now ordinary and acceptable raw material for laughter. He claims that this shift indicates a change in the society's collective memory, one that advocates a 'normalization' of the traumatic memory of the Holocaust. What began as a self-reflective critical look at Holocaust memory, and later developed into an exploration of other cultural fields, has become raw material, 'just another subject', demanding no unique treatment.[35]

In my opinion, there are no chronological phases: Holocaust jokes were told secretly during the 'taboo' period, Holocaust humour that comments on social and political issues began in the 1990s and continues until the present and, in the past years, we can still find Holocaust skits criticizing Holocaust memory agents, political and social uses of the Holocaust. There is no chronological development but rather a hybrid use of the many functions of humour. In addition, in my opinion, in contemporary Israel, Holocaust humour cannot function only as raw material for laughter. The trauma is integrated so well in the Jewish-Israeli soul that every use of Holocaust humour has a context. For people growing up in a society drenched in Holocaust anxiety, and living with the feeling of being on the verge of a second Holocaust, every humouristic use of the subject has deep roots in these fears. Therefore, black humour regarding the Holocaust in contemporary Israel is still first and foremost a defence mechanism in a society that acts out the Holocaust.

Regarding Holocaust humour in Israel in general, or humour which uses the Holocaust as "raw material," I do not think that they indicate a 'normalization' of the traumatic memory of the Holocaust. On the contrary, the frequent use of Holocaust references regarding Holocaust-related topics and especially general topics strengthens the presence of the Holocaust in the Israeli present and indicates abnormality. It points to the fact that the young generations who try to break free from the acting out of the Holocaust which created an abnormal state of constant victimization in Israel, in a way, find themselves locked in the same mental 'prison', as they revive the trauma in the Israeli present. They try to break the fear factor, by turning Holocaust-related themes into everyday funny, trivial events. But, by doing so, they preserve the Holocaust as one of the major themes in Jewish-Israeli life.

In conclusion, the analysis of the satirical texts in this chapter shows that both sides of the political map politicize the Holocaust and also use it in order to protest against social issues. The Israeli left-wing uses Holocaust humour in order to protest against the right-wing's politicization of the Holocaust but, at the same time, politicizes the Holocaust in order to support its own ideology. Thus, the satirical debate both ridicules the way in which the Holocaust is used in Israel by the hegemony and creates a critical gaze that allows one to condemn that phenomenon, but also serves as another facet of that politicization, thus increasing the dominance of the trauma in the Israeli present.

Notes

1. Bar-Tal, *Living with Conflict*; Evron, *From Athens*; H. Yablonka, *Harhek mehamesila: hamizrahim vehashoah [Off the Beaten Track: The Mizrahim and the Holocaust*] (Tel Aviv: Miskal-Yedioth Aharonot Books, 2008) [Hebrew]; M. Zuckermann, *Shoah baheder haatum* [*Holocaust in the sealed room*] (Tel Aviv: private publishing, 1993) [Hebrew]; I. Zertal, *Hauma vehamavet* [The Nation and Death] (Tel Aviv: Dvir, 1993) [Hebrew].

2. But, alongside this narrative, there are, in those early decades, very prominent artists who tried to create awareness of both traumas: the Holocaust and the *Nakbah* (the Arab catastrophe in the 1948 war), and even raise very disturbing questions regarding the moral outcome of the IDF's behavior in 1948. See L. Steir-Livny, 'The Link between the Holocaust and the Israeli-Arab Conflict in Israeli Culture, 1950s-1970s', in L. Aleksandrowicz-Pedich & M. Pakier (eds), *Jewish Identity in Pre- and Post-Holocaust Literature and Culture*, (Frankfurt: Peter Lang GmbHN Internationaler Verlag der Wissenschaften, 2012), pp.157-168.
3. B. Kimmerling, *Mehagrim, mityashvim, yelidim* [Immigrants, Settlers, Natives] (Tel Aviv: Am Oved, 2004). [Hebrew], pp.185-493; N. Gertz, *Sipur mehasratim* [*Motion Fiction: Israeli Fiction in Films*] (Tel-Aviv: The Open University Press, 1993) [Hebrew]. See pp.175- 288; Shohat, Israeli Cinema, pp.234-266.
4. Gertz, *A Different Choir*, pp.175-288.
5. *Intifada* – an Arabic word that means 'to shake off' and describes a violent outburst, civil uprising against the Israeli government in - the territories Israel conquered during the Six Day War of 1967. This refers specifically to the territories in which many Palestinians live: the West Bank and Gaza.
6. For example, Evron, *From Athens*; Y. Elkana, 'Bizchut hashichecha' ['The Need to Forget'], *Ha'aretz*, March 2, 1988 [Hebrew]; Zukerman, *Holocaust*; Zertal, *The Nation;* B. Kimmerling, 'The Continuation of the Israeli-Palestinian Conflict by 'Academic' Means: Reflections on the Problematiques of Publishing Books and Reviewing Them', *Contemporary Sociology*, Vol. 35, No. 5 (September 2006), pp.447-449; Bar-Tal, *Living with the Conflict*. Analysis and criticism of the post-Zionist notions regarding Holocaust memory in Israel can be found, for example, in D. Mechman, *Post zionut vehashoah[Post-Zionism and Holocaust]* (Ramat Gan: Bar Ilan University Press, 1997) [Hebrew]; Shapira, *New Jews*; D. Gutwein, 'The Privatization of the Holocaust: Memory, Historiography, and Politics', *Israel Studies*, Volume 14, Number 1 (Spring, 2009), pp.36-64; D. Ofer, 'The Past'; Porat, *The Smoke-Scented Coffee*.
7. The way the Israelis experience the connection between the Holocaust and the Arab threats to destroy Israel as a second Holocaust are known outside Israel. For example, the president of the USA, Barack Obama, showed this understanding in his famous 2009 speech in Cairo, Egypt, when he addressed the way Israelis view Arab threats to destroy Israel. His 'New Beginnings' speech showed an understanding of the way Israelis blend the Holocaust with the Israeli-Arab conflict: 'Around the world, the Jewish people were persecuted for centuries, and anti-Semitism in Europe culminated in an unprecedented Holocaust [...] Threatening Israel with destruction - or repeating vile stereotypes about Jews - is deeply wrong, and only serves to evoke in the minds of Israelis this most painful of memories, while preventing the peace that the people of this region deserve'. See: 'Remarks by the President at Cairo University, 6-04-09', The White House, Office of the Press Secretary 4 June 2009 https://www.whitehouse.gov/the-press-office/remarks-president-cairo-university-6-04-09 Accessed 20 June 2009.
8. Steir-Livny, *Let the Memorial Hill Remember*, pp. 79-112.
9. On the changing memory of the Holocaust in Israel in the last three decades, see for example: Ne'eman Arad, 'Israel and the Shoah'; Ofer, *We Israelis remember*; Porat, *The Smoke-Scented Coffee;* Steir-Livny, *Let the Memorial Hill.*
10. On collective memory, see: Halbwachs, *Collective Memory*; Young, *The Texture of Memory*; J. K. Olick & J. Robbins, 'Social Memory Studies: from 'Collective Memory' to

the Historical Sociology of Mnemonic Practices', *Annual Review of Sociology* 24, (1998), pp.105-140; E. Hobsbaum & T. Renger, *The Invention of Tradition* (Cambridge: Cambridge University Press, 1993).

11. *Megilat Esther* – one of the five scrolls in the *Writings* (*Ketuvim*) part of the Jewish *Tanakh* (the Hebrew Bible). The *Megillah* forms the core of the Jewish festival of *Purim*.
12. Shushan was the capital city of ancient Persia.
13. Haman was the one who plotted to kill the Jews Jews but, in the end, he and his sons were executed.
14. A *grager*, or noisemaker, is used during readings of the Book of Esther on Purim.
15. I use Limor Shifman's definition of 'meme': '(a) a group of digital items sharing common characteristics of content, form, and/or stance, which (b) were created with awareness of each other, and (c) were circulated, imitated, and/or transformed via the Internet by many users.' 'Hitler Rants' meme is defined by her as part of a group called 'egalitarian memes'- memes that are based on a certain formula or genre. Surfers relate to a certain formula and modify the text. See L. Shifman, *Memes in digital culture* (Cambridge: MIT Press, 2013), p. 41.
16. Shifman, *Memes in digital culture*, pp.138-141.
17. Ibid, p.136.
18. See Chapter 9.
19. Shifman, *Memes in digital culture*, pp.138-141.
20. Ibid.
21. B. Ravid, ''Netanyahu al neum sgan haramatcal yair golan: dvaraiv mekomemim vegormim lezilut hashoah' ['Netanyahu on the speech of the deputy chief of staff Yair Golan: his remarks are outrageous and cheapen the Holocaust'], *Haaretz*, 8 May 2016 [Hebrew] http://www.haaretz.co.il/news/politics/1.2937286 Accessed 20 June 2016.
22. *Asaf Harel*, 9 May 2016 http://10tv.nana10.co.il/Article/?ArticleID=1188351
23. S. Goldstein, and D. Rephael, 'Kmo bashoah' ['Like in the Holocaust'], *Maariv*, 5 August 2005 [Hebrew] http://www.raful.co.il/archives/846 Accessed on 15 June 2007.
24. In reaction to the skit, right-wingers disseminated on their websites and news sites a picture of the producer of the program, Muli Segev, wearing an SS uniform.
25. Season 3, Episode 16 http://www.dailymotion.com/video/x3pkold_%D7%92%D7%91-%D7%94%D7%90%D7%95%D7%9E%D7%94-%D7%A2%D7%95%D7%A0%D7%94-3-%D7%A4%D7%A8%D7%A7-16_tv
26. Pre-state Israel under the British Mandate. The Jewish national home was not an independent authority but had special rights under the Mandate. In the *Yishuv*, the dominant party was *Mapai*.
27. J. Tydor Baumel-Schwartz, *Perfect Heroes: The World War II Parachutists and the Making of Collective Israeli Memory* (Wisconsin: University of Wisconsin Press, 2010).
28. *The Jews are coming*, in the skit 'Hannah Szenes in a last brief before parachuting' https://www.youtube.com/watch?v=AzPgQXiJD1w
29. Tydor Baumel-Schwartz, *Perfect Heroes*; Steir-Livny, *Two Faces in the Mirror*, pp. 96-103.
30. A. Bender, 'Hapitaron shel ketzale lemehapsei miklat' ['Ketzale's Solution for Asylum Seekers: A Work Camp'], *NRG*, March 23, 2010 http://www.nrg.co.il/online/ 1/ART2/ 085/436.html [Hebrew] Accessed 20 May 2012.
31. *Minyan* refers to the ten Jewish adults required for certain religious activities.
32. The photograph caused turmoil and received mixed responses, some utterly appalled at it and others supported it. A day later, due to the turmoil, the image was removed from the program's Facebook page.

33. A. Ziv, *Personality and Sense of Humor*.
34. A. Sover, *Bedarco shel haadam hazohek* [*The Pathway to Human Laughter*] (Jerusalem: Carmel, 2009). See especially pp. 23-25, 55-57.
35. Zandberg, 'Ketchup Is the Auschwitz of Tomatoes'.

8

Holocaust Humour from the Perspective of the Ethnic Conflict

Memorial sirens were first sounded in Israel in November of 1949, during the funerals of soldiers who had fallen in 1948 war battles. This action was initiated by several Israeli local councils, taking an example from what was then customary in Britain. This custom was adopted the following year for the national memorial services held for casualties of the War of Independence and when the 'Day of Remembrance for IDF soldiers' was established in 1951, the memorial siren was included as part of the day's services. In 1951, the Israeli Knesset also decided upon establishing a memorial day to commemorate the Holocaust, then called the 'Day of Holocaust and Ghetto Uprising'. Given as this decision did not constitute an official law, this memorial day was not commemorated throughout the country in an orderly and extensive manner. Therefore, in 1959, the Knesset passed the 'Holocaust and Heroism Remembrance Day Law'. thereby determining the day's nature. Among other things, the law stated: 'Remembrance Day shall be marked throughout the State by a two-minute silence, during which all work and all road traffic shall be suspended; there shall be memorial gatherings, assemblies, and commemorative functions in Army camps and educational institutions'.[1] At present, the day is marked by a siren sounded at 10 am, followed by memorial services in various locations throughout Israel. Memorial services are also held on the evening of Holocaust and Heroism Remembrance Day.[2]

Even though Holocaust humour, satire and parody appeared in Israeli culture from the 1990s, the siren on Holocaust and Heroism Remembrance Day was a taboo subject until the first episode of the second season of the successful TV series *Zaguri Empire* (Herzliya Studios, HOT Telecommunication Systems, 2014-2015). Writer Maor Zaguri, a Mizrahi Jew (his grandparents immigrated from Morocco to Israel in the 1950s) who grew up in Beersheba,[3] created a daily comedy-drama series which is, to a large extent, autobiographical, revolving around the life of a family of Jewish-Moroccan descent living in Beersheba: Albert 'Beber', the patriarch, a grouchy man trying to earn a living, Vivienne, his wife, trying to keep the family intact, and their eight children - Aviel, Avishag, Eviatar, Miriam (Miri), Avi, Avishay, Abir and Avigail - who are constantly getting into trouble. The series quickly became a hit in Israel.[4] The second season's first episode, focuses on Holocaust and Heroism Remembrance Day.

Until the siren goes off, the family is busy with everyday affairs: fighting, making up and trying to manage the family's *falafel*[5] business. When the siren begins, Beber, Vivienne, Grandmother Alegria, Aviel, Eviatar, Miri and Avigail are all at home. Aviel runs into the living room and stands at attention. 'What's that, *qassams* again'? asks Grandmother Alegria. 'It's not *qassams*, it's the siren', shrieks Avigail, the youngest daughter. 'Aviel, Aviel, they don't want to stand up, come on, make them', she screams to her brother, as the camera pans around the family members who remain seated. Beber is in his armchair; Vivienne, Alegria and Miri are slouched on the sofa. Upon hearing her daughter's pleas, Vivienne stands up, an act which seems to be mainly for her daughter and not in honor of the siren, and continues knitting while she's standing, an act that symbolizes her detachment from what is supposed to be a very serious and pathos ridden moment.

In the furious dialogue that develops between Beber and Aviel, Beber refuses to stand up for the siren. Beber, who feels like he has been marginalized by the Ashkenazi hegemony, states that once people start acknowledging the adversities experienced by Jews of North African descent in Israel, he will show his respect to the trauma of the European-descended Jews. Aviel, his son, yells at him, trying to convince him to stand up, but Beber refuses.

When Avigail sees how her family treats the siren, she runs out of the house crying. The camera moves between the various members of the family: Beber, still-faced, sitting in his armchair, Miri and Grandmother Alegria who continue to nibble, Eviatar, combing his hair in the shower and displaying a complete lack of interest, Abir on the toilet, minding his business with an emotionless facial expression, Avi, Avishay and Avishag standing still in various locations outside the house with straight faces until the siren stops.

The family's behaviour and especially Beber's statements in the episode caused quite a turmoil in Israeli public discourse. Many writers and commentators were debating (in newspapers and on social media) whether the Holocaust should have been linked to ethnic issues; whether Beber's monologues are not a form of disrespect toward the Holocaust; whether it was appropriate to address Holocaust and Heroism Day in such a comic disrespect.[6] Yet, in fact, the question whether the creators of *Zaguri Empire* had been wrong or not in linking Holocaust humour with the ethnic conflict is

irrelevant. The issue brought up in this episode is, in fact, an integral part of an ongoing debate in Israel in recent decades regarding the Mizrahi-Ashkenazi rift: dealing with issues, such as how the Mizrahim were absorbed when they immigrated, their treatment by the Ashkenazim in the past and the present, their representation in Israeli culture and their part in the collective memory of the Holocaust. This very complex debate which has many facets was and is reflected, especially in the last two decades, in serious discussions, in academic research, but also in satire, comedy, and parody, in general, and in relation to the Holocaust, in particular.

The Ethnic Conflict in Israel: Two Schools

While sitting in his armchair, Beber explains that he has nothing to do with this Ashkenazi tragedy, 'It's not my family that perished [...] It is not my people', and focuses on the hardships of the Mizrahim's integration by the Ashkenazim: 'My people came to this land from wealth, palaces and splendor and they [the Ashkenazis] destroyed our lives. I truly apologize for them [the Nazis] not killing us too [...] When we came to Israel, they [the Ashkenazim] took out all their aggression from what the Germans did to them on us, those *wuswusim*'.[7]

Beber also criticizes the lack of commemoration of the Mizrahim's suffering: 'We were living in the mud. Mud. But is there a *Ma'abarot*[8] Remembrance Day? No. Just the Holocaust'. Beber then goes on to claim that Israel was and is a racist country. Aviel, on the other hand, tries to defend the concept of a shared Jewish destiny by saying, 'It's the people of your nation. Stand up', and argues that no one can compare the Mizrahim's suffering to the Holocaust. He mocks Beber's 'wallowing' and feelings of deprivation, and says that Beber's behaviour only perpetuates discrimination.

The intense dialogue between Aviel and Beber reflects two main contradicting perceptions in Israeli discourse and research regarding the days of mass immigration from Asia and North Africa to Israel, the manner in which these immigrants were absorbed, and the status of the Mizrahim in Israeli society to date.

As of the late 1940s and until the 1960s, hundreds of thousands of Jews from North Africa and Asia immigrated to Israel in several immigration waves. Researchers, politicians, journalists and public figures, particularly since the 1980s, have been trying to analyze the nature of the difficult encounter between them and Israeli society. Researchers are unanimous in their view that during the first decades of Israel, Mizrahi culture was marginalized. The immigrant absorption policy during the first decades of

Israel was centralistic, stemming from the viewpoint that Israel must melt the various cultures into one homogenous Israeli entity. But actually, the melting pot policy reflected the desire to preserve the western cultural tone which dominated the pre-state Jewish settlement (*Yishuv*) and to impose it on all Jews in Israel. In such a cultural climate, the heritage of most Asian and North African descendants was mostly left out. Yet, there are many disagreements regarding the absorption processes and its outcomes, and the opinions form two main schools.

Proponents of the first school claim that the socioeconomic gap between Ashkenazim and Mizrahim is mainly a result of systematic discrimination: the Mizrahim were deliberately directed toward the bottom layers of society. According to this persuasion, the orientalist perceptions are still maintained in current Israeli society. Thus, after almost 70 years after the great waves of immigration, it is still a 'white' society, marginalizing the Mizrahim.[9] Scholars of the second school claim that there was no deliberate policy of discrimination. According to them, the dichotomy formed by researchers of the first school ignores the complicated and fragile state of Israel in its formative years. Many of these researchers also claim that though the gaps have yet to disappear, the Mizrahim's status in society has greatly improved: Mizrahim are now an integral part of all leading systems, they have entered into the middle and upper class, the percentage of inter-ethnic marriages (between Ashkenazim and Mizrahim) has risen and, among the second and third generations, many view themselves as Israelis, with no specific ethnic identification.[10]

In the first season, director Maor Zaguri emphasized that Aviel was sent from his Beersheba home to a boarding school. He struggled to put his Moroccan heritage behind, adopting the norms of his Ashkenazi friends. He also replaced his surname with a more Ashkenazi sounding one – Gur – and pursued a promising career as an officer in the IDF's Artillery Corps. During the first season, Aviel has an Ashkenazi girlfriend named Shahar, a soldier who symbolizes the world to which he aspires to belong. He is once again torn from his environment when he is called to return to his home, where he has not visited since he joined the army, to see his grandfather, Pinto, on his deathbed. Aviel is in constant conflict with his father about every possible issue. He does not believe in the deliberate marginalization and in the continued existence of racism. He looks at his family as an outsider: unable to cut himself off from his roots and simultaneously unable to accept the codes dictated by his father. Aviel is a reflection of the second, more forgiving school, whereas Beber represents the first school, fervently holding on to the accusations of past and present discrimination, and racism. He protests by remaining seated when Israeli society demands from him to stand up.

Israeli Culture and North African Descendants

Further in the heated dialogue between Beber and Aviel, the issue of the representation of Mizrahim in Israeli culture comes up: 'You tell me… Mr Gur', says Beber, while mockingly swinging his hand at Aviel, 'Why do I need to know all their locations by name? All about their history and their writers and their poets? The cities where they lived'? 'Because that's the history of the Jewish people', screams Aviel. 'And I'm not the history of the Jewish people'? continues Beber. 'Why, do they know anything about my history? Do they know anything? Do they teach you anything about my *shtetl* in Africa'? 'You're this big. This big'! Aviel gestures a tiny space between his fingers. 'Crybaby. Entire families were killed just for being Jewish and there he is whining about his *shtetl* in Africa'. Miri and Vivienne observe with interest. 'I used to stand up for the siren every year, but after seeing that the Ashkenazim couldn't care less about what I went through, I stopped and no one is going to make me do it. Why don't they make shows and memorials about me, when the dinosaur director[11] makes a movie about the *Egoz* ship?[12]. Then, and only then, will I stand up'. 'He has a point, Aviel', says Vivienne. 'You disgust me, all of you', says Aviel and turns to Beber. 'No wonder your son was in jail, 'cause just like you, he has zero values'. Aviel says he is leaving, Vivienne tries to stop him. 'You go and don't bother coming back', mumbles Beber to himself.

Beber's arguments address the problematic manner in which Mizrahim have been represented in Israeli educational and cultural systems: during the first decades of the State of Israel, they were scarcely represented. When they were represented, they were often associated with negative stereotypes. For example, in the *Bourekas Films*[13] they were associated with backwardness, crime, unemployment and illiteracy. In many of these movies, the Mizrahim were depicted as superstitious, lazy and poor.[14] In the educational system, Asian and North African Jews were marginalized in the history books and their few mentions presented them as primitive and backward.

But, as of the 1980s, as the image of the New Jew, in particular, and the Zionist ideology, in general, dissolved and, as post-modern and post-Zionist currents began appearing, Israeli identity, isolated from its Jewish origins both from the east and from the west, no longer seemed reasonable. Israeli culture has become more and more a mosaic of memories and identities, where markers of foreignness, be it European, Asian or North African are longed for, comprising a basis for one's identity and an integral part of Israeli identity.[15] Many examples of how this identity is being reconstructed in

Israeli culture can be found in the works of Mizrahi artists in theater, literature, cinema, poetry and popular music which have become part of Israeli mainstream in the last decades.[16] Mizrahi history and identity, and their past and present manifestations continue to engage young Mizrahi artists and activists who instigate protests. In this cultural atmosphere, the series has created debates as to whether Zaguri is perpetuating negative stereotypes associated with the Mizrahim and is even reinforcing them, himself being part of that community, or whether he is dismantling those stereotypes while presenting a more complex and wide image of the Moroccan family.[17]

The two schools, which were previously mentioned, also address this issue of the representation of the Mizrahimin Israeli culture. Researchers of the first school argue that these changes are minor: Israel continues to be a racist society, viewing Mizrahim as second-class citizens. The second school observes these changes as evidence that the obstacles of the first decades are gradually making their way towards a dialogue. Beber represents this first school. As he sees it, nothing has changed: Mizrahi history is still underrepresented and Israeli culture is still dominated only by an Ashkenazi narrative.

Satirizing Mizrahi Detachment from the Holocaust: a Polysemic Reading

While Beber's detachment from the commemoration of the Holocaust is conscious, the case is different with Avigail, his daughter. Like Aviel, she thinks it is obvious that one ought to stand up during the siren in order to pay respect to the victims of the Holocaust, and tearfully runs away from home when her family members do not align with that norm. However, the following scene shows that even this family member, who displays a strong emotional reaction to the siren, is far from understanding the historical event. A tearful Avigail sits down next to Mr Levy, the Holocaust survivor. 'Mr Levy, you're from "Ashkenazland", aren't you'? asks Avigail. 'That's right', laughs Mr Levy, 'you may call it Europe'. 'Ok and sorry for the nerve, but were you around for the Holocaust'? 'Around'? laughs Mr Levy, 'Yes, you might say I was around'. He reveals the number tattooed on his arm. Avigail asks if she can touch it and Mr Levy tells her **they** did it to him in Auschwitz. She then tells him that her family does not care, that they are disrespectful, know nothing and do not stand still during the siren. He laughs in response and looks at her dearly, 'a man ought to do whatever he pleases in his own house. Whatever he feels. If he doesn't feel sad, why should he pretend like he's weeping'? 'I could kill them, I mean not really kill them', Avigail is startled by her own words. 'It's a figure of speech' [...] Mr Levy starts laughing and Avigail joins. While Beber compares the wrongful doings of the Ashkenazim toward the Mizrahim with those of the Nazis toward the Jews, thus portraying a 'cultural Holocaust' - hatred toward the Ashkenazim and detachment from their world - Avigail portrays emotional identification, a desire to honor and commemorate, regardless of the ethnic rift. Yet the statements made by Avigail, who supposedly represents the side of the family that does see itself as emotionally connected to the trauma attests to immense ignorance and, in fact, despite seemingly contradicting Beber's standpoint, actually reinforces the feeling of Mizrahi detachment from Holocaust consciousness.

Until recent decades, the Holocaust in North Africa was rarely discussed. The Holocaust was perceived and commemorated solely as an Ashkenazi trauma. Thus, Mizrahim were marginalized not only in the general Israeli culture, but also in the realm of Holocaust commemoration.[18] Mizrahi authors of the first immigrant generation, such as Sami Michael, Eli Amir and Amnon Shamosh have expressed their deep identification with European Holocaust survivors. They have included the Holocaust in the plots of their stories and showed profound empathy toward the survivors and their pain.[19] The second- and third-generation Mizrahim display identification with the memory of the Holocaust in Israel alongside a rejection of the issue as a form of reaction against the manner in which Mizrahim were marginalized both from Israeli identity, in general, and from the commemoration of the Holocaust, in particular. The sense that Israeli Ashkenazim have made the Holocaust a dominant component of Israeli identity, thus excluding the Mizrahim – not only from the particular memory of the Holocaust but also from 'Israeliness'in general - constantly reappears throughout the recent decades in the works of researchers, artists, authors and public figures.[20] The main trends that can be identified are varied: there are those, especially in documentary cinema, who seek to revisit the trauma of the Holocaust in North Africa, and thereby introduce North African Jews into the collective memory of the trauma of the Holocaust.[21] Other artists, especially in literature and poetry project Nazi representations onto the Ashkenazim, or portray absurd situations in which Mizrahim are so eager to be a part of Holocaust memory that they start to feel and behave as if they were there. These representations reflect both their engagement with the trauma of the Holocaust and their own trauma, caused by their exclusion from the memory of the Holocaust (symbolizing their marginalization in Israeli society). These texts reveal the hurt of the second- and third-generations born to immigrants from North Africa and Asia, who grew up in a society where the Holocaust is a fundamental trauma, were influenced by it and internalized its memory, but have never been made part of it.[22]

Beber's statements and his family's behaviour comically reflect notions that appear in serious debates on the subject: the comparison between Ashkenazim and Nazis, and the feelings that the Mizrahim were never included in the memory and therefore, do not understand its meaning. Beber's refusal to stand up is preceded by a scene in which three of the family sons are amusing themselves by imitating Hitler, after he was greeted by his daughter Avishag with 'Happy Holocaust Day'! and after his son, Abir, says, 'Ooh, the Holocaust, why are you making such a big deal out of it'? all of which break the sacredness of the Holocaust myth. In this way, Zaguri inserts his critique on the place given to Mizrahim in Israeli society while trying to show, through humour, the harsh consequences of a culture that 'explained' to the Mizrahim that they have no part in this memory.

The Mizrahi feeling of detachment from the Holocaust and, simultaneously, the constant engagement in it had already appeared before *Zaguri Empire* in different skits. For example, in the skit 'The Nazi and Pizza Delivery Boy' ['Hanazi veshaliach hapizza'], written by the group of comedians *Situation Spoon* [*Matzav kapit*], a young Nazi in Berlin enthusiastically listens to a Hitler speech as a Mizrahi pizza delivery boy named Udi Halima rings his doorbell, carrying a pizza tray meant for Shimon Haziza (all Mizrahi names) on Sprinzak St. in Holon.

'Holon'?! screams the Nazi, 'Can't you see you're in Berlin'? 'I can't believe this', says the messenger. 'And I was wondering why I was having a hard time finding the place and why I was spending so much on gas [...]' He keeps addressing the Nazi as *Haziza* (thus giving him a Mizrahi identity) and suggesting that he eat the pizza 'topped with black olives'. 'I hate blacks', yells the Nazi and smashes the pizza. 'Call me Haziza or Hatuka (another Mizrahi surname) one more time and I'll finish off what we didn't do in 1945'.

Halima mocks the Nazi's armband ('What is that? Looks like what my son put on for the scouts') and also wonders about the Nazi's obsession with red flags ('What is that? Are you *Hapoel* [an Israeli football team] fan'?) and the Hitler posters hanging around the house ('Come on, what was his name? The one with the moustache? Oh Chaplin, I couldn't understand one word he was saying'.). When giving the Nazi salute, Halima mistakenly thinks the Nazi wants to give him a religious blessing (in the manner that the Sephardic rabbis do) and places the Nazi's hand on his head. When Halima asks if he could use the toilet, the Nazi jokingly replies that he has no toilet at his home, 'only showers'. Halima ignores his words and begins walking toward the bathroom. 'Make us two coffees', he instructs the Nazi. 'Don't you worry – I'll put something on the gas', replies the Nazi joyfully and winks at the crowd.

This skit seemingly affirms the old perceptions of the Mizrahi detachment from the Holocaust: the Mizrahi delivery boy has no understanding of the place and the situation into which he has entered and the concepts are completely foreign to him. But, as a matter of fact, the skit undermines those views of detachment, as it consists a form of *acting out* – blending time and space (Mizrahi Israeliness and Nazi Germany), showing, as in *Zaguri Empire*, that even Mizrahim who have no biological connection to the Holocaust and who are seemingly far from the subject, cannot escape the Holocaust which lives in present day Israeli society.

Holocaust remembrance as a major Ashkenazi character of ethnic identity has appeared in a humouristic way also on Israeli sitcoms. The sitcom *Traffic Light*, for example, used the echoes of the Holocaust in order to depict the vast cultural differences between Ashkenazim and Mizrahim. Before their wedding, Tali of Tunisian descent and Amir of Hungarian descent, have had nightmares revolving around it. As an Ashkenazi, Amir is scared the wedding will have 'Arab' features (such as, shooting in the air, typical of Arab weddings in Israel) while Tali has a nightmare about a cold and distant Ashkenazi wedding where, instead of partying and celebrations, people are reciting the names of those killed, as they do in Holocaust and Heroism Remembrance Day memorial ceremonies.

In the television comedy *Naor's Friends*' [*Hahaverim shel naor*] (Israeli Channel 10, 2006-2011), one episode revolved around the question, 'Can a Mizrahi man have a relationship with an Ashkenazi woman whose grandparents are Holocaust survivors'? Naor Zion, a Mizrahi male, is the maker and star of the show that tells the story of four friends in their twenties living in Tel Aviv. In one episode, he meets an Ashkenazi young woman whose grandparents are Holocaust survivors, and falls for her. According to the episode, being the granddaughter of Holocaust survivors strengthens the Ashkenazi stereotype (In Israeli humour, women of Polish origin are often considered as cold, nagging, and bossy). Her name is Ya'ara and her surname is Warsaw. Naor says that her name makes him want to 'act like a partisan and start an uprising'. His friends warn him that dating her will 'start well and end like the Holocaust', but he refuses to listen. As time goes by, he learns that his friends were right. The sequence depicting their relationship includes scenes in which she is cold to him, makes him clean the house while she doesn't lift a finger, makes comments about every little thing, and replaces all the furniture in his house so it will be more pleasing to her taste. She is aggressive, bothersome, and intolerable. Throughout the sequence, the *Hymn of the Partisans* plays in the background. While having dinner at her house, he meets her mother, a second-generation Holocaust survivor, who mocks him and treats him in a racist manner. Naor decides to end the relationship, and returns to his Mizrahi friends. Through this comic episode, harsh and radical perspectives on an Ashkenazi-Mizrahi relationship in Israel are presented, and the incapability of holding a dialogue is demonstrated. In the binary division between the two worlds, the Holocaust is an Ashkenazi marker of identity. This episode seems like a kind of a late revenge on the Ashkenazim who did not let the Mizrahim enter the realm of Holocaust commemoration: a Mizrahi satirist ridicules their world while using Holocaust associations. But what seems to be a detachment of the satirist from the Holocaust can be understood as the opposite: in the same way as in *Zaguri Empire*, through this episode, a young Mizrahi satirist proves that the trauma and its echoes engage him.

The humouristic portrayal of Mizrahim being dragged into the domain of the Holocaust while displaying a lack of knowledge regarding historical occurrences also appeared in the skit show, *Am sgula* [*The Chosen People*] (Keshet Broadcasting, Channel 2, 2011), which revolves around situations in the lives of the characters, played by members of the comedy trio *Ma Kashur* – three Mizrahi comedians who play the lead roles in the skits. A central series of skits on the show is about two Mizrahi high school students (Shalom Michaelshvili and Asi Israelof), both named *Yossi* (who are depicted with an exaggerated, fixated set of negative stereotypic characteristics: ugly, ignorant, inarticulate and vulgar), and who join a high school delegation journey to the concentration camps' memorial sites in Poland in order to make their move on the beautiful and Ashkenazi Moran ('What's up Moran'? they repeatedly scream throughout the skits with a ridiculous accent). Yossi and Yossi substitute the engagement with the horrors of this tragic space with a series of emotionless clichés ('How sad. Inconceivable, it's the saddest thing ever', they mumble at each other inarticulately at the beginning of each skit). They see the journey as an opportunity to get to Moran ('We have to prepare. How?' 'We'll bring vodka and *condons*' [The use of the wrong word is deliberate and is intended to emphasize their ignorance]). They have no real interest in the Holocaust, they express no true sorrow or pain, and are mostly busy fighting, trying to pick up Moran, and searching for video and online games in order to pass the time.

In a skit called, 'They Didn't Have Facebook in the Holocaust' [Lo haya facebook bashoah], after going through the necessary clichés quickly ('How sad', 'Totally'), Yossi informs Yossi that things are bad: he has not logged on to Facebook for two days. 'All the sheep on my farm are probably already long dead', he complains, referring to the online game *Farmville* he plays. 'How sad', they mutter, 'inconceivable'. In this manner, the satirists emphasize that to Yossi and Yossi what happened during the Holocaust and what happens on a Facebook game are the same. 'How am I going to get to Facebook now? There were no computers in the Holocaust', whines Yossi.

But they suddenly hear the guide explaining about the computers in the Auschwitz Museum, where they can put in their surname and find information about their family roots. They use the computer to send their friends messages through Facebook in the style of Hey, what's up...'.

In the skit, 'The Germans Lost' ['Hagermanim hefsidu'], Yossi and Yossi, still on the journey, are made to watch a film about the war, looking bored. 'When is this going to end', one asks, 'it depends, if they broadcast the entire war now or just the highlights', the other says. They begin to quarrel over who is a better PlayStation player, and when the teacher calls the students to gather near the Eternal Flame, they connect their PlayStation to the projector used to screen films about the Holocaust in order to settle their argument on the spot. The camera simultaneously pans between the Ashkenazi students silently standing near the Eternal Flame and the two Yossis playing.

In the skit, 'Blessed Is the Match' ['Ashrei hagafrur'], Yossi claims: 'If I was alive then, I would have joined the parasites, the ones who fought in the woods'. 'They weren't called parasites'! Yossi scolds him, 'They were called partiNazis' (in this way manifesting their ignorance)]. Next to them, Moran, the beautiful Ashkenazi teenager that they are pursuing sings the Hebrew classic *A Walk to Caesarea*[23]; Yossi and Yossi are scheduled to perform after Moran. They pass the time drinking and trying to flirt with her. They get on stage, Yossi lights a match while the other Yossi commences singing, 'Ashrei Hagafrur' [*Blessed is the match consumed in kindling flame*] (another famous Holocaust song that accompanies many ceremonies). He blows at Yossi's match in order to extinguish it, yet his alcohol-filled mouth sets the match on fire, further burning Yossi's shirt who is screaming, '*Fire, My Brother, Fire*'.[24] 'Yossi was burnt in the Holocaust', weeps his friend, while melancholic music is playing in the background.

In these 'Yossi and Yossi' skits, humour is used in order to vent frustration, and as a social cohesion tool for a marginalized group. They seemingly display the Mizrahim's lack of understanding of the Holocaust as well as a lack of sensitivity toward it, showing another manifestation of the hegemonic argument regarding the detachment of the Mizrahim from the Holocaust. Alternatively, the skits can be interpreted as a form of resistance, undermining these perceptions: the fact that Mizrahi comedians repeatedly engage in the issue suggests that they are actually profoundly interested in it rather than detached from it. In addition to and along with claims according to which exaggeration of the vulgarization of stereotypes shatters them,[25] the Mizrahi characters in the skits are an inclusive collection of overstated negative stereotypes, and therefore these skits break the stereotypes rather than confirm them. They speak against common concepts in society regarding Mizrahim and their emotional detachment from the Holocaust in order to rebel against these concepts, make them absurd and shatter them. They confront a society which pushed them and their relationship to the trauma aside, by creating characters of Mizrahim infiltrating the 'forbidden' domain and replacing the sacred memory with humouristic disintegration.

A more blunt discussion in this blend of detachment from the Holocaust and intense engagement in it can be found in the satire show, *The Nation's Back,* which is loaded with Holocaust jokes. Given as the panelists on the show are part Mizrahi and part Ashkenazi, they often use humour in order to mock Orna Banai, the panelist of Mizrahi descent, and her lack of connection to the Holocaust. The Ashkenazi panelists emphasize that the Holocaust is their sole property. When a conference of immigrants from North Africa was held in Israel, in which the Holocaust in North Africa was discussed, the comedians reacted by orientalizing one of the most prominent songs played in Israel on Holocaust and Heroism Remembrance Day: *The Shtetl is Burning.* They replaced the melancholic melody with an oriental pop beat, accompanied by ululations and hand claps that often accompany pop songs sung by Mizrahi singers. The contradiction between the upbeat and joyous music and the difficult words, along with the associations Israelis have with this song immediately linking it with the Holocaust and Heroism Remembrance Day created a dissonance, a lack of congruence which produced humour. Yet it is clear that the obvious and ostentatious appropriation of the Holocaust and the emphasis on the Mizrahim's exclusion was a technique of 'upside-down logic' meant to go against these perceptions and emphasize their absurdity.

Another very prominent representation of the so-called detachment of Mizrahim from the Holocaust but showing their appeal to the trauma, appeared in the comedy-crime series *The Arbitrator* [*Haborer*] (HOT Telecommunication Systems, 2007-2014) which tells the story of Israeli criminals, most of whom are of Mizrahi descent. In the fifth episode of the third season, one of the most preposterous and exaggerated characters on the show, Naomi 'Spoon' (Mirit Balaban), the daughter of a Mizrahi crime family who has repented and found God, decides to travel to Poland. She scolds her husband for not wanting to join her with a series of absurd sentences:

> Shame on you. Have a bit of culture! We're going to fall on the graves of the righteous[26] People in the Holocaust went to sleep in fear, they were terrorized in their own homes, they were humiliated for years and couldn't live peacefully [...] I know they're Ashkenazim. If there had been some Moroccans in the Holocaust, trust me it wouldn't have come to that. Wow wow wow, the things I would have done to them

> had I been in the Holocaust, all the Kapos would have been sent to the hospital by the end of the first day. Like someone could wake me up at four in the morning and tell me to go take a shower in the snow???? [...] I'd tell them: pal, all Holocausts come to an end and you're on my list!!!

Presumably, these representations display a lack of understanding of the horrors of the Holocaust as well as insensitivity toward them on the part of the Mizrahim. They therefore can be seen as another manifestation of the argument regarding the detachment of the Mizrahim from the Holocaust; alternatively, they can be interpreted as a form of resistance, undermining these perceptions and proving the infiltration of the Holocaust commemoration into the lives of Mizrahim who have no biological connection to the trauma.

In conclusion, the various representations of the Holocaust in current Mizrahi humouristic texts reflect the manner in which offspring of immigrants from Asia and North Africa try to cope both with the trauma of the Holocaust as well as their exclusion from its commemoration. The creators use aggressive humour, black humour and self-deprecating humour in order to vent frustration, mirror the worldviews of those who grew up in a society where the memory of the Holocaust was constantly implanted into their minds, yet they were marked as those who had no part in it.

The satiric texts that represent detachment can be interpreted in a polysemic way: on the one hand, they can be read as reaffirmation of the Holocaust as an Ashkenazi trauma. On the other hand, the repetitive preoccupation with Holocaust memory by young Mizrahi artists can be read as the opposite. The Holocaust is a living part of the young Mizrahim's identity. By discussing it, in a serious and a humouristic manner, they emphasize its presence in their lives.

Notes

1. 'Hok yom hazicaron lashoah velagvurah' ['Holocaust and Heroism Remembrance Day Law'], 1959, *The Knesset*, http://main.knesset.gov.il/About/Occasion/Pages/ShoahLaw.aspx. [Hebrew]
2. Jewish memorial days and holidays begin the evening before.
3. Beersheva – a city in the periphery of Israel (in the south).
4. The series aired in early April 2014. On 29 April, 2014, after only nine episodes were

aired, the show already had three million views on HOT's VOD system, and was crowned the most successful launch in the history of HOT cables. The company also reported that the series had an outstanding opening in social media networks, with tens of thousands of followers on Facebook and Instagram. See L. Averbach, 'Zagury emperia – hahashaka hahazaka beyoter betoldot Hot' ['The Drama Series 'Zaguri Empire' – the Strongest Launch in the History of HOT'], *Globes*, 29 April 2014 http://www.globes.co.il/news/article.aspx?did=1000934953 Accessed 2 May 2015 [Hebrew]

5. *Falafel* – a popular Middle Eastern dish: fried balls of hummus.
6. Arguments regarding this episode revealed just how charged this issue is in Israeli society. There were those who justified Beber and those who were appalled by his conduct. See, for example, R. Alpher, 'Hashoah shel beber' ['Beber's Holocaust: 'Zaguri Empire' Nearly Became the Most Subversive Drama on Television'], *Ha'aretz*, 4 February 2015 http://www.haaretz.co.il/.premium-1.2556660 Accessed 5 March 2015 [Hebrew]; A. Shushan, 'Zaguri empire goremet nezek lemizrahim' [''Zaguri Empire' Is Causing Damage to the Mizrahim'], YNET, 1 February 2015 http://www.ynet.co.il/articles/0,7340,L-4620771,00.html Accessed 5 March 2015 [Hebrew]; R. Parshani, 'Beregashot meoravim' ['With Mixed Emotions: the Empire Strikes Back'], *NRG*, 10 February 2015 http://www.nrg.co.il/online/47/ART2/675/259.html Accessed 5 March 2015 [Hebrew]; A. Hatuka, 'Stereotipim, shoah, hishtaknezut' ['Stereotypes, Holocaust, Ashkenazification: Dismantling the 'Zaguri Empire'], *Haokets*, 10 May 2015 http://www.haokets.org/2015/05/10/%D7%A1%D7%98%D7%A8%D7%99%D7%90%D7%95%D7%98%D7%99%D7%A4%D7%99%D7%9D-%D7%A9%D7%95%D7%90%D7%94-%D7%94%D7%A9%D7%AA%D7%9B%D7%A0%D7%96%D7%95%D7%AA-%D7%9E%D7%A4%D7%A8%D7%A7%D7%99%D7%9D-%D7%90%D7%AA-%D7%B4/ Accessed 5 March 2015 [Hebrew]; D. Gavriely-Nuri, 'Zaguri lo omed bazfira' ['Zaguri Does Not Stand Up on Holocaust Remembrance Day and He Is Right'], *YNET*, 4 February 2015 http://www.ynet.co.il/articles/0,7340,L-4622511,00.html Accessed 5 March 2015 [Hebrew]; C. Sapir Weitz, 'Haperek shel zaguri' ['The Zaguri Episode Elicits the Question: Has the Commemoration of the Holocaust Also Been Privatized in the Israel of 2015?'], *Ma'ariv*, 12 February 2015 Accessed 5 March 2015 [Hebrew]; J. Doov, 'Ad yom hashoah' ['Don't touch Holocaust and Heroism Rememberance Day' Zaguri's Disrespect Crossed the Line'], *NRG*, 4 February 2015 http://www.nrg.co.il/online/47/ART2/674/031.html Accessed 5 March 2015 [Hebrew]; A. Hershkovitz, 'Zfirat hatra'a' ['Warning Siren: 'Zaguri Empire' Opens Its Second Season''], *Mako*, 3 February 2015 http://www.mako.co.il/culture-tv/local-Zaguri-Empire/Article-c56d0a7ee9f4b41006.html Accessed 5 March 2015 [Hebrew].
7. A derogatory name for Ashkenazim.
8. The *Ma'abarot (*absorption camps) were built in the late 1940s and the beginning of the 1950s as temporary housing for new immigrants from Europe, North-Africa and Asia. Conditions in the camps were terrible with crowding and poor hygiene.
9. For example, see S. Svirsky, *Lo nehshalim ela menuhshalim* [*Not Backwards but Subordinated*] (Haifa: Machbarot leMechkar, 1981) [Hebrew]; S. Svirsky, *Hinuch beisrael* [*Education in Israel*] (Tel Aviv: Breirot, 1990) [Hebrew]; Y. Peled and G. Shafir, *Mihu israeli* [*Who is an Israeli: the dynamics of complex identity*] (Tel Aviv: Tel Aviv University, 2005) [Hebrew]; B. Kimmerling, *Ketz shilton haahusalim* [*The End of the Ashkenazi Hegemony*] (Jerusalem: Keter, 2001) [Hebrew]; S. Shalom Chetrit, *Hama'avak hamizrahibe'israel: bein dikui keshihrur, bein hizdahut lealternativa, 1948–2003* [*The Mizrahi Struggle in Israel: Between Oppression and Liberation, Identification and*

Alternative, 1948–2003], (Tel Aviv: Am-Oved/Ofakim Series, 2004) [Hebrew]; H. Hever et al (eds) *Mizrahim beisrael* [*Mizrahim in Israel: a renewed debate*] (Jerusalem: Van-Leer Institute and HaKibbutz HaMeuhad, 2002) [Hebrew]; E. Shohat, *Mizrah umaarav* [*East and West in Israeli Cinema*] (Raanana, The Open University, 2007) [Hebrew]; E. Shohat, '*Zichronot asurim*' ['Forbidden Memories'], *Keshethamizrah* 2, Bimat Kedem leSafrut 13, 2010 [Hebrew]; D. Mishani, *bechol hainyan hamizrahi yes eize absurd* [*The Mizrahi Debate is Absurd*] (Tel Aviv: Am Oved, 2006) [Hebrew].

10. For example, see Y. Tsur, 'Eimat hakarnaval' ['The Terror of the Carnival: the Moroccans and the ethnic problem in Young Israel'] *Alpaim* 19 (2000), pp.57-82 [Hebrew]; E. Amir, 'Hasliha vehatoda' ['Forgiveness and Gratefulness'], *Alpaim* 16 (1998), pp.186-191 [Hebrew]; S. Smooha, 'Rav tarbutiyut bahevra haisrelit' ['Multiculturalism in Israeli society'], in: I. Yovel (ed), *Zman yehudi hadash* [*New Israeli Time*] (Jerusalem: Keter, 2007), 4, pp.221-228; L. Eliav and Y. Alfi, *Mishnei evrey hamaabara* [*From both sides of the Ma'abara*] (Tel-Aviv: Maariv, 2006); A. Molcho, 'Ta'anat hahaslala' ['The claim of subordination in Israeli Education'], *Israeli Sociology*, 13, 1 (2011), pp.9-54; S. Plotzker, 'Lehafsik lispor levanim veshhorim' ['Stop Counting Whites versus Blacks'], *Yediot Aharonot*, 15 January 2012, p.21 [Hebrew].
11. He is referring to Steven Spielberg and *Schindler's List* (1993).
12. *Egoz* was the name of a ship that carried Jewish emigrants from Morocco to Israel in the 1960s when the immigration of Moroccan-Jews to Israel was forbidden by the Moroccan authorities. In January 1961, the ship sank and all 44 Jewish immigrants who were on board drowned. Opposed to Beber's claim regarding the cultural disregard of the Egoz ship, a mini-series regarding the ship and its sinking was broadcast on the Israeli First Channel. In Israel, there are street names that commemorate the ship as well as several monuments.
13. *Bourekas Films* - A genre that was very dominant in Israeli cinema in the 1960s and 1970s. These films mainly dealt with the Ashkenazi-Mizrahi conflict in a comic way.
14. Shohat, *East and West*; R. Yosef, 'Ethnicity and Sexual Politics: The Invention of Mizrahi Masculinity in Israeli Cinema,' *Theory and Criticism*, 25, (Fall 2004), pp.31-62. There were only a few Mizrahi film directors who presented in the 1970s a more profound look at Mizrahi society and its roots. See Shohat, *East/West*.
15. A. Shapira, 'Lean halcha shlilat hagalut' ['The Denial of the Diaspora'], *Shvut* (2004), p.13-61.
16. L. Steir-Livny, 'Hacomback shel hagalut' ['The Comeback of the Jewish Diaspora in Israeli Culture'], in *Identity in transition in Israeli culture, A book in honor of Prof. Nurith Gertz* (Raanana: The Open University, 2013), pp.461-481 [Hebrew].
17. L. Abazon, 'Zaguri empire: primitivim aval optimim' ['Zaguri Empire: Primitive But Optimistic'], *Mako*, 8 April 2014 http://www.mako.co.il/culture-tv/local/Article-0d7a6dd6abf3541006.htm Accessed 1 May 2015 [Hebrew]; S. Shiloni, 'Zagury empire nafla bepach haotentiyut' ['The Zaguri Empire Fell into the Authenticity Trap'], *YNET*, 9 April 2014 http://www.ynet.co.il/articles/0,7340,L-4508186,00.html Accessed 1 May 2015 [Hebrew]; N. Hadas, 'Zagury empire menapezet et hadeot hakdumot' ['The Zaguri Empire Smashes Prejudice'], *Ha'aretz*, 25 April 2014 http://www.haaretz.co.il/.premium-1.2302878 Accessed 1 May 2015 [Hebrew]; A. Melamed, 'Zaguri empire: Lo gazanit meguvenet' ['The Zaguri Empire: Not Racist, Diverse'], *YNET*, 20 May 2014 http://www.ynet.co.il/articles/0,7340,L-4521659,00.html Accessed 1 May 2015 [Hebrew]; I. Hefetz, 'Mashehu rakuv bemamlechet zaguri' ['Something Is Rotten in the State of Zaguri'], *Haokets*, 11 May 2014 http://www.haokets.org/2014/05/11/%D7%9E%D7%

A9%D7%94%D7%95-%D7%A8%D7%A7%D7%95%D7%91-%D7%91%D7%90%D7%99%D7%9E%D7%A4%D7%A8%D7%99%D7%99%D7%AA-%D7%96%D7%92%D7%95%D7%A8%D7%99/ Accessed 1 May 2015 [Hebrew]; M. Kigel, 'Imperia' ['E-m-p-i-r-e: All About Why You Need to Adopt the Zaguri Family'], *NRG*, 6 June 2014 http://www.nrg.co.il/online/47/ART2/
584/359.html Accessed 1 May 2015 [Hebrew]; M. Alush-Levron, 'Zaguri poremet et simlat haarmon' ['Zaguri Unravels the Hegemon's Robe'], *Ha'aretz*, 6 February 2015 http://www.haaretz.co.il/.premium-1.2558299 Accessed 1 May 2015 [Hebrew].

18. For example, see I. Avrahami, 'Kehilot yehudei tunis beyamey hakibush hagermany' ['Tunisian Jews under Nazi Occupation'], Peamim 28 (1986), pp.107-125 [Hebrew]; I. Avrahami, 'Yehudei tunis' ['Tunisian Jews'], Shorashim bamizrah, 3, Ramat-Efal: Yad Tabenkin (1989), pp.273-293 [Hebrew]; I. Avramski-Blai, Pinkas hakehilot: luv-tunis [Libya-Tunisian Communities Writings] (Jerusalem: Yad Vashem, 2007) [Hebrew]; L. Goldstein, 'Antishemiut bezfon africa' ('Antisemitism in North Africa prior to WWII'), Yad Vashem 50 (2008), pp.10-11 [Hebrew]; I. Abramson, 'A Double Occlusion: Sephardim and the Holocaust', In: Z. Zohar (ed.), Sephardic and Mizrahi Jewry: From the Golden Age of Spain to Modern Times (New York and London: New York University Press, 2005), pp.285-300; S. Ward, 'The Holocaust in North Africa and the Sephardic World', The International Sephardic Journal 1(1) (2004), pp.72-86; R. Satloff, Among the Righteous: Lost Stories from the Holocaust's Long Reach into Arab Lands (Public Affairs, 2006); Yablonka, Off the beaten track.
19. Ibid.
20. Yablonka, *Off the Beaten Track*, pp. 268-289; T. *Hajbi, Mishlahot tichon lepolin* [*High school delegations to Poland*], Seminar paper, Culture Department, Sapir Academic College, 2013 [Hebrew].
21. Yablonka, *Off the Beaten Track*, pp. 268-289.
22. Steir-Livny, *Let the Memorial Hill Remember*, pp. 113-148.
23. See Chapter 7.
24. A word play on another classic song often performed at Holocaust and Heroism Remembrance Day ceremonies.
25. Shifman, *Televised Humor*, pp. 143-150.
26. This is a religious practice of North African Jews who travel to the graves of well-known religious figures, believing that visiting their graves will bring them luck.

9

The Downfall of the Führer: Lampooning Hitler's Image

Jokes about Hitler were already told underground during the Nazi regime.[1] Charlie Chaplin portrayed him in a ridiculous manner during the Second World War in *The Great Dictator* (1940). After the War, Mel Brooks made a caricature out of his image in *The Producers* (1968). From the 1990s, he is mocked in films and contemporary sitcoms which ridicule his character or attach Hitler-like mustaches to characters they want to make fun of, or to emphasize their violent behavior.[2] In the last two decades, the internet has become a wide cultural field for Hitler jokes, satire and parody. The online dimension of the Holocaust by now is a decisive aspect of the culture of remembrance and there is considerable public engagement with information that is available on the internet about the history and the remembrance of the Holocaust and it has far-reaching consequences on how people mediate the history and remembrance of the Holocaust.[3]

In regard to Hitler's image, the internet broadened the possibilities of mocking the Führer, and the varied examples of visual and textual representations reveal that he has become an internet icon. There are sites dedicated to cats with black markings under their noses that look like Hitler (also known as *Kitler*).[4] A website called *Things that look like Hitler* was established in 2012 to document features, such as houses, vegetables, etc. that look like Hitler. Other sites dedicated to his image that appeared in 2010 describe him as a cool hipster (*Hipster Hitler*) living in today's urban society. The site has tens of thousands of fans and has begun to sell T-shirts, based on the plots of the daily life of the hipster.[5] There are many internet memes which take advantage of his character or ridicule him in order to create a sophisticated play on words. For example, 'Hi Hitler' is one of the captions in these memes: a corruption of the infamous Nazi salutation, 'Heil Hitler'. There are also many textual forms of making fun of Hitler, especially in web-based satirical journals and the *Uncyclopedia* (a mock online 'encyclopedia') offering irrelevant and crude humouristic 'information' on various topics. For example, in describing Hitler's adolescence, it says in the *Uncyclopedia* that he started a small garage band

and wrote songs such as 'Dachau side of the moon' and 'Hitler baby one more time'.[6]

The sites use different forms of humour, including irony, parody and satire, and receive immense attention (both negative and positive). Although making fun of Hitler is not a phenomenon that is unique to the internet, the internet has intensified this trend and opened it to the masses, allowing them to take part. Gavriel Rosenfeld gives tens of examples of humouristic Hitler clips, sites and memes in his book. He claims that there are an estimated 61,000 Hitler-related image macros that are currently listed on the meme generator, and thousands more exist on competing meme-generating sites. Hitler has become the subject of infinite forms of humouristic digital distortion. In the many examples one can find, there are countless versions of *Disco Hitler*. This is a mash-up of a famous photograph of Hitler by Heinrich Hoffman, an item from contemporary popular culture (a disco ball) and funny captions in many different languages (an example for a caption: 'I said "a glass of juice", not "gas the Jews"'). Another successful meme is *Advise Hitler* (a knockoff of the famous *Advise dog* meme) which features Hitler's head set against the backdrop of a black, white and red color wheel with user-generated captions of phrases or bad advice that are meant to elicit laughs. Other similar memes are *Bedtime Hitler* (a pajama-clad Führer riding a toboggan across a nighttime sky with funny captions), *Chilling Hitler* (the Führer relaxing on a patio with funny captions) and more. In addition to appearing in countless memes and web games, Hitler stars in many humouristic clips online. Countless music videos have combined images of Hitler with familiar songs. Some use home movies of the Führer or parts of his speeches edited in the rhythm of the song or played forward and backward, making it appear as if Hitler is dancing.[7]

Hitler Rants Memes

One of the most successful video memes is the *Downfall Parodies*, also known as *Hitler Rants* or *Hitler Reacts* meme. *Hitler Rants* parodies began appearing in August 2006. A Spanish web surfer took a scene from the dramatic German feature film *Downfall* (Oliver Hirschbiegel, 2004) showing Hitler ranting at his staff as the end of the Second World War approaches and added parodic subtitles in Spanish, as if Hitler were criticizing Microsoft's flight-simulator. An English-speaking surfer uploaded the English subtitles for this parody, making the joke accessible to many other flight simulator fans on YouTube. From that time on, more and more surfers created their own parodies, and today there are hundreds of parodies in English, Spanish, Chinese, Japanese and many other languages.[8] These parodies discuss various subjects: politics, the economy, sports, technology and gaming, culture and everyday trivialities, topical events and trivial news or gossip. The parodies in English that have attracted the highest number of viewers present Hitler Rants when he gets banned from Xbox live[9], when he is furious that Usain Bolt Breaks 100m World Record[10] and when he cannot stand the vuvuzela at the 2010 Fifa World Cup.[11]

The Downfall director, Oliver Hirschbiegel, said that he had seen many of the parodies and could see the merits of the idea. *Constantin Film*, the production company of *The Downfall* was less pleased, and when the meme spread, *Constantin Film's* managers began sending takedown notices to YouTube in April 2010. Martin Moszkowicz, head of film and TV at *Constantin Film* in Munich, stated that he finds many of the parodies distasteful and trivial in light of the seriousness of the Holocaust and the Second World War. However, the surfers did not give up. In order to bypass YouTube's visual-based copyright detection software, many contributors began applying the 'mirror effect' on their parody uploads, flipping the original clip before adding subtitles.[12] In October 2010, the Downfall Parodies Forum users reported that *Constantin Film* put an end to its YouTube blockade on *The Downfall*-derived parody videos, even placing advertisements on some of them.[13] The YouTube channel of these parodies is very successful, and there are online technical explanations on how to create your own *Hitler Rants* parody.[14] This meme is a unique phenomenon because internet memes are usually short-lived, while the *Hitler Rants* meme has been online for more than a decade now, with new videos continuously emerging.[15]

The huge success of the meme, and the fact that every surfer can easily prepare this type of parody have caused several incidents over the years. For instance, in December, 2010, Jefferies Investment Bank executive Grant Williams was fired after sharing a *Hitler Rants* parody in a company newsletter email. In January 2012, Tom Harris, a Scottish Labour Party Member of Parliament uploaded a *Hitler Rants* parody to his personal YouTube channel, criticizing Scottish National Party leader Alex Salmond. The video was seen as a direct comparison of Salmond to Hitler, and the negative public response forced Harris to resign from his position.[16]

Hitler Rants parodies started appearing in Hebrew in 2009, and became hugely popular. In Israel, the parodies are used to protest against political issues, Israeli wars, military service, religious coercion, etc. They also engage in the little, irritating details of daily life in Israel, like skiing on Mount Hermon which has enough snow (usually for only) a few days a year, the lack of cannabis to smoke, Israeli reality shows, Israeli rudeness, and so on. In addition, they are very popular as inside jokes: high school classes make

Hitler Rants parodies for their end-of-school parties; IDF units create them to mark course graduations; high-tech employees send each other such parodies highlighting their specific companies' internal work issues, and so on.

The parody that became the greatest success in Israel (according to view numbers in March 2016) is 'Hitler is looking for a parking space in Tel-Aviv.' It attracted more than 220,000 viewers. In this parody, Hitler rants about the city's infamous traffic problems: he is angry that his colleagues could not find a parking space anywhere in Tel Aviv and had to park in a bikers' parking area. They therefore got a parking ticket of $65 that he has to pay, as their leader. He orders, 'those of you who live in Tel Aviv and have private parking spaces, or don't have a car' to leave the room, and in a crazed monologue begins complaining about his parking problems. He yells that the parking inspectors are vicious thieves:

> They are all one big Mafia! What are they thinking???? They don't have a shred of humanity!! A shred of humanity!! They are worse than the SS!! And all the money goes to the corrupt municipality. They have been renovating the same tile near city hall for seven years!

When a Nazi officer explains that the Tel Aviv municipality has good intentions, and is now planning to add a third traffic lane, Hitler cuts in brutally. 'Why the hell do I need a third lane??? They should build a public parking space!!' The Nazi officer tries again: 'But Sir, they built a public parking lot…,' but it doesn't help. Hitler goes wild, screaming that in this new parking lot, one can park only from 18:30 pm until 6 am:

> I arrived 10 minutes after 6:00 am and already found a parking ticket on the window of the car– $65! They towed my brother's car three times in one week. I pay more for parking tickets than I pay for gas!! And all the money goes to the fucking mayor! He has been the mayor for ten years!! Who does he think he is??? He is worse than Stalin!! And don't even start talking to me about public transportation! Two hours! Two hours I was waiting at the bus station! I hate those buses! And then two buses arrive at the station together! What am I supposed to do?? Ride them both?? And then there is a traffic jam, because some stupid woman driver tried to park by reversing her car, and crashed into a traffic light that anyway is green for only 3 seconds! She should have her license revoked for good! Maybe I'll sell my Volkswagen and that's it. I can sell it for five-six thousand NIS. Maybe someone is interested? Maybe….We'll split the parking ticket. It's not worth

> having a car in Tel-Aviv. I think I'll just take my stuff and go. I'm sick and tired of this fucking city. There is a parking place in Petah Tikva [a small town in Israel near Tel Aviv].

'Hitler is looking for a parking space in Tel-Aviv' was so successful because large audiences could relate to it. *Hitler Rants* parodies that had appeared previously mostly addressed narrow subjects that interested specific audiences; they were original, but not every Israeli could relate to them because of the specific content and insider jokes (such as, the rivalry between football teams in Israel). The parking problem in Tel Aviv is a subject every Israeli knows, understands and to which he/she can relate. The clever script is funny because it is also so accurate. Working carefully on matches between the original dialogue of the scene in *Downfall* and the Hebrew script (such as, using the reference to Stalin at the exact moment Hitler says 'Stalin' in the original scene, or translating words from German which most of the Israeli audience does not understand to curses in Hebrew that sound the same). These adjustments increased the amusing feeling that Hitler was indeed ranting and raving about the parking problems in Tel Aviv. Since then, *Hitler Rants* meme in Hebrew has spread like wildfire.

The reactions to *Hitler Rants* parodies in Israel are mixed. The opponents claim that these parodies indicate that Jewish-Israelis have no respect for Jewish history, and that this is an educational problem. The creator of 'Hitler is looking for a parking space in Tel Aviv' claims that he felt very bad when he heard that there were some Holocaust survivors who were offended by the parody. But then, he received many comments from people who told him that their grandmother or grandfather, Holocaust survivors, watched the parody, laughed and enjoyed it. He claims that the parody does not include offensive content and does not even mention Holocaust survivors; the only group that could be offended by it are Tel Aviv's city parking inspectors.[17] In any case, the opponents' reactions did not hurt the popularity of the *Hitler Rants* parodies and they are, by now, a proven success in Hebrew.

The success of the meme echoes a combination of several theories of humour: mainly the superiority theory, the relief theory and the incongruity theory. At the basis of the superiority theory is the idea that the person who is laughing feels superior to the person who is the object of the laughter, and laughter can be a tool used to actively diminish (or degrade) that person. The laughing person feels as though he has won the battle. Laughter can give a feeling of superiority over others, not only to individuals, but also to groups. People enjoy the feeling of belonging to a group superior to other groups.[18]

Another component which has an impact on the intensity of laughter and enjoyment is the emotional relationship between the person laughing and the object of the laughter. If the object of laughter is an enemy, the intensity of the laughter and enjoyment increases. Along these lines, this meme shows Hitler unable to face the trivial aspects of daily life, failing to find a solution to the parking problem. The scene always ends with Hitler sitting, looking defeated, his head slouched. In comic situations such as these, Hitler's failure to do anything about the problem that bothers him, besides ranting, increases the comic effect of the situation.[19]

Hitler's most known visual images were portrayed in Leni Riefenstahl's film, *Triumph of the Will* (1934). In this film, Hitler was presented as a type of a god, photographed from a low angle, in front of hundreds of admirers, as if he had immense, even mystic, powers.[20] In the *Hitler Rants* parodies, this 'god' becomes a niggling, even pathetic individual who is stressed out by the irritating details of everyday life. *Hitler Rants* deconstruct the power that he and the Nazis might still hold over the present as a malevolent force, knock Hitler from a pedestal, and take away his power to frighten others.[21] These farcical portrayals neutralize Hitler's menacing identity and allow viewers to feel superior to the Nazi leader.[22]

The incongruity theory refers to putting together conflicting ideas which show the incongruence between what is expected - the familiar and the known - and the real object found in the situation.[23] It claims that the laughter is the outcome of an encounter between two contradictory spheres. Jokes, according to Elliott Oring,[24] are based on incongruity, or a mismatch between two different perceptions. The meeting point between the two different perceptions of reality is where the joke's basic meaning is found. The basic meaning of the joke cannot be a narrative sentence, but only an opposition between contrasts. Palmer[25] addresses it as an encounter between the reasonable and the unreasonable. Watching Hitler yell is reasonable but the subtitles showing that he falls apart in the face of daily trivialities is unreasonable. The 'comic gap' refers to the level of incongruity between the extraordinary situation perceived by the audience and what is familiar and known to them. The meme has an additional humouristic feature: inversion – a pursuer becoming pursued, but not by mighty and powerful forces, but rather by the pettiness of everyday life.[26] Hitler becomes a comic character because of the contradiction between the myth (our knowledge about Hitler), the visual image (Hitler and his colleagues in a bunker during the Second World War) and the text, which address completely different, mundane and trivial matters, and are driving him off balance. Gilbert[27] claims that the *Hitler Downfall* parodies became popular because of the 'imitation, exaggeration, and incongruity' they produced, turning Hitler into an 'unapologetic buffoon'.

In order for a joke to be funny, its hearers should be of common cultural or social knowledge upon which the incongruity of the joke is built.[28] In the case of the *Hitler Rants* parodies, former familiarity with the text to which the videos intertextually relate is not obligatory. Even people who have not watched the film can understand that this is a dramatic occurrence being ridiculed. The comedy is based on the gap between this knowledge, the visual information and the subtitles.

The relief theory claims that laughter helps to relieve stress and anxiety for individuals and groups. Freud claimed that this is the way the individual can release aggression in an acceptable manner. In the case of *Hitler Rants*, the devaluation and relief is also a form of revenge: the dictator who murdered millions is depicted as a little man who cannot deal with the challenges of everyday life. The immense contrast between his diabolical image and his breakdown in response to the trivialities of life induces laughter. According to Kaplan[29], humour can liberate viewers of Hitler parodies from the horrifying reality of the dictator's regime. Similarly, Gilman[30] notes that laughing at the Hitler regime can provide a means of exhibiting control over the situation, where previously, there was none.[31]

Another motif is repetition: humour which is based on repetition occurs when the recurring theme is comic to begin with. Each repetition of the same theme increases the comic gap. Laughter intensifies respectively, in accordance with the number of repetitions.[32] The meme features the same bunker scene, where Hitler reacts with outrage to a different issue each time.

The *Hitler Rants* meme is a combination of parody and satire. Parody imitates the style of someone or something else in an amusing way, creating a distorted imitation of something real in a funny way.[33] Satire reflects the evils of society in a humouristic way in order to change them. Gilbert argues that Hitler as a vehicle for social and political commentary is disquieting precisely because parodists are not just playing with a film text or the figure of Hitler; they are playing with wider cultural narratives and political problematics, even as the parodies are not about Hitler per se.[34]

Researchers of culture who were asked to explain this phenomenon have different opinions: Kotler claims that the meme has an important role in the lives of the individuals who are facing the depressing reality; while creating and repeatedly watching the videos does not solve the problem, it does allow the viewer/creator to let off steam and release anger, and maybe evoke action. The makers of the meme and/or the viewers sharing links to the meme with friends are not changing reality *de facto*, but are taking an active part in protesting against it, while displaying involvement which allows them to feel as though some things are in their hands and as though they have the power to change them.[35]

Others claim that in today's world of mass media which floods us with texts and visual images, one has to shout as strong as one can in order to be heard, otherwise the protest will get lost in the sea of other protests. Others claim that there is a built-in comic potential in the real historical image of the Führer, which explains why Hitler is made into a laughing stock much more than other dictators. Some claim that this is an opportunity to gloat about Hitler, to show him in an inferior situation, in which he falls apart in the face of trivial problems. Others see the parodies as a sign of maturity: the ability to face the Holocaust in a different way than the canonic memory. Some see it as a sign of normalization: the young generation wants to abandon the perception of the Holocaust as taboo, as untouchable, and this is one way to achieve it.[36]

Rosenfeld claims that the success of these images, sites and memes reflects the emergence of a new internet 'law': the more popular the meme, the more likely it will be 'Hitlerized'. In Rosenfeld's opinion, for web surfers, it is like adding spices to food. Adding a Hitler mustache, hairstyle, or Nazi uniform to a meme automatically lends it a powerful kick of irony and sensationalism. This practice has become an automatic reflex that has been applied to all kinds of themes. For example, if there are image macros in which 'serious' people's heads are photoshopped into bodies of supermodels, popstars etc., it is only a matter of time before the head of the Führer appears there. In other cases, Hitler's mustache or a Nazi uniform are added to children's cartoons like *Hello Kitty*, company logos, etc.[37] Rosenfeld claims that humouristic memes with Hitler themes and their related offshoots (for example, the countless memes that have been ironically Hitlerized) confirm the internet's importance in fostering a normalization of Hitler's and Nazism's memory. He suspects that many young web users have probably begun to see Hitler as a familiar, amusing and reassuring internet presence. The enthusiastic embrace of ironic Hitlerization by ordinary web users points to the rejection of moralistic methods of representing the Nazi past. Hitler's transformation into a humouristic icon promotes the process of normalization.

Rosenfeld recognizes that the *Hitler Rants* meme reflects the prominent humour theories of superiority, relief and incongruity, but he does not see them as legitimate representations, and claims that they promote the universalization of the Nazi past. In his opinion, normality threatens to undermine morality. The more that people become accustomed to laughing at the subject of Nazism, the greater the danger that, in due time, no one will take it seriously anymore. He doubts that web users can address the serious representations of the subject as well as the humouristic representations, and claims that the humouristic representations will cloud the serious ones. In his opinion, it is hard to imagine that people can regularly consume information in both serious and comic modes and not be affected at a deeper level.[38]

In my opinion, these explanations (and worries) might be relevant for the influence of *Hitler Rants* parodies in the world, but Israel, by its nature, is a separate space regarding Holocaust memory and awareness. In Israel, these parodies in Hebrew are a part of an inner dialogue and have a special and important meaning as defence mechanisms, as a tool for venting and a social tool.

While the *Hitler Rants* meme is not unique to Israeli culture, in Israel the parodies are created and consumed in a capacity and intensity that exceeds any other place in the world. I have checked the statistics for the number of *Hitler Rants* videos and views per speakers in the four languages in which the highest number of *Hitler Rants* videos were made: Hebrew, English, Spanish and Polish. For Polish speakers, one of each 6.7 Polish speakers viewed a *Hitler Rants* parody; for Spanish native speakers, one of 7.5; for English speakers one of each 4.84, while one of 4.14 Hebrew speakers viewed a *Hitler Rants* parody. The numbers also show a huge difference between Hebrew speakers who created *Hitler Rants* videos and Polish, English and Spanish speakers who created these videos. The number of Hebrew speakers who created *Hitler Rants* videos is 10 times higher than Polish speakers, 24 times higher than English speakers and 40 times higher than Spanish speakers. The number of viewers per Hebrew language speakers, and the number of parodies per Hebrew language speakers are proportionately much greater than other languages.[39]

As noted previously, Holocaust memory is an integral part of the Israeli education system. Jewish-Israelis learn about the Holocaust from kindergarten until the end of high school. The subject of the Holocaust is included in the matriculation exams and, while in high school, many pupils travel with their class to the former concentration camps in Poland. Therefore, Rosenfeld's concern that humouristic representations will cloud serious ones is not relevant in Israel. The *Hitler Rants* meme cannot cloud over the intense serious knowledge regarding the Holocaust in Israel.

In addition, as mentioned in other chapters of the book, in the last two decades, humouristic representations of the Holocaust in Israeli culture have intensified. The creators use humouristic texts as defence mechanisms, as a social and political protest against collective memory agents in Israel, and for venting their socio-political-economical frustration. The *Hitler Rants* meme adds yet another layer to the struggle since they differ from other aspects of Holocaust humour and satire in Israel.

As noted, memes' researchers claim that internet memes are more than just simple jokes, they go beyond general silliness, and are to be taken seriously.[40] The fact that *Hitler Rants* meme in Hebrew is created and consumed in a capacity and intensity that exceed any other place in the world demonstrates the mental need of the young generations to struggle against the 'acting out' of the Holocaust as well as dismantle the symbols of fear in a society that is forced to relive the trauma. With respect to political satire, Gehring[41] explains that parody is a means of expressing 'creative criticism'. Hariman[42] points to the vitality of political comedy within an 'engaged' public culture. He notes that parody, in particular, is a way of creating, expressing, and sustaining public discourse. These parodies are an outlet for what some might see as the most trivial of grievances, but also for a political and social protest regarding very important issues and, in that sense, YouTube is a political medium.[43]

Kotler believes that the *Hitler Rants* meme indicates which cultural, economic and political current events are engaging Israeli society, what is enraging and upsetting the Israelis, and what they aspire to change. She argues that the Hebrew versions of the meme convey more social and political protest than the English version. In her research, she claims that the ten most viewed videos in Hebrew include the following: searching for a parking space in Tel-Aviv, Tel Aviv is within the range of Hamas rockets, difficulties getting drugs, disappointment with iPhone 4s, Hitler gets angry about the winner of the first season of the Israeli 'Big Brother' (an issue which caused a stir in the discussion of the ethnic conflict between Ashkenazim and Mizrahim in Israel), Hitler gets angry about getting invited to yet another wedding, Hitler gets angry about a cell phone company malfunction, Hitler reacts to the law prohibiting the use of Nazi symbols, Hitler gets angry about an Israeli politician (Yair Lapid), and Hitler gets angry about Jerusalem. That is, out of the ten most viewed videos, three addressed political-security issues (rockets, legislation, Yair Lapid), three addressed universal matters (parking, iPhone, weddings) and four addressed social affairs. In comparison, the ten most viewed videos in English include the following: Hitler gets banned from Xbox Live, Hitler's angry reaction to the iPad, Hitler gets angry about iPhone 4S, Hitler gets banned from *Runescape* (an online fantasy game), Hitler gets fired from *McDonald's*, Hitler rants about *League of Legends* (a multiplayer online game), Hitler goes to *McDonald's*, Hitler finds out that President Obama is not a US Citizen, Hitler can't complete *Super Mario Bros*, and Hitler gets angry studying chemistry. That is, six of the most viewed videos are about technology (computer games and electronic devices), two are about *McDonald's*, one is about education and only one is political (referring to President Obama). This short examination indicates that for Israelis, the phenomenon has become, more so than in other places, a tool enabling them to complain mainly about social-political issues.[44]

Holocaust survivor Danny Chanoch, who himself uses black humour as a defence mechanism,[45] argues that the *Hitler Rants* meme is a part of the young generation's reaction to the habitual way of establishing the memory of the Holocaust in Israel. He claims that this should make the agents of this memory in Israeli society reevaluate themselves.[46] As mentioned, in Israel, the terms 'second-generation Holocaust survivors' and 'third-generation Holocaust survivors' refer not only to the offspring of Holocaust survivors; they represent the Jewish-Israelis who were born in and after 1945 in Israel, and grew up in an environment that focused on the Holocaust as one of the most important features in Jewish-Israeli identity.[47] Therefore, *Hitler Rants* parodies as well as many other humouristic and satirical texts regarding the Holocaust that appear in Israeli culture from the 1990s are an example of the way humour is used as a defence mechanism by the Jewish-Israelis suffering from secondary traumatic stress[48] in order to try to lessen reactions of tension and anxiety concerned with the Holocaust. Figley claims that, in order to reduce symptoms that appear in PTSD and in secondary traumatic stress, one has to refrain from stimulations that are a reminder of the trauma. In Israel, refraining from Holocaust references is almost impossible, but there are other ways. In *Hitler Rants* parodies, the surfers silence (symbolically and actually as one) the original soundtrack that features Hitler, the Third Reich, and the behaviour of absolute evil and, by doing so, silence the traumatic events. This is a provocation against the canonic memory of the Holocaust in Israel which replicates the Holocaust into Israeli everyday life, and a defence mechanism against the anxiety it creates.

Moreover, satirical programs like *The Chamber Quintet*, *It's a Wonderful Country* and *The Nation's Back* also use Holocaust satire in order to protest against the hegemonic Holocaust remembrance in Israel.[49] However, *Hitler Rants* parodies that address current issues add an important component of instant responses to the struggle against hegemonic remembrance. They are distinct from the television skits because the web enables surfers to express their protest immediately, without the need to wait for a specific broadcast each week.

Furthermore, there are many disputes in research on whether television attempts to preserve, even in this multicultural era, a sort of tribal campfire. Does it provide opportunities to undermine the hegemonic codes? Or should we address television as a polysemy reading, typified by a combination of hegemonic and subversive positions?[50] These questions become more complex where humourous skits are concerned due to polysemic nature of humour and the multiple meanings it inherently possesses.[51] The satirists on

Israeli television programs like *The Nation's Back* and *It's a Wonderful Country* have to think twice before using Holocaust satire, and then often have to apologize, even while on-air and sometimes after the show when dealing with letters of complaint. This set of apologies weakens the struggle against the hegemonic commemoration of the Holocaust and helps reassure its boundaries. The social media platforms free *Hitler Ra*nts from consideration of any aspect of hegemonic powers, and this turns these platforms into a significant and central tool in the struggle against the repetition compulsion of the trauma. In this battle against the hegemonic memory of the Holocaust, Hitler, who is supposed to remain the symbol of evil in the young generations' consciousness turns into a friend, a buddy, the one who says what the 'common Israeli' thinks.

Ridiculing Hitler in Israeli Contemporary Art

Up to the 1990s, only a few artists used the symbols of the Third Reich and its key characters in their work. However, since the 1990s, it has become a more common subject. For example, Roee Rosen (born 1963) is an artist who has participated in many exhibitions in Israel and abroad. His controversial exhibition in the Israel Museum in 1997, *Live and Die as Eva Braun*, caused turmoil and a broad public discussion regarding the commemoration of the Holocaust in Israel. *Live and Die as Eva Braun* opened again in 2016 in the Tel Aviv Museum in a retrospective of Rosen's works.[52]

Live and Die as Eva Braun consists of 66 works on paper and a text in ten segments. Addressing the viewer as a potential client, the text promises and describes the ultimate entertainment experience: becoming Eva Braun, Hitler's lover, during the last days of the Second World War, experiencing intimacy with the dictator, the suicide and a short trip to hell. The viewer was invited to take part in Hitler's death, to take away the Führer's control of his own death.[53] *Live and Die as Eva Braun* stirred up a scandal when first exhibited at the Israel Museum, and was later exhibited in other places in the world.[54] In *Live and Die as Eva Braun*, number 2 in 1995, acrylic, pastel and gesso on paper, Rosen represents a sketch of an innocent-looking child with a Hitler mustache and a pair of scissors cutting his hair. The image, like the entire exhibition, subverts under binary divisions of innocent and evil, good and bad, 'humanizes' little Hitler as a child while hinting at the humiliation that was part of life in the concentration camps where, upon arrival, the inmates' hair was cut.[55]

Boaz Arad is a famous Israeli artist who shows his works in solo exhibitions and group exhibitions in museums and leading galleries across the world.[56] He also teaches art at the Midrasha School of Art and at the Bezalel Academy of Art and Design in Jerusalem, and is the curator of the *Midrasha* Gallery in Tel Aviv. In many of his works, he engages with the image of Hitler and the symbols of the Third Reich.[57] His works sometimes address the subject through black humour and aggressive humour that contain a sense of revenge.

Arad's first video works are a series centering on the figure of Hitler. These works were made between 1999 and 2002 using archival material. The short films are a kind of private revenge of Arad who allows himself to show Hitler masturbating (*100 Beats*, 1999), apologize in Hebrew (*Hebrew Lesson*, 2000) or play with his mythic mustache (*Mustache*, 1999 and *Marcel Marcel*, 2000).[58]

In *Moustache,* for example, Arad deprives Hitler of the one thing you cannot erase without destroying him as an image (apart from his speaking voice): the moustache. The void, the absence of that which makes Hitler into Hitler leaves the viewers with a charisma-free bureaucrat. Indeed, he continues with his speech, but something of his determination is lost. In Arad's case, the humiliation involves shaving. In light of the horrifying images from the violent shaving of Jews' hair in concentration camps, there is a type of revenge here. This provides the cue for the carnivalesque moment. In *Marcel, Marcel,* the moustache, the symbol of evil, becomes an independent entity. It is cut away from the body while its wearer continues his speech, becoming a fly buzzing around the face. It is a scrutiny of how the oppressor looks without the oppressor, without the moustache under which so many speeches were given.[59] Arad's preoccupation with the figure of Hitler peaked in his installation, *The Nazi Hunter's Room* (2007), a room in the center of which is the figure of an aging Hitler whose skin has turned into a rug, like the fur of a hunted bear.[60] The incompatibility of the head and the rug creates a humouristic image that also constitutes a kind of revenge: the Führer is shot dead, skinned and lies dead on the floor of an Ashkenazi house in Israel. This combination also symbolizes the strong presence of the Holocaust in the Israeli present.

As part of a graduate exhibition, Nir Avigad, an alumni of Visual Communication from the Bezalel Academy of Arts and Design, presented an altered portrait of Hitler as a hundred and fifty different icons. In the work, Hitler's facial features are once seen as a dog, once as a Babushka, once as the yin and yang symbol, and so forth, repeated a hundred and fifty times. As part of the project, Avigad started a website called *The Daily Hitler*, to which he uploaded a new Hitler icon every day. Avigad, trying to explain his work, stated the following:

> Just as Marilyn Monroe is an icon of beauty, the Dalai Lama is an icon of peace and Mother Teresa is an icon of kindness and mercy, so is Hitler an icon. Whether we'd like to admit it or not, he is an icon. An icon of evil. Yet there's a taboo on such icons. They can't be explored. Can't be developed. Can't be touched. Can't be a laughing matter.[61]

The humourous icons diminish the Führer's image and make him seem ridiculous, while also rendering him a cultural symbol rather than a human being. Quite expectedly, the exhibition caused turmoil amongst organizations of Holocaust survivors in Israel, but the work was still showcased in the exhibition.[62]

These representations emphasize the need to dismantle the fear and anxiety caused by the intense Holocaust remembrance in Israel, by ridiculing the major symbol of evil.

Lampooning Hitler on Israeli Television

Holocaust skits on Israeli TV do not usually deal directly with the Holocaust but rather with its remembrance and commemoration.[63] Hitler is almost absent from this discussion. It seems that Israeli TV is still reluctant to deal with the Führer himself in an era when humouristic texts about Holocaust commemoration appear more and more frequently. Over the last two decades, there are only few examples mocking Hitler on television: in the nonsense comedy show *Pini the Great* [*Pini Hagadol*] (Bip channel, 2003), an episode was broadcast in which an actor was dressed up as Hitler while singing songs from children's television shows. In the skit show, *Not in front of the children* [*Lo lifne hayeladim*] (Channel 10, 2007-2009), in a skit called 'Judith', a young woman (Yael Sharoni) goes out on a date with a man (Idan Alterman) whose hair is carefully combed sideways, who keeps 'reminding her of someone'. Only when he eats a piece of chocolate cake which leaves a mark on the gap between his nose and his lips (creating a shape which highly resembles Hitler's moustache) does she realize whom he reminds her of, which leads her to escape, while he screams 'Judith, Judith', pointing in her direction with a gesture reminiscent of the Nazi salute. According to these skits, the trauma of the Holocaust is integrated within Israeli present day life. The subtext of the skit reflects research findings that Israeli media, the educational and cultural fields, and public discourse in Israel frame the

Holocaust as a current, ongoing local trauma rather than as an event that ended decades ago in another place.[64]

One of the few examples that refers directly to Hitler is the skit, *Hitler in Vienna*, in the satire, *The Jews are Coming*. It takes place in the Vienna Academy of Art in 1907. A painter, whose face we cannot see, stands behind his large painting of flowers and a group of three professors criticize it. Two professors with a strong German accent think the painting is interesting: 'Nice', starts the first, 'there is something pretty and interesting in this exciting colorfulness'. 'It is not bold, but not conservative', says the female professor. 'And what do you think, Mr. Weiss (a Jewish family name)'? she asks the third professor, who sits between them looking bored and yawns. He kills the painting aggressively: 'Flowers, vase, it has the chic of an old-age home'. 'It's not good?' the painter that we cannot see asks hesitantly. 'Good? My son can draw something better and he has no hands, a tram ran over him', mutters Weiss in contempt. 'O.K. I understood, thank you', says the painter. 'What did you understand'? asks Weiss huskily, 'What are you, an artist or a ragpicker? Ahh??? Don't be such a loser!! If you want to be an artist, you should connect to your feelings. Don't you have any anger in you'? he yells at him. The painter takes down the picture and we see that it is Hitler (with the famous mustache, hairdo and a German accent). 'I'm sorry Sir, but I'm not an angry person', he tells Weiss politely. 'You didn't bring with you a painting that shows anger'? Weiss continues. 'No. everything I have is paintings of kittens', Hitler replies. Weiss almost throws up. 'Kittens is actually nice', says the woman professor. 'Thank you', says Hitler and turns to go. 'What do you mean "thank you"'?? yells Weiss, 'get angry at me, god dammit, get mad!! I'm trampling on your future here'!! Hitler is embarrassed, moves uncomfortably in his place, 'Maybe I'm a bit angry', he says softly. 'You're a bit angry', repeats Weiss cynically. 'Get angry'!!!! he yells, 'Get angry!!! I say that you have no talent, that your work sucks!! Get mad at me god dammit, get mad'!! Hitler looks frightened, 'Yes, I think I'm upset', he continues politely. Weiss doesn't let go, 'Get mad at me, god dammit, get mad!! I'm the one that separates you from your fantasy'. Hitler looks puzzled, thinking about Weiss' words. Weiss gets up; he looks very intimidating as he is photographed from a low angle. He orders Hitler, 'Say "Weiss, I hate you"'!! '"Weiss, I hate you"', says Hitler calmly. 'I pee on your dream', Weiss says and encourages him to demonstrate hatred. 'Do you hate me? My family? C'mon say it'!! Hitler says he loathes Weiss' family. In this scene, the soundtrack plays 'the Valkyrie dance' as Weiss turns Hitler into an angry man and says 'Do you hate, my friend? I fucked your sister'. Hitler bursts out, the close-up presents him as the audience knows his mimics from the propaganda films, yelling, 'I hope they'll burn. I'll blow up all of you'!!! 'Great, great, that's what I'm looking for', says Weiss and sits down, 'now take this anger and do something with it. I promise you that in the future there won't be a single person who won't know the name…ahhh what is your name'? 'Adolf Shikelgruber'. 'Shikelgruber??? Change the name into something more catchy'. Hitler salutes and leaves. The professors compliment Weiss on the wonderful process.[65]

This skit adds to the attempt to dismantle the anxiety caused by Hitler's image, by portraying him as a humiliated confused 'little man'. But the self-deprecating humour is quite unusual because it 'blames' the Jews for their destiny. According to the skit, a Jewish professor is the one who changes the nice, polite, young Hitler and turns him into an angry, hating, frustrated individual.[66]

One of the common theories adopted by many researchers is that for humour to happen, it must come as a surprise. *The Jews are Coming* 'Hitler in Vienna' skit is primarily based on the element of surprise[67]: the audience does not know the identity of the painter. Once his identity is revealed, each word takes on a different meaning.

One of the most basic human needs is having control over one's environment. Control means knowing what is happening in your existential environment at any given moment: the better the control, the better the odds of survival. The saying 'knowledge equals power' is a result of this primary human quality. Humour inherently tends to adhere to those significant qualities of human nature. Knowing means being on the right side of things. Not knowing is a flaw, and flaws make for good platforms for humour. Not knowing is a situation in which one or more details are not revealed to the person or persons involved in the situation. The observer is unaware of the 'hidden detail', which appears at the end of the act. This sub-genre includes two options: the first is that the person performing the action is not aware of the latent detail and the second is that neither is the observer. It will become known to them at the end of the process.[68]

In the aforementioned skit, the 'hidden detail' is twofold. At the beginning, the viewers do not know the identity of the painter and, as his character is revealed, the meaning of the skit changes. In addition, Weiss, the art professor, is unaware of the future. Therefore, his statements regarding the anger and hatred Hitler must feel towards his family and his friends convey a meaning which his character is unable to comprehend. This gap creates the humour.

Hitler as a buffoon who does not understand his own doing is portrayed in the skit 'The cancellation of the Holocaust' in the show, *A Place for Worries* [*Makom ledeaga*] (Matar Productions, 2008-2010, Channel 10). This skit represents Jews in line in a concentration camp using all the known images from Holocaust films: bent, miserable women, children and men with the yellow star on their ragged clothes, as Tobias Ebbrecht terms it: a series of well-known, repetitive Holocaust narratives and visuals that have appeared so often in western popular culture that they have almost become clichés.[69] One Jew (Maayan Blum) standing in line is happy and cheerful, whistling a happy tune. He is sure they are about to enter real showers and then go to work (and he is happy because, 'the work is liberating'). His friend in line, who doesn't understand how he can be so cheerful, explains to him that he is wrong: they are about to be killed. The happy Jew cannot grasp it. It seems too illogical because 'it is immoral to kill Jews. It is racism'. The happy Jew is determined to explain their mistake to the Nazi officer (Dvir Benedek) who approaches as threatening music is heard. The happy Jew explains to the vicious officer that he cannot kill them, 'It is immoral to kill Jews. It is racism'. The officer who at first laughed a vicious laugh nods his head, scratches his hair and is completely puzzled by this announcement. 'Oh no', he mumbles and asks the Jew's permission to check the order again. In the following sequence, the message is transferred from one officer to another, up the Nazi hierarchy. All the senior officers learn, to their amazement, that 'it is immoral to kill Jews. It is racism'. Finally, Hitler himself receives a phone call regarding this matter. Hearing that 'it is immoral to kill Jews. It is racism', he is shocked. The skit that uses every possible cliché of a dramatic Holocaust film shows the camera approaching Hitler's face, as threatening music is heard in the background, in order to explode the visual through incongruity, 'It is true', Hitler mumbles into the phone with an embarrassed look, 'so tell them to stop it'. The camera returns to the concentration camp: through the huge speakers, the Nazi officer apologizes to the inmates, explains that a mistake has taken place and that the Nazis have realized that 'it is immoral to kill Jews. It is racism'. He sends everyone back home and wishes them farewell, 'Thank you, goodbye, and I hope this war will end and peace will come'. While the sugary song from the film and musical, *Annie*, 'The sun will come out tomorrow' is playing in the background, the Jews and Nazis shake hands and go their separate ways.

As opposed to internet memes that mock Hitler, this skit dismantles the 'absolute evil' in another way: through using fantasy, black humour and absurdity created by the incongruity of combining themes from Holocaust films with Hollywood melodramas that have happy endings. This dismantling of Hitler's image is another struggle against Israeli collective memory agents who insist on reliving the Holocaust in the present in order to create a constant feeling of victimization.

In conclusion, objectors to the humorous, satiric and parodic representations of Hitler see them as a threat to the serious moral remembrance of the Holocaust. In my opinion, the Hebrew texts mocking

Hitler represent the exact opposite: in a society drenched in Holocaust awareness, they are yet another important defence mechanism for the young generations who live in a society that relives the trauma of the Holocaust in the present. Those who seek to remove themselves from the constant anxiety imposed on them by collective memory agents create humouristic contents which put up a barrier between the Jewish-Israelis and the trauma, keeping the horrors at distance and diminishing the ultimate epitomes of evil, thus allowing the anxiety to be relieved, if only temporarily. They do not threaten the serious discussions regarding Hitler which, in Israel, are an integral part of the educational system and of everyday life. In addition, paradoxically these humouristic representations increase Hitler's presence in Israeli daily life, turning him into an integral part of the Jewish-Israeli contemporary collective identity.

Notes

1. R. Herzog, *Dead Funny: Humor in Hitler's Germany* (New York: Melville House, 2011); S. Lipman, 'Can A Swastika Be Funny?' *The Jewish Week,* Online: https://forums.spacebattles.com/threads/can-swastikas-be-funny.129890/. Accessed February 20, 2014; Wisse, *No Joke*, pp. 143-181; Levin, *Through the tears;* Ostrower, *Without Humor we would have Killed Ourselves,* pp. 49-97.
2. Steir-Livny, *Let the Memorial Hill Remember*, pp. 37-78.
3. A. Reading, 'Clicking on Hitler: The virtual Holocaust @ Home', in: Barbie Zelizer (ed.) *Visual Culture and the Holocaust* (Rutgers University Press, 2001), pp. 323-337;E. Pfanzelter, 'At the crossroads with public history: mediating the Holocaust on the Internet', *Holocaust Studies. A Journal of Culture and History*, 21/4 (2015), pp 250-271; V. G. Walden, 'New Ethical Questions and Social Media: Young People's Construction of Holocaust Memory Online', *Frames Cinema Journal* http://framescinemajournal.com/article/new-ethical-questions-and-social-media-young-peoples-construction-of-holocaust-memory-online/ Accessed 1 June 2015.
4. http://www.catsthatlooklikehitler.com/cgi-bin/seigmiaow.pl
5. For example, in one of the plots he wears a T-shirt with a play on words 'I love Juice' and sips from a cup. See:http://hipsterhitler.com/animation/
6. Rosenfeld, *Hi Hitler*, pp.292-339.
7. Macros are photographs with superimposed texts on which the surfers can add captions. Image macros juxtapose images and texts in ironic or absurd combinations between visual and text and within the photograph. See Rosenfeld, *Hi Hitler*, pp. 292-339.
8. G. Ben-Ari, G, *'Hitler matza hanaya',* [*'Hitler Found a Parking Space'*] *Yediot Aharonot*, 26 February 2010, http://e.walla.co.il/?w=/267/1819879 Accessed 30.3.2014 [Hebrew].
9. 'Hitler gets banned from Xbox Live', https://www.youtube.com/watch?v=sfkDxF2kn1I - 9,307,093 views by 7 March 2017.
10. Usain Bolt Breaks 100m World Record and Hitler Reacts, https://www.youtube.com/watch?v=9xUS30-RFf0 - 3,792,676 views by 7 March 2017.

11. Hitler and the vuvuzela at the 2010 Fifa World Cup, https://www.youtube.com/watch?v=z-Ln_rqPpPk - 3,588,504 views by 7 March 2017.
12. J. Dubs, 'Downfall / Hitler Reacts', *Know your Meme*, 2009 http://knowyourmeme.com/memes/downfall-hitler-reacts Accessed 7 September, 2014.
13. Dubs, 'Downfall / Hitler Reacts'.
14. Regarding the problem of the use of the copyrighted material in '*Hitler Rants*' parodies, see, A. Schwabach, 'Reclaiming Copyright From the Outside In: What the Downfall Hitler Meme Means for Transformative Works, Fair Use, and Parody,' *Buffalo Intellectual Property Law Journal*, 2012, http://papers.ssrn.com/sol3/papers.cfm?abstract_id=2040538 Accessed 1 February 2016.
15. S. Kotler, *Folklore beidan hainternet: hainterakzua bein hamemim hitler mitazben vehatarbut haisraeli* [*Folklore in the Age of Internet: The Interaction Between Hitler Gets Angry Memes and Israeli Culture*], a thesis as part of the requirements for a Master's degree, supervised by Prof. Hagar Salamon, Hebrew University of Jerusalem, 2015 [Hebrew].
16. Dubs, 'Downfall / Hitler Reacts'.
17. Ben-Ari, 'Hitler Found a Parking Space'.
18. Sover, *Humor: The Pathway to Human Laughter*, p. 29.
19. Ibid, pp. 97, 104.
20. I. Avisar, 'Tiud veitzuv shel todaa historit besirtey taamula' ['Documentation and Visualization of Historic Aearness in Propaganda Films'], *Zmnaim*, 39-40, 1991, pp. 38-47.
21. R. C. Reimer , 'Does Laughter Make the Crime Disappear?: An Analysis of Cinematic Images of Hitler and the Nazis, 1940-2007,' (September 2009) Feature Articles Issue 52 http://sensesofcinema.com/2009/feature-articles/does-laughter-make-the-crime-disappear-an-analysis-of-cinematic-images-of-hitler-and-the-nazis-1940-2007/ Accessed 2 November 2015.
22. Reimer, 'Does laughter'.
23. Sover, *Humor: The Pathway to Human Laughter*. pp.19-20.
24. E. Oring, 'Jokes and the Discourse on Disaster', T*he Journal of American Folklore* Vol. 100, No. 397 (Jul. - Sep., 1987), pp.276-286.
25. J. Palmer, *The Logic of the Absurd* (London: BFI, 1987).
26. See Sover, *Humor: The Pathway to Human Laughter*, p.28,92.
27. C. J. Gilbert, 'Playing with Hitler: Downfall and Its Ludic Uptake', *Critical Studies in Media Communication,* Vol. 30, No. 5, (December 2013), pp.407-424.
28. See Milo, 'Black Humor in Folk Songs of Israeli Soldiers'.
29. L. Kaplan, 'It will get a terrific laugh:' On the problematic pleasures and politics of Holocaust humor', in H. Jenkins, T. McPherson, & J. Shattuc (eds), *Hop on Pop: The politics and pleasures of popular culture* (Durham and London: Duke University Press, 2002), pp.343-356.
30. S. L. Gilman, 'Is Life Beautiful? Can the Shoah be funny? Some thoughts on recent and older films', *Critical Inquiry*, Vol. 26, No. 2 (Winter, 2000), pp.279-308.
31. Ibid.
32. Sover, *Humor: The Pathway to Human Laughter*, p.125-127.
33. 'Parody'. In Merriam Webster online dictionary. http://www.merriamwebster.com/dictionary/parody. Accessed 2 June 2015.
34. Gilbert, 'Playing with Hitler'.

35. Ibid.
36. Ben-Ari, 'Hitler Found a Parking Space'; A. Caril, E. Shif, & A. Shavit, 'Zohakim mitahat lasafam: humor hashoah mehahamishia hakamerit vead eretz nehederet' [Holocaust Humor: from the *Hahamishia Hakamerit* to *EretzNehederet*], *Walla*, 2 May 2011 http://e.walla.co.il/?w=/267/1819879 Accessed 2.10.2014 [Hebrew]; I. Dolev, 'Ma pitom hitler' ['Why Hitler?'], *Haaretz*, Musaf Haaretz, 9 April 2010, pp. 36-38 [Hebrew].
37. Rosenfeld, *Hi Hitler*, pp.292-339, especially pp.305-339.
38. Ibid.
39. L. Steir-Livny, 'Hitler Rants on YouTube Parodies inHebrew', *The European Journal of Humour Research*, Vol 4, No. 4, pp. 105-121.
40. C. Lankshear, & M. Knobel, (eds), *A New Literacies Sampler* (New York: Peter Lang, 2007), pp. 1-24; L. Shifman, 'An anatomy of a YouTube meme', *New Media and Society*, 14 (2) (2012), pp.187-203; Shifman, *Memes in digital culture, pp.* 119-150.
41. W. D. Gehring, *Parody as film genre,* (Westport, CT: Greenwood Publishing, 1999).
42. R. Hariman, 'Political parody and public culture, *Quarterly Journal of Speech*, 94, 3 (2008), pp.247-272.
43. Gilbert, 'Playing with Hitler'.
44. Kotler, *Folklore in the Age of Internet*.
45. See in Chapter 4.
46. Dagan and Dishon, 'Holocaust-Nostalgia'.
47. See Chapter 3.
48. Figley, *Compassion Fatigue*, pp. 1-20.
49. Shifman, *Televised Humor*, pp.143-150; Zandberg, 'Critical Laughter'; Steir-Livny, *Let the Memorial Hill Remember;* Steir-Livny, 'Holocaust humor, satire, and parody'.
50. P. Bourdieu, *Distinction: A Social Critique of the Judgement of Taste* (London: Routledge, 1984a); P. Bourdieu, P, 'The Field of Cultural Production, or: The Economic World Revered' *Poetics* 12 (1984b), pp.311-356; J. Fiske, *Television Culture* (London and New York: Routledge, 1987); S. Hall, S. *Representation (London*: Open University Press and Sage, 1997).
51. Shifman, *Televised Humor,* pp.143-150*;* J. Meyer, 'Humor as a Double-Edged Sword: Four Functions of Humor in Communication,' *Communication Theory* 10. 3 (2000), pp.310-333; O. H. Lynch, 'Humorous Communication: Finding a Place for Humor in Communication Research', *Communication Theory*, 12.4, (2002), pp.423-445; Brook, 'Virtual Ethnicity'; M. Bakhtin, *Rabelais and His World*, trans. Hélène Iswolsky, (Bloomington: Indiana University Press, 1993). On the ambivalent perception of Holocaust satire in Israel, see Zandberg, 'Critical Laughter'.
52. S. Litman, 'Behazara leva Braun' ['Back to Eva Brown'], *Haaretz*, 25 January 2016 http://www.haaretz.co.il/gallery/art/.premium-1.2830419 Accessed 26 January 2016.
53. A. Azulay, 'Mi haya maamin ata kore germanit' ('Who could believe you can read German'), *Theory and Criticism* 15 (Winter, 1999), pp. 49-62.
54. R. Rosen, *Live and Die as Eva Braun* http://roeerosen.com/tagged/Live-and-Die-as-EvaBraun Accessed 1 March 2016.
55. R. Rosen, http://roeerosen.com/image/15944447327 Accessed 1 March 2016.
56. B. Arad, *The ArtLab*http://www.theartlab.co.il/mentors/boaz-arad/ Accessed 1 March 2016.
57. D. Arieli-Horowitz, 'Boaz Arad – Voozvooz', History and Theory, Bezalel, 4 (Spring, 2007) https://bezalel.secured.co.il/zope/home/he/1173510036/1176612903 Accessed 1 March 2016.

58. S. Edelstein Israeli Art Now http://boazarad.net/wp-content/uploads/2010/texts/Boaz%20Arad%20IAN%20en.pdf Accessed 2 March 2016.
59. G. Ben-Ner, Boaz Arad: VOZVOZ, The Center for Contemporary Art, Tel-Aviv 2007 Synchronization of a Moustache http://boazarad.net/wp-content/uploads/2010/texts/Synchronization%20of%20a%20Moustache.pdf Accessed 2 March 2016.
60. Edelstdein, *Israeli Art Now*; Arieli-Horowitz, 'Boaz Arad'.
61. A. Ronco, 'Hitler in Jerusalem', *City Mouse Online*, 20 July 2008 [Hebrew]. http://www.mouse.co.il/CM.articles_item,610,209,25690,.aspx Accessed 2 April 2016.
62. Ibid.
63. Shifman, *Televised Humor*, pp.143-150; Zandberg, 'Critical Laughter'; Steir-Livny, *Let the Memorial Hill Remember; L.* Steir-Livny, 'Holocaust humor, satire, and parody on Israeli television', *Jewish Film and New Media*, 3/2, (Fall, 2015), pp.193-219.
64. Meyers, Neiger, and Zandberg, *Communicating Awe*.
65. https://www.youtube.com/watch?v=DVINXflQU4I
66. This self-deprecating, self-accusation appeared in another skit of *The Jews are Coming*. In the seventh episode in the second season, in the skit, 'Jews vote for Hitler', three well-dressed intelligent Jews are sitting in a fancy café in Berlin in 1932 and discuss the upcoming elections. Two of them had heard vague wonderful things about Hitler and try explaining them to the third Jew who hasn't heard about Hitler. They describe Hitler as a war hero with a firm ideology who wrote a book and wants to change Germany. When the third Jew tries to ask the other two questions about Hitler beyond the shallow clichés ('What is the book about? What is his ideology'?), it turns out that they know nothing. They describe the book as 'long', the ideology as 'strong', and it is clear that they do not understand anything. They are shallow people who do not check the facts and get carried away by the superficial elements that symbolize an intellectual. At the end of the scene, all three of them, including the third Jew, who is superficial enough to be persuaded by their stories, wave at the Nazi parade that goes by. See: 'Jews vote for Hitler', The Jews are Coming, 1.4.2016 https://www.youtube.com/watch?v=aZzHVyGUGZo
67. Sover, *Humor: The Pathway to Human Laughter*, p. 29.
68. Ibid.
69. Ebbrecht, 'Migrating Images'.

10

Holocaust Jokes in Contemporary Israeli Websites: Characters and Developments

In his book, *Jokes and Their Relation to the Unconscious* (1905), Sigmund Freud made a breakthrough in the research of humour and laughter, and continued to engage in the matter in an article called *Humor* (1928).[1] Freud argued that in the same way that dreams compensate for unresolved affective states which occurred in reality, and treats them or repairs them, jokes are also a tool through which people can touch issues around which they are blocked or inhibited, such as sexuality and aggression. The joke, claims Freud, is a tool which can bypass the censor, a kind of manmade mask in order to get around the prohibitions. The joke is like a defensive shield, allowing people to manifest their aggressive impulses without being criticized or punished for them by society.

The chapters in this book have so far demonstrated that most humouristic, satirical and parodic texts in Israel engage in the commemoration of the Holocaust, its transgenerational transmission, its politicization, commercialization, instrumentalization, its impact on the ethnic conflict in Israel, and more. But, for the most part, the various texts avoid touching the dark core of the Holocaust itself. Holocaust jokes in Hebrew are a genre in itself, an exception which does not prove the rule. They pertain to the Holocaust itself and humourously refer to both the murderers and the Jewish victims.

The main part of this chapter, will explore the themes of Holocaust jokes in several contemporary Israeli leading websites on the subject.[2] The chapter will examine whether the themes of the contemporary Israeli websites jokes in Hebrew differ from those of the Holocaust jokes written and told by Jews under the Nazi regime; whether they address different issues, or express different perceptions of the trauma.

The analysis of the Holocaust jokes appearing on websites in Hebrew reveals that for the most part, the same Holocaust jokes appear over and over again on multiple sites, at times with slight changes and, at times, in exactly the same form. They present several main areas of discussion, some of which appeared during the Holocaust and some of which are new.[3]

Israeli Jokes whose Themes Appeared during the Holocaust

The themes which emerged in jokes during the Holocaust and also appear in Holocaust jokes in contemporary Israeli websites include humour that revolves around hunger, death, eradication as well as famous myths, such as using Jewish corpses to manufacture soap. This self-deprecating, black humour can be understood as a defence mechanism for the offspring of the victims: a way to deal with the past trauma while removing it a bit from the collective soul.

There are very few jokes dealing with the yellow badge, ridiculing the Jewish mark of disgrace, for instance: One German boy wanders around the ghetto and sees another boy wearing a yellow badge. The German boy asks him, 'Say, are you Jewish?' and the Jewish boy replies: 'No, I'm a sheriff...'

Other jokes engage in the mass murder. For instance, a joke opens with the question,

'How can you fit six million Jews into a car?'

'Two in the front, two in the back and the rest in the ashtray...' [numbers vary between different versions of the joke on various sites but the general idea remains the same].

Some jokes focus on the absurd. For instance,

> 'What sign was hanging at the entrance to the gas chambers?'
> 'Caution! Watch your step'
>
> 'What's an extraordinary Jew during the Holocaust?'
> 'A living Jew...'

The jokes often revolve around Jews who turned into ash after their cremation, with an emphasis on chimney jokes. For example, a boy is sitting on a chimney over the camp's incinerators, while Hitler passes by and asks,

> 'Son, what are you doing up there?'
> 'I'm waiting for my parents.'

Another joke goes as follows,

> 'Why were the Jews considered to be magicians during the Holocaust?' 'Do you know any other people who can walk in through the door and leave through the chimney?'

A similar joke asks,

'How is the Holocaust connected to Santa Claus?'

'Santa enters through the chimney and leaves through the door, in the Holocaust they entered through the door and left through the chimney [...]'

The humouristic discussion of the extermination holds an entire group of jokes dedicated to oven jokes. Among others, there is the following joke,

'What's the difference between Jews in the oven and a pizza in the oven?'

'The pizza doesn't scream...'

The joke has several variations, including,

'What's the difference between a Jew and plum pie?'

'The pie doesn't scream when you put it in the oven [...]'

Another joke reads, two Nazis are walking through the extermination camp, while one says to the other,

'It smells like caramel around here'.

'Yes, they're burning the diabetics today[...]'

One of the myths which emerged during the Holocaust was the usage of Jewish bodies in order to manufacture soap. Ostrower learned that soap jokes already began appearing during the Holocaust (for instance, some Jews displayed some self-humour by saying that if they were to turn into soap, they would prefer it to be a nicely fragranced one).[4] The myth infiltrated into Israeli culture in its earliest days and often served as an insult in Hebrew against Holocaust survivors and/or people who were seen as 'Diaspora Jews', meaning pale and weak. There are many Holocaust jokes in Hebrew referring to the myth as if it were part of the reality of the Holocaust. For example, two Jews are fighting in a gas chamber. One throws a bar of soap at the other, who immediately protests: 'Hey, we said no parents involved'!

Another example,

'What did it say on the ingredients of soap manufactured during the Holocaust'?

'Made with natural ingredients, such as distilled water, Jacob, Moses, David [...]'

The hunger, lack of hope and determinism, which were given a humouristic tone during the Holocaust, also appear in Israeli jokes concerning children during the Holocaust. For instance, Hitler comes up to one of the children in the ghetto and asks him, 'How old are you?' The excited child replies: 'I'll be seven next week'. Hitler responds: 'Aren't we optimistic'? Another joke goes, A young boy approaches Hitler and asks him, 'Say, what will I be when I grow up'? Hitler replies, 'I don't know, perhaps a shoe, perhaps a bar of soap, perhaps a picture [...]'

Death seems to be at the core of more Israeli jokes compared to hunger and starvation jokes. One of the only jokes about children and hunger describes Hitler walking through the ghetto as he encounters a child. He asks him, 'Son, how much do you weigh'? and the boy replies: 'Five kilograms'. Hitler continues walking and sees another boy. Hitler asks him, 'Son, how much do you weigh'? and the boy replies: 'Four kilograms'. Hitler continues his walk, sees another boy and asks him, 'Son, how much do you weigh'? the boy replies, 'Seven kilograms' and Hitler says, 'Fatty...'

While the aggressive function of humour was an integral part of the jokes which appeared during the Holocaust, aggression, whether due to frustration or a sense of superiority, rarely appears in Holocaust jokes in Hebrew. Within the category of Hitler jokes, there are some jokes which link him with his murderous actions, such as,

'Why did Hitler commit suicide'?
'Because he received the gas bill [...]'

and

'Why wasn't Hitler a good pupil'?
'Because he had concentration problems [...]'

while other jokes depict Hitler as a powerful man, making fun of his victims. For instance, Hitler grabs three Jews and tells them, 'Well, jump into the chemical pool right now and swim to the other side or I'll kill you right on the spot'! The three obviously do not have much choice. They jump into the pool, they swim and swim and swim; the first one loses his hand and teeth, the second one's eyebrow falls off, the third one loses his leg, but they continue swimming [...] they reach the other side of the pool and get out, exhausted, missing half their body parts [...] then, finally, Hitler tells them, 'Whoa, good for you, really! Ok then [...] let's hop into the showers and head home'. In another joke, Hitler wanders around the ghetto as he sees a boy jumping. He asks the boy, 'Son, how high can you jump'? The boy replies, 'One meter'. Hitler says, 'Let's see'. The boy jumps and Hitler hands him one loaf of bread. By evening, the rumor about Hitler going around handing out a loaf of bread for every meter jumped spreads around the ghetto. As of the next day, everyone starts jumping. Hitler walks around the ghetto again and asks one boy how high he can jump. The boy replies, 'Two meters'. He jumps and Hitler gives him two loaves of bread. He approaches another boy and asks, 'Son, how high can you jump'? The boy replies, 'Five meters'. He jumps and receives five loaves of bread. Hitler walks up to another boy and asks, 'Son, how high can you jump'? The boy replies, 'Ten meters', and Hitler says, 'Kill him, he can jump over the wall'.

As opposed to jokes during the Holocaust that ridiculed Hitler (and opposed to other representations in Israeli culture that turn him into a buffoon),[5] and opposed to Hitler being ridiculed in Israeli TV satire, art and new media, there are very few Holocaust jokes on Hebrew internet sites that ridicule Hitler. Most of the jokes are self-deprecating. They ridicule his victims and keep him in the position of the vicious Führer.

Ostrower mentions that one of the functions of humour during the Holocaust was sexual, venting frustration through obscenities and sexual discussions.[6] This theme scarcely appears in Israel's Holocaust jokes. The most prominent example of a Holocaust joke with sexual characteristics also involves the soap myth mentioned earlier. One boy sees his friend masturbating with soap in the ghetto. The boy asks him, 'What are you doing'??? and the friend replies, 'Shagging your mother'.

Unique Elements in Contemporary Israeli Holocaust Jokes

My analysis of the Holocaust jokes in Hebrew discovers that the unique elements in contemporary Israeli Holocaust jokes relate to several fields: some jokes combine the Holocaust with current technology (which did not exist in the 1940s), some use a play on words, combining concepts taken from Holocaust and Hebrew words and expressions, some engage in the outcomes of the Holocaust (things that Jews under the Nazi regime could not have known), and some link between the Holocaust and current terror attacks in Israel.

Holocaust and Technology

One genre of jokes juxtaposes the Holocaust with media devices that did not yet exist or were not common during the Nazi regime. An example of such a jokes is,

'What does a child in the Holocaust who doesn't have batteries for his Walkman do?'

'Connects it to the fence'.

Another widely spread joke: One day, Hitler was standing on a mountain, ordering Jews to get into peculiar poses and then, throwing them off the mountain. Eichmann asked him, 'Hitler my friend, what are you doing'? Hitler, amused, replied, 'Don't interrupt me, I'm playing Tetris…' (the joke appears in various places in various different lengths, but the idea of presenting the extinction of the Jews as a game of Tetris appears in all of them).

Play on Words in Hebrew

In her book, Ostrower presents the intellectual function of humour, which included, for example, a play on words and meaning, and using words and expressions taken from Polish and German.[7] In Hebrew, the intellectual function of humour is comprised of a large portion of the Holocaust jokes that combine concepts related to the Holocaust with words and expressions from Israeli culture. These jokes demonstrate the uniqueness of Israeli language and culture. The incongruity between concepts from the Holocaust and concepts from Israeli culture generates humour. There are many examples of such a use of humour. For instance, an example for intellectual humour is:

'How did they call the kindergarten in the Holocaust'?

'Shoahton'.

This play on words is a combination of the Hebrew word for Holocaust, *Shoah*, and the diminutive suffix *'on'* (similar to the suffix 'et/ette' in English).

Other jokes use typical dishes associated with Israeli culture in order to create the pun, for instance,

'What kind of food did they have in the Holocaust'?

'Shoaharma' [a combination of *Shoah* and the popular meat dish *Shuarma*].

Many jokes borrow words and concepts from Israeli culture and position them in the realm of the Holocaust and its myths. For example, one of the best known Israeli children's song is *The Soap Cried Loudly* by Miriam Yalan-Shteklis. The first line of the song is, 'The soap cried loudly, Danny (a very common Israeli name) does not want me anymore'. The joke which uses this song as a reference is as follows, 'The soap cried loudly, Hitler does not want me anymore'. Another joke involves *Hayehudim* (literally: The Jews), a very famous rock band in Israel. The joke asks,

'What was the most popular band in the Holocaust'?

'The Jews'.

One of the favorite foods among Israeli children is schnitzel (fried chicken breast covered with bread crumbs). In Hebrew, the word 'schnitzel' resembles the word 'nitzol', the Hebrew word for Holocaust survivor. A joke relying on this resemblance:

'What did people in the ghetto eat during the Holocaust?'

'Schnitzols …' [a mix of the Hebrew 'Holocaust survivors' and 'schnitzels']

'Concentration hour' is a familiar Hebrew term in kindergartens in Israel, referring to a time when the kindergarten teacher gathers all the children around her in order to do some common activity, yet the word concentration is also associated with the term 'concentration camp'. This produced the following joke:

'What did the kindergarten teacher do in the Holocaust'?

'Concentration hour…'

Baguette is a famous kind of bread, both in Israel and worldwide. Adding the vowel 'o' to the word generates a word combining baguette and ghetto. A famous joke in Hebrew asks:

'What was the name of the most famous bakery in the Holocaust?'

'Baghetto…'

Shlomo Artzi is a very well-known singer in Israel. One of his most famous songs is called *According to the Trains' Movement*. The related joke asks:

'What song was a favorite at the ghetto'?

'*According to the Trains' Movement…*'.

Bamahane is the IDF's official magazine. However, it includes the word *Mahane*, meaning camp, which is associated in Hebrew not only with a military camp but also with the Holocaust's concentration camp.

'What was the most popular newspaper in the Holocaust'?

'*Bamahane*'.

As part of the integration of the Holocaust into Israeli culture, there emerged a group of jokes combining the Holocaust with titles of famous TV shows in Israel, whose names have twofold meanings associated with the Holocaust. For instance:

'Which TV show did children watch during the Holocaust'?

'*The Train of Surprises…*'

'What was the favorite TV show in the extermination camps'?

'*A Matter of Time…*'

'What did the elderly like to watch during the Holocaust'?

'*Zehu Ze*!' (literally translates as: *That's it*!).

The Results of the Holocaust

Other jokes in Hebrew engage in the outcomes of the Holocaust and therefore could not have appeared during the Holocaust. For instance, jokes that relate to the number 'six million', have many different versions.

'Why did Israel beat Poland in football'?

'Because it has six million die-hard fans'.

Another version of the joke:

'Why can Hitler be a football star'?

'Because he has six million die-hard fans'.

Another joke describes Hitler and Eichmann sitting on top of a mountain. Hitler throws a Jew off the mountain and bursts out laughing, but Eichmann sits still. Hitler asks Eichmann: 'Why aren't you laughing?' Eichmann replies, 'Hitler, for the six millionth time, it's not funny'!

A sub-group of these jokes are Anne Frank Jokes. Anne Frank jokes form a category in itself within the new Israeli Holocaust jokes revolving around its outcomes. Anne Frank only became a myth in the decades after the end of the Second World War. Her father, Otto Frank, the only man among those hiding in the attic to survive, received her diary when he returned to Amsterdam after the war from Miep Gies who worked for his company and facilitated the group of Jews in hiding. For a long time, Frank objected to the publication of the painful personal diary and considered only allowing a narrow group of friends and relatives to read it. But after contemplating for a long time, and after having made some changes along with a close friend, he finally gave his consent. The diary was published in 1947 in Dutch, by an unknown publisher. At first, the book did not gain much success. However, slowly but surely, the book's audience of readers expanded, and a second edition was soon published and sold out. The diary was published in English in the USA in 1952, with an introduction written by Eleanor Roosevelt. In 1955, the stage adaptation of the book on Broadway quickly became a blockbuster. As of the mid-1950s, the diary became a global asset: 1959 saw the premiere of the film, *The Diary of Anne Frank* (George Stevens), which was also, like the play on which it was based, widely successful. The Anne Frank House opened in the year 1960. This is the same house where the family members hid during the war, and it has hundreds of thousands of visitors every year. The diary was translated into more than fifty languages, and approximately 30 million copies of it, in various languages, have been sold worldwide. Anne Frank's name appears on plazas and streets, coins and stamps, awards, conferences, exhibitions and monuments. Through its universalization, the diary has become a symbol of human suffering in general, rather than a specific symbol of the Holocaust and Jewish suffering.[8]

For the reasons stated above, Anne Frank was not mentioned at all in jokes made by Jews during the Holocaust. Related Holocaust jokes in Hebrew mostly refer to the hiding place and the diary. For instance,

'What are the last words in Anne Frank's diary'?

'Just a minute, there's someone at the door….'

'How do we know that Anne Frank was not gay'?

'She never came out of the closet'.

'What did Anne Frank tell Hitler when he asked her on a date'?

'Wait, I need to check my diary'.

Holocaust Remembrance in Israel

Another group of new Holocaust jokes in contemporary Israel websites revolve around its commemoration in Israel. The jokes illustrate the acting out of the trauma in the present, hence reinforcing the claim that for Jewish-Israelis, the Holocaust is not an historical event that ended many years ago in a different place. For example, *The Ghetto Fighters Kibbutz* [*Kibbutz Lohamei HaGeta'ot*] was founded in northern Israel after the establishment of the State, and its founding members include partisans and ghetto fighters. A joke about the kibbutz goes as follows:

'Why did they put up an electrical fence in Kibbutz Lohamei HaGeta'ot'?

'In order to make the survivors feel at home'.

Another joke emphasizes that the blurred boundaries between past and present do not only characterize survivors but rather Israelis in general, along with Germans who continue to live their lives according to the Nazi code:

A group of Israelis fly to Germany in order to visit the concentration camps and see all the historical places. After having landed they get on a bus, which breaks down on the way. The driver says, 'Wait, let me get us some help', and then walks around until he sees a house and knocks on the door. A Nazi-looking German opens the door, holding a beer and bratwurst, and the driver says to him, 'I need help, I have a group of Israelis stuck back out there, could you help me'? The German replies, 'No, I can't, my microwave is too small'. It is noteworthy that this joke comprises a representation of the perception according to which there is no 'other Germany'. It also clearly demonstrates how the past infiltrates the present. Such a blend is also unknowingly represented, as noted, in the intellectual Holocaust jokes in Hebrew, creating wordplays by using concepts from Israeli culture, and inserting the world of the Holocaust into current Israeli discourse and television.

Holocaust and Contemporary Terror Attacks

The most powerful representation of this blend lies in another group of new Holocaust jokes in contemporary Israel websites, associating the Holocaust with Palestinian terror attacks of recent decades, in which terrorists blow themselves up within large crowds of Israelis. These jokes, which naturally were not a part of the reality of the Holocaust are a part of the projection of the Holocaust onto the Israeli-Palestinian conflict.[9] These jokes present the Palestinians as the successors of the Nazis and the Israeli Jews as eternal victims – those who were victimized by the Nazis in the past are victimized by the Palestinians in the present. For example,

'What's common to terror attacks and what did the Holocaust tried to prevent'?

'Human overpopulation' [in Hebrew, the expression for human overpopulation literally translates as 'population explosion'].

One of the most difficult terrorist attacks in the history of Israel occurred at Tel Aviv's Dolphinarium on 1 June 2001, in which 21 people were killed. The joke referring to the incident, also serving the intellectual function of humour, creates a wordplay based on the similarity between the name 'Adolf' and the first syllable of the word 'Dolphinarium'.

'Which three Adolfs massacred Jews?

'Adolf Hitler, Adolf Eichmann and Adolf-inarium' [sounds like, The Dolphinarium].

Jokes with Historical Errors

Another group of jokes, which only emerged after the Holocaust, are jokes including historical errors, mostly failing to differentiate between what happened in the ghettos and what happened in the concentration camps, treating those two domains equally, and projecting onto the ghettos events which only took place in concentration camps or in a specific concentration camp. These jokes did not exist during the Holocaust because, back then, Jews had good knowledge of the places in which they were imprisoned by the Nazis. The ghettos had no electric fences and the only place in which numbers were tattooed on the arms of the prisoners was Auschwitz. But the jokes in Hebrew often create a unification between ghettos and concentration camps into one large mixture of electric fences and number tattoos.

'What does a Jew do in the ghetto when his batteries run out'?

'Clings to the fence'.

'Who was the most popular kid in the ghetto'?

'90210' (the code of the prestigious neighbourhood Beverly Hills, CA and a famous TV show).

Another version of the same joke

'Who was the richest Jew in the ghetto'?

'90210'.

144 is the number for the Israeli telephone service center through which one can obtain telephone numbers of Israeli residents.

'Who knows the telephone numbers for everyone in the ghetto'?

'Number 144'.

Another erroneous joke referring to numbers tattooed goes,

'How do you pick up a girl in the ghetto?

'You ask her – can I have your number?'

A different version of the joke goes: Two Jewish girls are talking in the ghetto. Suddenly a man comes running and snatches the loaf of bread one of them was holding in her hands. The other says to her, 'Aren't you going to try and chase him'? She replies, 'Don't worry, I have his number'.

The soap, as noted, one of the main myths in the concentration camps, is sometimes also combined with the world of the ghettos in Hebrew jokes, for instance,

'What game did they play in the ghetto'?

'Sick, dying, dead, soap...' ['Sick, dying, dead' is an Israeli children's game].

Between European Holocaust Jokes and Israeli Holocaust Jokes

Ostrower's research on Jewish humour during the Holocaust found that it fulfilled all five main functions of humour: the aggressive function (including humour stemming from frustration), the sexual function, the social function, the intellectual function and the function of humour as a defence mechanism, including black humour and self-deprecating humour (which was the most apparent). In addition, she found that a form of scatological humour was added to the sexual function of humour, and that food-related humour was added to the function of humour as a defence mechanism.[10]

The analysis above shows that some of these functions were passed on to Israeli Holocaust jokes, some disappeared and some new ones, which did not exist before, emerged. Most of the jokes on Hebrew websites also have the function of serving as defence mechanisms; the absolute majority of the jokes are black humour and self-deprecating humour. The intellectual function of humour can also be found in jokes based on a play on words in the Hebrew language. However, Israeli Holocaust humour rarely expresses the sexual function of humour.[11] A social function was not found either, and it is particularly interesting to learn that aggressive humour is absent from Hebrew Holocaust jokes. While the Jews who were humiliated by the Nazis used humour also in order to produce a false sense of superiority for themselves, Jewish-Israeli websites do not engage in that whatsoever. There are mainly self-deprecating black humour jokes that describe the victims' lives. Very few jokes ridicule Hitler, while most of them actually illustrate the Nazis as superior. There are no jokes concerning mutiny or uprising, while the only joke referring to *The Ghetto Fighters Kibbutz*, which was founded by rebel fighters, actually revolves around the electric fence surrounding the kibbutz, thus erasing the powerful spirit of mutiny and fighting. Moreover, Israeli innovations, that is, jokes concerning the outcomes of the Holocaust, combining concepts from the Holocaust and Israeli culture, only indicate a deep sense of continued victimhood. There is no superiority in the jokes, but rather a penetration of the trauma into the Israeli present, by the use of a play on words, combining the Holocaust with concepts taken from Israeli popular culture and comparing them to terror attacks against Israelis.

According to Ostrower, jokes under the Nazi regime were essential, given the existential lack of hope and the lack of security and certainty regarding the next day. The jokes saved people from sinking into depression, soothed the longing for freedom and for the family, comprised an expression of self-defence, provided encouragement, hope, and sense of a coming end to the war.[12] Adir Cohen argues that

> Jokes are not naïve, but are rather a cultural index. In Israel, Holocaust jokes are part of a process of self-therapy. It is not disparagement, nor rudeness. These jokes indicate an immense fear of being in a situation which resembles the Holocaust.[13]

The themes appearing in Holocaust jokes in contemporary Israeli websites suggest that humour continues to serve as a defence mechanism, indicating that for Jewish-Israelis, the Holocaust is not an historical event that ended in the 1940s, but a continued trauma. The jokes indicate that the sense of victimhood is very much alive and refuses to release its grip. More than seventy years after the war ended, the fear of the Holocaust is still alive and present in Israeli society, even for those living for years and years in an independent country with a strong army.

Thus, opposed to the claims that the immigration to Israel changed the bases of Jewish humour and, opposed to the notions that living in an independent state stopped the need for self-deprecating humour, the analysis of the themes of Holocaust jokes in contemporary Israeli websites in comparison with Holocaust jokes that were created in Europe during the Holocaust show that, as Wisse claims, parts of Jewish humour were integrated into Israeli humour. Therefore, Jewish humour and Israeli humour are not two contradictory spheres and Israeli humour has Jewish traits.[14]

Unlike humour researchers claiming that Israeli humour is more aggressive than Jewish humour,[15] Holocaust jokes in Hebrew versus Holocaust jokes from the 1940s indicate that Israeli humour is much less aggressive and much more victim-like. Even though there are differences between Holocaust jokes in Hebrew and Holocaust humour, satire and parody in other cultural fields, their analysis shows similarities: Israeli society is living the Holocaust in the present, with an ongoing sense of victimhood. Humour helps as a defence mechanism in trying to overcome the heavy burden while reflecting sensations of ongoing fear and of daily life soaked in Holocaust memory and intimidations regarding a second Holocaust.

Notes

1. Freud, *Jokes and Their Relation to the Unconscious*; Freud, 'Humor'.
2. The websites analyzed are:
   http://www.bdihot.co.il/topic/%D7%A9%D7%95%D7%90%D7%94/
   http://www.2all.co.il/web/Sites/joke_no_censorship/PAGE2.asp
   https://www.fxp.co.il/showthread.php?t=2945976
   http://www.kipa.co.il/community/show/7345473
   http://www.inn.co.il/Forum/Forum.aspx/t139413
   https://www.facebook.com/CorrectingJokes/
   http://www.ynet.co.il/Ext/App/TalkBack/CdaViewOpenTalkBack/0,11382,L-1472448-3,00.html
   http://www.hydepark.co.il/topic.asp?topic_id=899457&forum_id=8947
   http://www.tapuz.co.il/blog/ViewEntry.asp?EntryId=52987&r=1
3. Naturally, there are jokes which simultaneously belong to several categories. Here, I provide examples for the different categories.
4. Ostrower, *Without Humor we would have killed ourselves.*
5. See Chapter 9.
6. Ostrower, *Without Humor we would have killed ourselves,* pp. 121-132.
7. Ostrower, *Without Humor we would have killed ourselves,* pp. 139-146.
8. For more information on this matter, see for example: M. Gies, *Anne Frank Remembered: The Story of the Woman who Helped to Hide the Frank Family* (New York: Simon and Schuster, 1987); M. Müller, *Anne Frank: The Biography* (New York: Metropolitan Books: Henry Holt, 1998); Carol Ann Lee, *A friend called Anne: one girl's story of war, peace,*

and a unique friendship with Anne Frank. New York: Viking, 2005; D. Porat, 'Arbaim shana shel maavak: hayoman shel anna frank imachhishei shoah' ['Forty Years of Struggle: Anne Frank's Diary and Holocaust Deniers, 1958-1998'], in: The Holocaust – the Unique and the Universal, essays presented in honor of Yehuda Bauer (Jerusalem, 2001), pp.160-183 [Hebrew].

9. For further discussion, see Chapter 7.
10. Ostrower, *Without Humor we would have killed ourselves,* pp. 323-326.
11. The absence of the sexual function from Israeli Holocaust humour is surprising, since Israeli culture definitely did associate the Holocaust with sexuality. Female Holocaust survivors have often been thought of as having used their bodies in order to survive, as can be seen in cultural texts as of the 1940s and until today. For more information, see:Steir-Livny, 'The threefold exile' [Hebrew].
12. Ostrower, *Without Humor we would have killed ourselves,* pp. 323-326.
13. Tuli Shragai and Hilit Levi, 'Shoah – ma mazhik beze?' ['Holocaust: What's funny about that?'], Walla!, 18 April 2001 http://news.walla.co.il/item/54337 Accessed 2 May 2002.
14. See for example, in the introduction and especially Ruth Wisse's analyses of the Jewishness of Israeli humour: Wisse, No Joke.
15. See in Chapter 1.

Conclusions

The combination of Holocaust memory with humour, satire and parody have been a matter of heated controversy in the western world. There are debates expressing harsh criticism against Holocaust humour, seeing it as a destructive representation which shallows and trivializes the trauma.[1]

This book has claimed that Israel is a distinct, unique domain within this debate. While most of the world sees the Holocaust as an historical tragedy, in Israel, the Holocaust is viewed as a constitutive event, whose echoes linger on, and which has a profound, ongoing influence on the collective identity.[2] The intensity with which the memory of the Holocaust has penetrated into the consciousness of the generations that were born in and after 1945 and its blending with the present, in a country already living by the sword, have often led to feelings of anxiety, distress and fear.

The way Holocaust memory was shaped in Israel provides evidence for Israeli society as post-traumatic and in a condition of acting out. The book claims that the new humouristic, satiric and parodic representations of the Holocaust are, in fact, defence mechanisms created by many second- and third-generation Holocaust survivors to dismantle the acting out of the trauma. Members of the young generations try to create a mental wall between Jewish-Israelis and the Holocaust, and to detach themselves a bit from the trauma, in the hope that it will enable them to move the memory to a 'healthier' way of dealing with it: working through. Jewish-Israelis, who live in a society in which Holocaust memory is intensive and creates constant anxiety seek to lessen reactions of tension and anxiety, even for a few minutes, and they do so through humour. The new representations confront official memory agents who treat the Holocaust as an ongoing trauma in the Israeli present, and these new representations seek to create a mental barrier demarcating past from present.

Some of the young generations also use Holocaust humour, satire or parody as a subversive social tool to protest against Holocaust canonic commemoration, its manipulation and other issues regarding general life in Israel: political, ethnic, economic, and more. Since the Holocaust is such a main feature in the young generation's identity, these are the glasses through which they relate to their Israeliness, criticize it and try to change it. In these instances, humour is also used as a venting tool to release feelings of angst. Since Holocaust humour is still not a norm in Israel, the humouristic texts regarding the Holocaust give their creators and their audience the feeling of a group united against the 'others' and, in this way, humour is also used as a social cohesion tool to reinforce opposition voices in Israel. This use of Holocaust humor to protest Holocaust commemoration and manipulation as well as various phenomena in Israeli society is not only a way to vent frustration and to create social cohesion but it also serves as defence mechanism: this kind of protest breaks down the elements of fear that were and are integrated into the Jewish-Israeli collective soul, and creates a (temporary) mental barrier between the individuals who are laughing and the trauma.

As mentioned[3], Ziv divided the functions of humour into five central groups: the aggressive function of humour (including humour stemming from frustration, and humour stemming from a sense of superiority), the sexual function of humour, the social function of humour, the function of humour as a defence mechanism (including black humour and self-deprecating humour), and the intellectual function of humour.

In this book, I have shown how Holocaust humour, satire and parody in Israel reflect four functions of humour (as there is almost no use of the sexual function in Holocaust humour): intellectual humour which is based on absurdities, wordplays and nonsense mocks the serious acting out of the Holocaust; humouristic texts allow their users and consumers to release feelings of frustration in a society which keeps the Holocaust alive: they serve as defence mechanisms against the profound anxiety evoked by the canonic memory which emphasizes constant victimization. Moreover, Holocaust humour, satire and parody are a social and political tool attempting to rectify and change society, to point to its general shortcomings and at the specific manipulations which are conducted in the commemoration of the trauma.

Opposed to the notion that Israeli humour is very different from Jewish humour,[4] the book has shown that Israeli humour, as Wisse claims, has Jewish traits: the black humour and self-deprecating humour of the persecuted is still a part of the Jewish State. The threatened Jews come comically together.[5]

Opposed to the notion that Holocaust humour, satire and parody in Israel constitute cheapening mechanisms, the book has shown that most of the humour does not deal with the atrocities but with Holocaust commemoration, and is mostly nurtured by pain and criticism. The texts reviewed in this book indicate that the postmemory of the trauma is a central and integral part of the second- and third-generation Holocaust survivors' identity.

As noted, research claims that the representations of the Holocaust in popular culture are dangerous and consist of cheapening mechanisms, that these representations bring a shallowness to the memory of the trauma, blunt the possibility of feeling empathy towards the victims of the Holocaust, and trivialize the mass murder. The analyses in this book have showed that Holocaust humour, satire and parody in Hebrew indeed simplify the complex narratives of the Holocaust, and turn complex experiences into a line of symbols, but these do not blunt the possibility of feeling empathy towards the victims of the Holocaust nor do they trivialize the mass murder. On the contrary, they emphasize how much the second- and third-generation Holocaust survivors in Israel live the trauma in the present as their own open wound (and not only the victims'). These humoristic 'simplifications' actually contribute to the dominance of Holocaust in the Israeli contemporary sphere and, in that sense, help to deepen its memory. The texts do not trivialize the mass murder, they demonstrate that the Jewish-Israelis are still afraid of it, and black humor and self-deprecating humour is a way to overcome this fear that does not fade over the years.

Scholars point to the fact that a mark of Holocaust memorialization and representation in the present is the repetition of the same few images and symbols, which appear to convey the essence of the Holocaust.[6] Holocaust humour, satire and parody in Hebrew appear to contain more diverse symbols. The texts do indeed refer to the well-known symbols that are a major part of Holocaust visual and linguistical representations in the western world, such as trains, railway cars, barbed wires, six million, 'Arbeit macht frei' ['Haavoda meshachreret'], Auschwitz, Hitler, Anne Frank, yellow badge, the expressions 'We shall not forgive, we shall not forget' ['Lonislah velo nishcach'] and 'One cannot compare' ['Asur lehashvot']. But in addition, Holocaust humour in Israel refers to much more varied subjects. According to research, the most common Holocaust symbols in the world do not directly communicate its brutal violence.[7] The examples in this book have showed that, in Israel, self-deprecating humor does deal with the brutality and mass extermination [ghettos, tattoo numbers, striped prisoners' uniforms, gas, gaschambers, density, destruction, annihilation, soap, piles of objects (shoes, glasses, suitcases etc.), hunger, deportation, brutal dogs, barracks] and thus it emphasizes Israel as a unique sphere of Holocaust awareness.

The texts reviewed in this book indicate that the postmemory of the trauma is a central and integral part of the second- and third-generation Holocaust survivors' identity. The views of researchers and public figures speaking against any humouristic form of addressing the Holocaust, rejecting it and seeing it as disparaging or disrespecting the Holocaust ignore the important role of black humour and self-deprecating humour in dealing with secondary traumatic stress. It seems that for many second- and third-generation Holocaust survivors, a humouristic outlook on the trauma is a way of coping with it and with its powerful presence in the Israeli sphere. For them, trying to establish some normalcy, in an anomalous sphere, flooding the culture with humouristic images and concepts related to the Holocaust help disarm the acting out of the trauma of its threatening intensity. The overload of humouristic texts helps deconstructthe constant fear and chronic anxiety created by the collective memory agents of the Holocaust in Israel

The official agents of the canonic memory (politicians, educators, public figures, artists, etc.) who, through serious texts, preserve a constant state of victimization as well as the people who practice and consume Holocaust humour stand on opposite sides of the aisle and (consciously and unconsciously) fight each other. One side preserves a continuing state of fear and anxiety, while the other side wishes to dismantle it and work through the trauma. Instead of fearing, Holocaust black humour and self-deprecating humour hug the fear, laugh about it, by turning the trauma's representatives (Nazis, Hitler, trains, concentration camps, ghettos, extermination, gas, Anne Frank, etc.) into a familiar and laughable part of the daily life. This 'hug' wishes to keep afar the fear factors, but simultaneously inserts the trauma even more into everyday life.

The insertion of Holocaust humour into popular culture, the satiric and parodic critique on the commemoration of the Holocaust and its manipulation, the protest against general events and elements in Israeli culture through Holocaust black humour, the reaction to personal and Israeli events that have nothing to do with the Holocaust, through humoristic Holocaust associations strengthen, unknowingly (and probably unwillingly) the acting out of the Holocaust by completely blending the trauma into the present.This is a contradictory process of creating boundaries between past and present and at the same time assimilating the trauma even more into contemporary Israel.

The initiatives and the goals of the collective memory agents and those who practice Holocaust humour are completely opposing, but the results are, in a way, similar: both of them turn the Holocaust into an integral part of the Israeli present and maintain the unique, intense role of the Holocaust in the Jewish-Israeli collective identity.In the 'battles' over Holocaust commemoration in Israel, they are both collective memory agents who keep the Holocaust alive in Israeli daily life and each, in their way, strengthens the merge of the trauma within the Israeli public sphere.

In that sense, the various aspects of Holocaust humour are, in fact, a double-edged sword: through humour, some of the second- and third-generation Holocaust survivors fight the acting out of the Holocaust. But,at the same time, paradoxically, the multiple variations of Holocaust humour, which are integrated into popular culture and Israeli everyday life, strengthen, in another way, the acting out of the Holocaust in Israel.

Notes

1. See in the Preface and Chapter 3.
2. See in Chapters 3 and 4.
3. See in Chapter 10.
4. See in Chapter 1.
5. Wisse, *No Joke*.
6. O. B. Stier, *Holocaust Icons* (New Brunswick: Rutgers University Press, 2015); M. Hirsch, *The Generation of Postmemory: Writing and visual culture after the Holocaust* (New-York: Columbia University Press, 2012).
7. Stier, *Holocaust Icons*, p. 2.

Bibliography

Abazon, L. 'Zaguri empire: primitivim aval optimim' ['Zaguri Empire: Primitive But Optimistic'], *Mako*, 8 April 2014 http://www.mako.co.il/culture-tv/local/Article-0d7a6dd6abf3541006.htm Accessed 1 May 2015 [Hebrew].

Abramson, I. 'A Double Occlusion: Sephardim and the Holocaust', In: Z. Zohar (ed.), *Sephardic and Mizrahi Jewry: From the Golden Age of Spain to Modern Times* (New York and London: New York University Press, 2005), pp. 285-300.

Adorno, T. W. *Negative Dialectics* (London: Routledge, 2000).

Alexander, J. C. 'On the Social Construction of Moral Universals: The 'Holocaust' from War Crime to Trauma Drama,' in J. C. Alexander(ed), *Cultural Trauma and Collective Identity* (Berkeley: University of California Press, 2009), pp. 196-263.

Alexander, J. C. 'Toward a Theory of Cultural Trauma, in J. C. Alexander(ed), *Cultural Trauma and Collective Identity* (Berkeley: University of California Press, 2009), pp. 1-30.

Almog, O. *Hatzabar: dyukan* [*The Sabre: A Portrait*] (Tel Aviv: Am Oved, 1997) [Hebrew].

Alpher, R. 'Hashoah shel beber' ['Beber's Holocaust: 'Zaguri Empire' Nearly Became the Most Subversive Drama on Television'], *Ha'aretz*, 4 February 2015 http://www.haaretz.co.il/.premium-1.2556660 Accessed 5 March 2015 [Hebrew].

Altschuler, A. A Biography, *TEDx*, http://www.tedxjerusalem.com/speaker/adi-altschuler/ Accessed 1 July 2016.

Altschuler, A. 'Hazaa lemifgashim slternativim lezichron hashoah' ['A suggestion for alternative encounters to commemorate the Holocaust'], *YNET*, 7.4.2012 http://www.ynet.co.il/articles/0,7340,L-4216611,00.html Accessed 1 July 2016 [Hebrew].

Alush-Levron, M. 'Zaguri poremet et simlat haarmon' ['Zaguri Unravels the Hegemon's Robe'], *Ha'aretz*, 6 February 2015 http://www.haaretz.co.il/.premium-1.2558299 Accessed 1 May 2015 [Hebrew].

Amir, E. 'Hasliha vehatoda' ['Forgiveness and Gratefulness'], *Alpaim* 16 (1998), pp. 186-191 [Hebrew].

Anderman, N. 'A Graphic Story of a Holocaust Survivor's Son', Haaretz, June 2 2013 http://www.haaretz.com/jewish/features/.premium-1.527336 Accessed 4 June 2013 [Hebrew].

Andreas, H. 'Of Mice and Mimesis: Reading Spiegelman with Adorno,' in Barbie Zelizer (ed.) *Visual Culture and the Holocaust* (Rutgers University Press, 2001), pp. 28-44.

Arad, B. *The ArtLab* http://www.theartlab.co.il/mentors/boaz-arad/ Accessed 1 March 2016.

Arieli-Horowitz, D. 'Boaz Arad – Voozvooz', *History and Theory*, Bezlel, 4 (Spring, 2007) https://bezalel.secured.co.il/zope/home/he/1173510036/1176612903Accessed 1 March 2016 [Hebrew].

Ashkenazi, 'O. Ridiculous Trauma: Comic Representations of the Nazi Past in Contemporary German Visual Culture', *Cultural Critique*, 78 (Spring 2011), pp. 88-118.

Atlani, A. *The Ha-Ha Holocaust: Exploring Levity Amidst the Ruins and Beyond in Testimony, Literature and Film*, a thesis submitted in partial fulfillment of the requirements for the degree in Doctor of Philosophy, The University of Western Ontario, 2014 http://ir.lib.uwo.ca/cgi/viewcontent.cgi?article=3776&context=etd Accessed 2 October 2015.

Ausubel, N. *A Treasury of Jewish Humor* (New York: M. Evans and Company, 1951).

Averbach, L. 'Zagury emperia – hahashaka hahazaka beyoter betoldot Hot' ['The Drama Series 'Zaguri Empire' – the Strongest Launch in the History of HOT'], *Globes*, 29 April 2014 http://www.globes.co.il/news/article.aspx?did=1000934953 Accessed 2 May 2015 [Hebrew].

Avisar, I, 'Tiud veitzuv shel todaa historit besirtey taamula' ('Documentation and Visualization of Historic Aearness in Propaganda Films'), *Zmnaim*, 39-40, 1991, pp. 38-47 [Hebrew].

Avisar, I. *Screening the Holocaust* (Indiana: Indiana University Press, 1988).

Avrahami, I. 'Kehilot yehudei tunis beyamey hakibush hagermany' ['Tunisian Jews under Nazi Occupation'], *Peamim* 28 (1986), pp. 107-125 [Hebrew].

Avrahami, I. 'Yehudei tunis' ['Tunisian Jews'], *Shorashim bamizrah*, 3, Ramat-Efal: Yad Tabenkin (1989), pp. 273-293 [Hebrew].

Avramski-Blai, I. *Pinkas hakehilot:Luv-Tunis* [*Libia-Tunis Communities' Writings*] (Jerusalem: Yad vaShem, 2007) [Hebrew].

Azaryahu, M. *Tiksei medina* [*State Rituals*] (Beer Sheva: Bialik Institute, 1995) [Hebrew].

Azulay, A, 'Lehangish et hazicaron lecol ehad' ['Making the memory accessible for everyone'], *Israel Today*, 1.5.201 http://www.israelhayom.co.il/opinion/377587 Accessed 10 July 2016 [Hebrew].

Azulay, A. 'Mi haya maamin ata kore germanit' ['Who could believe you can read German'], *Theory and Critisicm* 15 (Winter, 1999), pp. 49-62.

Bakhtin, M. *Rabelais and His World*, trans. Hélène Iswolsky (Bloomington: Indiana University Press, 1993).

Balint, J. L. 'Remembering the Holocaust In Israel's National Living Room', *IsraelForever*, 7.4.2016 http://israelforever.org/interact/blog/remembering_the_holocaust_in_israels_national_living_room/ Accessed 10 April 2016.

Bar-On, D. *Bein Pahad leTikva* [*Between Fear and Silence: Life Stories of Five Families of Holocaust Survivors, Three Family Generations*] (Tel Aviv: Beit Lochamei Haghettaot and Kibbutz Meyuchad Press, 1994) [Hebrew].

Baron, L. *Projecting the Holocaust into the present: the changing focus of Contemporary Holocaust Cinema* (Mariland: Rowman & Littlefield, 2005).

Bar-Tal, D. 'Lama atem lo rozim shalom' ('Why don't you want peace?'), Haaretz, Musaf, 2.9.2016, pp. 54-56 [Hebrew].

Bar-Tal, D. *Lihyot im hasichsuch* [*Living with the Conflict*] (Jerusalem: Carmel, 2007) [Hebrew].

Bartal, U. 'Mehiroshima lesabra veshatila' ['From Hiroshima to Sabra and Shatila in comics and graphic novels'] *History and Theory* (15, 2010) [Hebrew] http://bezalel. secured.co.il/8/bartal15.htm Accessed 2 September 2013 [Hebrew].

Bartov, O.*Hayehudi bakolnoa* [*The Jew in Cinema*] (Tel Aviv: Am Oved, 2008) [Hebrew]

Baudrillard, J. *Simulakrot vesimulatzia* [*Simulacrum and Simulations*] (Tel Aviv: Resling, 2007). [Hebrew].

Ben-Ami, I. '*Hahumor hayehudi hamarokayi*', ['Jewish Moroccan Humour'], *Maroko Jewry: Chapters in the research of their Culture* (Jerusalem: Reuven Mas, 1976), pp. 127-135.

Ben-Amos, D. 'The 'Myth' of Jewish Humor.' *Western Folklore* 32.2 (1973), pp. 112–131.

Ben-Ari, G, '*Hitler matza hanaya*,' ['*Hitler Found a Parking Space*'] *Yediot Aharonot*, 26 February 2010, http://e.walla.co.il/?w=/267/1819879 Accessed 30.3.2014 [Hebrew].

Ben-Baruch, B. 'Hashoah bacomix' ['The Holocaust as reflected in Comics'], *History and Theory* (15, 2010) [Hebrew], http://bezalel.secured.co.il/8/baruch15.htm [Hebrew] Accessed 2 September 2013 [Hebrew].

Ben-Dat, A. *Bein humor letrauma bein etica leestetica[Between Humor and Trauma, Between Ethics and Aesthetics]*, Tel-aviv: Resling, 2015 [Hebrew].

Bender, A. 'Hapitaron shel ketzale lemevakshei hamiklat: mahane avoda' ['Ketzale's Solution for Asylum Seekers: A Work Camp,'] *NRG*, March 23, 2010, www.nrg.co.il/online/1/ART2/085/436.html Accessed 20 May 2012 [Hebrew].

Ben-Ghiat, R. 'The Secret Histories of Roberto Benigni's Life Is Beautiful,' in J. D. Zimmerman (ed), *Jews in Italy under Fascist and Nazi Rule1922-1945*, (Cambridge: Cambridge University Press, 2005), pp. 330-350.

Ben-Ner, G. *Boaz Arad: VOZVOZ*, The Center for Contemporary Art, Tel Aviv 2007 Synchronization of a Moustache http://boazarad.net/wp-content/uploads/2010/texts/Synchronization%20of%20a%20Moustache.pdfAccessed 2 March 2016.

Berger, A. L. & Berger, N. *Second Generation Voices: Reflections by Children of Holocaust Survivors and Perpetrators*. (Syracuse University Press, 2001).

Berger, L. 'Tribeca 2016 Women Directors: Meet Ferne Pearlstein – 'The Last Laugh'', *Indiewire*, 18 April, 2016 http://www.indiewire.com/2016/04/tribeca-2016-women-directors-meet-ferne-pearlstein-the-last-laugh-288342/ Accessed 1 May 2016.

Bergson, H. *Laughter: An Essay on the Meaning of the Comic*, (London: Macmillan, 1911).

Berrin, D. 'Roseanne plays Hitler for Heeb magazine', 3 August 2009, http://www.jewishjournal.com/hollywoodjew/item/roseanne_plays_hitler_for_heeb_magazine_20090803 Accessed 20 January 2010.

Bhabha, H. K. 'The Other Question: Stereotype, Discrimination, and the Discourse of Colonialism,' in H. K. Bhabha (ed) *The Location of Culture*, (London: Routledge, 1994), pp. 66-84.

Blacher Cohen, S. (ed), *Jewish Wry: Essays on Jewish Humor*, (Bloomington: Indiana University Press, 1987).

Blau, S., 'You must be joking!', *Index on Censorship*, Volume 34, Issue 2(2005), pp. 57-62.

Blau, S. 'Misheu amar shoa?' ['Somebody Said Holocaust?'], *Ha'aretz*, April 22, 2004, http://www.haaretz.co.il/news/health/1.961589 Accessed September 7, 2014 [Hebrew].

Boginski, Y. 'Skira historit shel hamusag nitzol shoah' ['A Historical Overview of the Concept of a Holocaust Survivor'] 1/24/2013, *The Knesset*, http://www.knesset.gov.il/mmm/data/pdf/m03154.pdf Accessed 1 January 2014 [Hebrew].

Bondi, R. & Naor, R. C. *Trapped: essays on the history of the Czech Jews, 1939-1945*. (Jerusalem: Yad Vashem Publications, 2008).

Bondi, R. *Shorashim akurim: prakim batoldot yahadut czechia, 1939-1945* [*Torn Roots*] (Yad Vashem u'beit terezinpp, 2002). [Hebrew].

Bourdieu, P, 'The Field of Cultural Production, or: The Economic World Revered' *Poetics* 12 (1984b), pp. 311-356.

Bourdieu, P. *Distinction: A Social Critique of the Judgement of Taste* (London: Routledge, 1984a).

Brook, V. *Something Ain't Kosher Here: The Rise of the 'Jewish' Sitcom* (New Brunswick, NJ: Rutgers University Press, 2003).

Burg, A. *Lenatzeaj et Hitler* [*To defeat Hitler*] (Tel-Aviv: Yediot Aharonot, 2007) [Hebrew].

Caril, A. Shif E. & Shavit, A. 'Zohakim mitahat lasafam: humor hashoah mehahamishia hakamerit vead eretz nehederet' [Holocaust Humor: from the *Hahamishia Hakamerit* until *EretzNehederet*], *Walla*, 2 May 2011 http://e.walla.co.il/?w=/267/1819879 Accessed 2.10.2014 [Hebrew].

Casher, A. 'Haim satira beyom hashoah hi legitimit?' ['Is Holocaust satire on Holocaust Remembrance Day legitimate'?] *Retro - Tik Tikshoret*, 5 May, 2016. https://www.youtube.com/watch?v=QKcLzLcMjLA Accessed 2 June 2016 [Hebrew].

Chaitin, J. 'Yeladim venechadim shel nizolim mitmodedim im haSshoah' ['Children and grandchildren of Holocaust survivors deal with the Holocaust'], in Z. Solomon and J. Chaitin (eds), *Yaldut bezel hashoah* [*Childhood in the Shadow of the Holocaust:Child Survivors and Second Generation*](Tel Aviv: Hakibbutz Hameuchad, 2007), pp. 304-336 [Hebrew].

Channel 7, 'Zikaron basalon – baslon shel hanasi' ['*Remembrance in the Living Room* – In the president's living room'] *Channel 7*, 3.5.2016 http://www.inn.co.il/News/News.aspx/321257 Accessed 1 July 2016 [Hebrew].

CNN Staff, 'Joan Rivers not apologizing for Holocaust joke', 1 March 2013 http://edition.cnn.com/2013/02/28/showbiz/joan-rivers-holocaust-joke/ Accessed 2 July 2016.

Cohen, A. *Haim bizhok* [*LivingLife with Laughter*] (Haifa: Amazia 1994) [Hebrew].

Cohen, A. *Sefer hahumour hayehudi hagadol* [*The Great Jewish Humor Book*] (Or Yehuda: Cineret, 2004) [Hebrew].

Cohen, G. *Beit lihiot: bein zicaron ishy lezicaron leumy* [*Beit Lihiot – between personal and collective memory*], Seminar (Sapir Academic College: Department of Culture, Creation and Production Department, 2011) [Hebrew].

Cooke, R. 'The Property by Rutu Modan – review', The Guardian, 15 July 2013 HYPERLINK "https://www.theguardian.com/books/2013/jul/15/the-property-rutu-modan-review%20Accessed%2020%20July%202013" https://www.theguardian.com/books/2013/jul/15/the-property-rutu-modan-review Accessed 20 July 2013.

Cramer, P. 'Defence mechanism in psychology today: further processes for adaptation', *American Psychologist* 55 (2000), pp. 637-646.

Dagan, H. & Dishon, G. 'Holocaust-Nostalgia: Rethinking Trauma and Nostalgia in Light of Pizza in Auschwitz', *Theory and Criticism*, 38-39 (Winter 2001), pp. 185-209 [Hebrew].

Davies, C. 'Exploring the Thesis of the Self-Deprecating Jewish Sense of Humor', In: A. Ziv & A. Zajdman (eds) *Semites and Stereotypes: Characteristics of Jewish Humor* (London: Greenwood Press, 1993), pp. 29-46.

Davies, C. *The Mirth of Nations* (New Brunswick, NJ: Transaction, 2010).

Demsky, J. 'Searching for Humor in Dehumanization: American Situational Comedies and Second/Third Generation Holocaust Representation', *Film and History Conference*, November 2015, Madison WI.

Des Press, T. 'Holocaust Laughter?', in Berel Lang (ed): *Writing and the Holocaust* (New York: Holmes and Meier, 1988), pp. 216-233.

Dolev, I. 'Ma pitom hitler' ['Why Hitler?'], *Haaretz*, Musaf Haaretz, 9 April 2010, pp. 36-38 [Hebrew].

Doov, J. 'Ad yom hashoah' ['Don't touch Holocaust and Heroism Remembrance Day' Zaguri's Disrespect Crossed the Line'], *NRG*, 4 February 2015 http://www.nrg.co.il/online/47/ART2/674/031.html Accessed 5 March 2015 [Hebrew].

Dundes, A. & Hauschild, T. *WesternFolklore*, Vol. 42, No. 4 (Oct., 1983), pp. 249-260.

Ebbrecht, T. 'Migrating Images: Iconic Images of the Holocaust and the Representation of War in Popular Film', *Shofar – An Interdisciplinary Journal of Jewish Studies* 28, No. 4 (Summer, 2010), pp. 86-103.

Egerton, J. H. *'Kush mir in tokhes!': Humor and Hollywood in Holocaust Films of the 1990s*, A Ph.D dissertation, submitted to The University of Texas at Austin, (2006) http://www.lib.utexas.edu/etd/d/2006/egertond25518/egertond25518.pdf Accessed 1 November, 2015.

Eilbirt, H. 'Jewish Humor: The Logic of Jewish Humor', *World Humor and Irony Membership Serial Yearbook* (1987), pp. 178-180.

Eilon, A. *Hayisraelim* [*The Israelis*] (Tel Aviv: Shoken, 1970) [Hebrew].

Elias, I. 'Lama marokaim ohavim lizchok al azmam', ['Why Moroccans love to laugh about themselves'], *Haaretz*, 18 February 2016 http://www.haaretz.co.il/gallery/.premium-1.2854321 Accessed 30 March 2016 [Hebrew].

Eliav, L. & Alfi, Y. *Mishnei evrey hamaabara* [*From both sides of the Ma'abara*] (Tel Aviv: Maariv, 2006) [Hebrew].

Elkana, Y.'Bizchut hashichecha' ['The Need to Forget'], *Ha'aretz*, March 2, 1988 [Hebrew].

Epstein, L. J. *The Haunted Smile: The Story of Jewish Comedians in America* (New York: Public Affairs, 2002); J. Boskin and J. Dorinson, 'Ethnic Humor Subversion and Survival,' *American Quarterly Special Issue: American Humor*, (37.1 1985), pp. 81-97.

Erll, A. & Rigney, A. (eds), *Mediation, Remediation, and the Dynamics of Cultural Memory* (Berlin and New York: de Gruyter, 2009).

Esterkin, Y. 'Az veachsahiv – al elo zrachim onim hatkasim haalternativim' ['Then and now – What needs does the alternative ceremony answer?'], *NRG*, 18 April 2012, http://www.nrg.co.il/online/47/ART2/358/706.html?hp=47&cat=306&loc=68 Accessed on 14 April 2012 [Hebrew].

Eyerman, R. *Cultural Trauma: Slavery and the Formation of African-American Identity* (Cambridge: Cambridge University Press, 2002).

Ezrahi, S. 'After Such Knowledge, What Laughter?' *Yale Journal of Criticism, special issue on the Holocaust and Interpretation*, 14.1 (2001), pp. 287-317.

Feldman, J. *Above the Death Pits, Beneath the Flag, Youth Voyages to Poland and the Performance of Israeli National Identity* (New York and Oxford: Berghahn Press, 2008).

Figley, C.R. 'Compassion fatigue as secondary traumatic stress disorder: An overview'. In: Figley CR, (ed). *Compassion fatigue: Coping with secondary traumatic stress disorder in those who treat the traumatized*, (Brunner-Routledge; New York, 1995), pp. 1–20.

Fiske, J. *Television Culture* (London and New York: Routledge, 1987).

Florenthal, A.R. 'Hayahasim bein mavet vehumor' ['The Relationship between Death and Humor'], *Humor Mekuvvan: Research Journal in Humor Studies*, 2 (January 2013), pp. 69-87 [Hebrew].

Frankl, V. E. *Man's Search for Meaning: An Introduction to Logotherapy* (New York: Simon & Schuster, 1984).

Freud, A. *Haani vemaganonei haganah* [*The I and defense mechanisms*] (Tel Aviv: Dvir, 1977) [Hebrew].

Freud, S. *Hatipul hapsichoanaliti* [*Psychoanalysis Treatment*], (Tel Aviv: Am Oved, 1988) [Hebrew].

Freud, S. *Jokes and Their Relation to the Unconscious* (The Standard Edition) (New York: W. W. Norton & Company, 1990).

Freud, S. *Meever laoneg vemasot aherot* [*Beyond Pleasure and other Works*], (Tel Aviv: Dvir, 1990) [Hebrew].

Friedman, H. H. & Weiser-Friedman, L. *God Laughed: Sources of Jewish Humor* (New Brunswick, NJ: Transaction, 2014).

Friesem, L. Mi 0 le 180 kamash (kilometer shoah) [From 0 to 180 Mph*(*Mile per Holocaust): Holocaust Tweets as an Act of Resistance], a seminar in the course Jews, Hebrews, Israelis: Cultural Aspects of Jewish Identity (Ra'anana: The Open University, 2017) [Hebrew].

Frosh, P. & Pinchevski, A. (eds), *Media Witnessing: Testimony in the Age of Mass Communication* (Basingstoke and New York: Palgrave Macmillan, 2009).

Fruchtman, A. *Zichron hashoah cetzir mercazi bahevra haisraelit berei haseret 'Made in Israel'* [*Holocaust Memory as a central core of the Israeli culture, as reflected in the filmMadein*

Israel], A seminar paper in the course 'Holocaust Survivors in Israeli Cinema,' The Open University, 2006 [Hebrew].

Gan, A. *From Sovereignty to Victimhood: An Analysis of the Victimization Discourse in Israel,* (Jerusalem: The Israel Democracy Institute, 2014) [Hebrew].

Garrick, J. 'The Humor of Trauma Survivors', *Journal of Aggression, Maltreatment & Trauma* 12. 1-2 (2006), pp. 169-182

Gavriely-Nuri, D. 'Zaguri lo omed bazfira' ['Zaguri Does Not Stand Up on Holocaust Remembrance Day and He Is Right'], *YNET*, 4 February 2015 http://www.ynet.co.il/articles/0,7340,L-4622511,00.html Accessed 5 March 2015 [Hebrew].

Giuseppe, S. "Josef Bau: Israel's Walt Disney and Mapmaker of Hell", The Krakow Post, 7 September 2012 http://www.krakowpost.com/5785/2012/09/josef-bau-israels-walt-disney-and-mapmaker-of-hell Accessed 2 September 2016.

Gehring, W. D. *Parody as film genre,* (Westport, CT: Greenwood Publishing, 1999).

Gertz, N. *Nizoley shoa zarim veaherim* [*A Different Choir: Holocaust Survivors, Aliens and Others in Israeli Cinema and Literature*] (Tel Aviv: Am Oved/The Open University, 2004) [Hebrew].

Gertz, N. *Sipur mehasratim* [*Motion Fiction: Israeli Fiction in Films*] (Tel Aviv: The Open University Press, 1993). [Hebrew].

Gilbert, C. J. 'Playing With Hitler: Downfall and Its Ludic Uptake', *Critical Studies in Media Communication* Vol. 30, No. 5, December (2013), pp. 407-424.

Gilman, S. L. 'Is Life Beautiful? Can the Shoah be funny? Some thoughts on recent and older films', *Critical Inquiry*, Vol. 26, No. 2 (Winter, 2000), pp. 279-308.

Godfrey Mark, *Abstraction and the Holocaust* (New Haven: Yale University Press, 2007).

Goldberg, A. 'Introduction,' in D. LaCapra, *Writing History, Writing Trauma* (Baltimore, MD: Johns Hopkins University Press, 2000), pp. 7-28 [Hebrew].

Goldstein, L. 'Antishemiut bezfon africa' ['Antisemitism in North-Africa prior to WWII'], *Yad Vashem* 50 (2008), pp. 10-11 [Hebrew].

Goldstein, S. & Rephael, D. 'Cmo bashoah' ['Like in the Holocaust'], *Maariv*, 5 August 2005 http://www.raful.co.il/archives/846 Accessed 15 June 2007 [Hebrew].

Gonshak, H. *Hollywood and the Holocaust* (Maryland: Rowman & Littlefield Publishers, 2015).

Greenspoon, L. G. (ed), *Jews and Humor* (West Lafayette, IN: Purdue University Press, 2011).

Grotjahn, M. 'Jewish jokes and their relation to masochism', in M.W. Mendel (ed), *A celebration of laughter* (Mara Books, 1970).

Gutman, I. R*esistance: The Warsaw Ghetto Uprising* (Boston: Houghton Mifflin, 1994).

Gutwein, D. 'The Privatization of the Holocaust: Memory, Historiography, and Politics', *Israel Studies*, Volume 14, Number 1 (Spring, 2009), pp.36-64.

Hadas, N. 'Zagury empire menapezet et hadeot hakdumot' ['The Zaguri Empire Smashes Prejudice'], *Ha'aretz*, 25 April 2014 http://www.haaretz.co.il/.premium-1.2302878 Accessed 1 May 2015 [Hebrew].

Hajbi, T. 'Mishlahot batei sefer tichon lepolin' [*High school delegations to Poland*], Seminar paper, Culture Department, Sapir Academic College, 2013 [Hebrew].

Hakim, D. 'Hayey saharah', ['The Life of Sarah'], *Haaretz*, 18 February 2003 http://www.haaretz.co.il/hasite/pages/ShArtPE.jhtml?itemNo=264761&contrassID=2&subContrassID=13&sbSubContrassID=0 Accessed 12 October 2014 [Hebrew].

Halbwachs, M. *On Collective Memory* (Chicago: The University of Chicago Press, 1992).

Halkin, H. 'Why Jews Laugh at Themselves', *Commentary* (1, April 2006) https://www.commentarymagazine.com/articles/why-jews-laugh-at-themselves/ Accessed 2 April 2016

Hall, S. 'Encoding/Decoding,' in S. Hall et al (eds), *Culture, Media, Language*, (London: Hutchinson, 1980): 128-138.

Hall, S. *Representation (London*: Open University Press and Sage, 1997).

Hall, S. 'The Question of Cultural Identity' In: S. Hall, D. Held, A. McGrew (eds), *Modernity and Its Futures (*Cambridge: Polity Press, 1992), pp. 274–316.

Hariman, R. 'Political parody and public culture, *Quarterly Journal of Speech*, 94, 3 (2008), pp. 247- 272.

Hatuka, A. 'Stereotipim, shoah, hishtaknezut' ['Stereotypes, Holocaust, Ashkenazification: Dismantling the 'Zaguri Empire'], *Haokets*, 10 May 2015 http://www.haokets.org/2015/05/10 Accessed 5 March 2015 [Hebrew].

Hazan, Y. 'Dor sheni lashoah' ['The second generation of the Holocaust: A questionable concept'], *Sihot: Israel Journal of Psychotherapy*, 1 (1987), 104-108 [Hebrew].

Hefetz, I. 'Mashehu rakuv bemamlechet zaguri' ['Something Is Rotten in the State of Zaguri'], *Haokets*, 11 May 2014 http://www.haokets.org/2014/05/11 Accessed 1 May 2015 [Hebrew].

Heller, R. 'Eretz nehederet pagu berigshot nizolei hashoa' ['Eretz Nehederet Hurt Holocaust Survivors'] *Ynet*, November 10, 2004, http://www.ynet.co.il/articles/0,7340,L-3002314,00.html Accessed October 21, 2014 [Hebrew].

Herman, J. L. *Trauma ve hachlama* [*Trauma and Healing*], (Tel Aviv: Am Oved, 1994) [Hebrew].

Hershkovitz, A. 'Zfirat hatraa' ['Warning Siren: 'Zaguri Empire' Opens Its Second Season'], *Mako*, 3 February 2015 http://www.mako.co.il/culture-tv/local-Zaguri-Empire/Article-c56d0a7ee9f4b41006.html Accessed 5 March 2015 [Hebrew].

Herzog, R. *Dead Funny: Humor in Hitler's Germany* (New York: Melville House, 2011).

Hever, H. et al. (eds) *Mizrahim beisrael* [*Mizrahim in Israel: a renewed debate*] (Jerusalem: Van-Leer Institute and HaKibbutz HaMeuhad, 2002) [Hebrew].

Hirsch, M. 'Past Lives, First Memories in Exile', *Poetics Today, Winter 17* (1996), pp. 659-67.

Hirsch, M. *The Generation of Postmemory: Writing and visual culture after the Holocaust* (New-York: Columbia university press, 2012).

Hobsbaum, E. & Renger, T. *The Invention of Tradition* (Cambridge: Cambridge University Press, 1993).

Imagor, T. 'Yom hazikaron lashoah velagvurah 2012' ('Holocaust Memorial Day 2012'), *City Mouse online*, April 18, 2012 [Hebrew].

Interview with Michel Kichka "My Holocaust family", *Europe Comics* http://www.europecomics.com/interview-with-michel-kichka/ 4 February 2016. Accessed 1 March 2016.

Juni, S., Katz, B. and Hamburger, M. 'Identification with the Aggression vs. Turning against the self: an empirical study of the turn of the century European Jewish humor', *Current Psychology* 14 (4, 1996), pp. 313-328.

Kaplan, B.A. *Landscapes of Holocaust Postmemory* (Routledge Research in Cultural and Media Studies 29. New York: Routledge, 2011).

Kaplan, L. 'It will get a terrific laugh: On the problematic pleasures and politics of Holocaust Humor,' in H. Jenkins, T. McPherson & J. Shattuc (eds), *Hop on pop: the politics and pleasures of popular culture* (Duke University Press Books, 2003), pp. 343-356.

Kauffman, J. 'Gallows humor and Jewish humor: A reading of 'The dance of Genghis Cohn' by Romain Gary', in A. Ziv (ed), *Jewish humor* (New Brunswick and London: Transaction Publishers, 1998), pp. 99-110.

Keidar Cohen, K. Ben-Ishay, S. and Dimri, S. 'Humor, Mental Resilience and Post-Trauma in Gaza Envelope Residents Following 'Operation Protective Edge', *The 2nd Multidisciplinary*

Conference for the Research of Humor, Seminar Hakibbutzim, 9 February 2016. Lecture. [Hebrew]

Kellermann, N. 'Transmission of the Holocaust Trauma', in Z. Solomon and J. Chaitin (eds), *Yaldut bezel hashoah* [*Childhood in the Shadow of the Holocaust:Child Survivors and Second Generation*](Tel Aviv: Hakibbutz Hameuchad, 2007), pp. 286-303 [Hebrew].

Kerner, A. *Film and the Holocaust: New Perspectives on Dramas, Documentaries and Experimental Films* (New York: Continuum Books, 2011).

Kichka, M. *Second Generation: Things I Never Told My Father* [*Hador hasheni dvarim shelo siparty leaba*] (Ben-Shemen: Modan & Hargol, 2013).

Kichler, Z. 'Hahumor shel bnei hador hasheni lashoah' ['Second-generation Holocaust humour'] *The New Memory of the Holocaust Conference*, The Open University, February 2015.

Kidron, C. 'Hahavnaya hahvratit shel dor sheni lashoah' ['The Social Construction of Second Generation Survivors: Support Group Narratives of Wounded Carriers of Memory'], in Z. Solomon and J. Chaitin (eds.), *Yaldut bezel hashoah* [*Childhood in the Shadow of the Holocaust*](Tel Aviv: Hakibbutz Hameuchad, 2007), pp. 261-285 [Hebrew].

Kigel, M. 'Imperia' ['E-m-p-i-r-e: All About Why You Need to Adopt the Zaguri Family'], *NRG*, 6 June 2014 http://www.nrg.co.il/online/47/ART2/584/359.html Accessed 1 May 2015 [Hebrew].

Kimmerling, B. *Ketz shilton haahusalim* [*TheEnd of the Ashkenazi Hegemony*] (Jerusalem: Keter, 2001) [Hebrew].

Kimmerling, B. *Mehagrim, mityashvim, yelidim*[*Immigrants, Settlers, Natives*] (Tel Aviv: Am Oved, 2004). [Hebrew], pp. 185-493.

Kimmerling, B. 'The Continuation of Israeli-Palestinian Conflict by 'Academic' Means: Reflections on the Problematiques of Publishing Books and Reviewing Them', *Contemporary Sociology*, Vol. 35, No. 5 (September 2006), pp. 447-449.

Klein, H. 'Hipus nizolei hashoah ahar mashmaut vezehut' ['The survivors' search for meaning and identity'], in: I. Gutman and R. Manber (eds), *Nazi Concentration Camps, Lectures and Discussions in the 4th Yad Vashem International historical conference* of Holocaust Researchers (Jerusalem: Yad Vashem, 1980), pp. 543-553.

Klein, J. 'Taharut karikaturot shoah beiran hofechet beinleumit' ('Holocaust caricatures exhibition becomes international'), *CFCA*, 2 June 2016 http://antisemitism.org.il/article/106368/%D7%AA%D7%97%D7%A8%D7%95%D7%AA-%D7%A7%D7%A8%D7%99%D7%A7%D7%98%D7%95%D7%A8%D7%95%D7%AA-%D7%A9%D7%95%D7%90%D7%94-%D7%A9%D7%9C-%D7%90%D7%99%D7%A8%D7%90%D7%9F-%D7%94%D7%95%D7%A4%D7%9B%D7%AA-%D7%9C%D7%91%D7%99%D7%A0%D7%9C%D7%90%D7%95%D7%9E%D7%99%D7%AA Accessed 1 July 2016.

Knafo, A. *Te im na'na* [*Tea with Na'na: The Jokes of Moroccan Jews*] (Tel Aviv: Bimat Kedem, 2014) [Hebrew].

Kotler, S. *Folklore beidan hainternet: hainterakzia bein hamemim 'hitler mitazben' vehatarbut haisraelit* [*Folklore in the Age of Internet: The Interaction Between Hitler Gets Angry Memes and Israeli Culture*], a thesis as part of the requirements for a Master's degree, supervised by Prof. Hagar Salamon, Hebrew University of Jerusalem, 2015 [Hebrew].

LaCapra, D. *Writing History, Writing Trauma* (Baltimore, MD: Johns Hopkins University Press, 2000).

Lankshear, C. & Knobel, M. (eds), *A New Literacies Sampler* (New York: Peter Lang, 2007).

Launstein, N. 'Nitzulei show' ['The Show of the Shoah'], *Yediot Aharonot*, 8 September 2010, pp. 22-24 http://www.youtube.com/watch?v=EUvo5OHH6o8 Accessed 3 March 2011 [Hebrew].

Lederhendler, E and Finder, G. N (eds). *A Club of their Own: Jewish Humorists in the Contemporary World*, (New York: Oxford University Press, 2016).

Levin, I. *Mibaad ladmaot* [*Through the tears: Jewish humor under the Nazi regime*] (Jerusalem: Yad Vashem, 2004) [Hebrew]

Lewis, P. 'Three Jews and a Blindfold: The Politics of Gallows Humor,' in A. Ziv and Zajdman, A. (eds) *Semites and Stereotypes* (Westport, CT: Greenwood Press, 1993), pp. 47-57.

Lewis, P. 'Three Jews and a blindfold: The Politics of Gallows Humor', in A. Ziv & A. Zajdman (eds) *Semites and Stereotypes: Characteristics of Jewish Humor* (London: Greenwood Press, 1993), pp. 47-58.

Lichfield, J. 'Anti-semitic' comedian Dieudonné M'bala M'bala has his show cancelled in France after Nicolas Anelka's inverted Nazi salute', 7 January 2014 http://www.independent.co.uk/news/world/europe/quenelle-comedian-dieudonn-mbala-mbalas-show-is-banned-in-france-9044504.html Accessed 1 July 2016

Lipman, S. 'Can A Swastika Be Funny?' *The Jewish Week*, Online: http://www.thejewishweek.com/features/can_swastika_be_funny. Accessed February 20, 2014.

Lipman, S. *Laughter in Hell: The Use of Humor during the Holocaust* (Rowman & Littlefield Publishers, 1993).

Lissak, M. 'Eda veadatiyut beisrael beperspectiva historit' ['Ethnicity in Israel in an historical perspective'], *Hevra likrat Shnot haAlpaim* [*Society towards the 21th century*] (Jerusalem: Magness, 1996) [Hebrew].

Litman, S. 'Behazara leva Braun' ['Back to Eva Brown'], *Haaretz*, 25 January 2016

Litvak-Hirsch, T. & Bar-On, D. 'Livnot et haHaim mehadash' ['Rebuild Your Life: A Follow-up Study on Intergenerational Transference of Trauma of the Holocaust'] *Megamot, Journal of Behavioral Sciences*, Vol. 45, No. 2, December 2007, pp. 243-271.

Loshitzky, Y. *Identity Politics on the Israeli Screen* (Texas: University of Texas Press, 2001), pp. 15-71.

Loshitzky, Y. *Identity Politics on the Israeli Screen* (Texas: University of Texas Press, 2001).

Lubin, O. *Isha koret isha* [*Woman Reading Woman*] (Haifa: Haifa University/Zmora Bitan, 2006) [Hebrew].

Lynch, O. H. 'Humorous Communication: Finding a Place for Humor in Communication Research', *Communication Theory*, 12.4, (2002), pp. 423-445.

Mar, B. 'Mendy cohn limed yiddish et sahkaney haben shel shaul' ['Mendy Cohn taught Yiddish to the actors of 'The Son of Saul"], *Haaretz*, 18 March 2016 http://www.haaretz.co.il/gallery/cinema/.premium-1.2884632 Accessed 18 March 2016 [Hebrew].

McEvers, K. "It's A Surviving Tool': 'Native' Tells Satirical Stories Of Life In Israel', *NPR*, 12 February 2016 http://www.npr.org/2016/02/12/464920474/its-a-surviving-tool-native-tells-satirical-stories-of-life-in-israel Accessed 11 April 2016.

Mechman, D. *Post zionot vehashoah* [*Post-Zionism and Holocaust*] (Ramat Gan: Bar Ilan University Press, 1997) [Hebrew].

Melamed, A. 'Zaguri empire: lo gazanit meguvenet' ['The Zaguri Empire: Not Racist, Diverse'), *YNET*, 20 May 2014 http://www.ynet.co.il/articles/0,7340,L-4521659,00.html Accessed 1 May 2015 [Hebrew].

Mendelson-Maoz, A. and Steir-Livny, L. 'Hibridiyut batelevizia haisraelit' ['Hybridity in Israeli television – the first Israeli-Arab sitcom'], *Media Frames* [*Misgarot media*] 6, pp.31-59. [Hebrew].

Meyer, J. 'Humor as a Double-Edged Sword: Four Functions of Humor in Communication,' *Communication Theory* 10. 3 (2000), pp. 310-333.

Meyers, O. Neiger, M. & Zandberg, E. *Communicating Awe: Media Memory and Holocaust Commemoration* (New York: Palgrave Macmillan Memory Studies, 2014).

Miller, G. 'Zarfat: Antishemiut bazerem hamercazy' ('France: Mainstream Antisemitism'), *CFCA*, 1 November, 2013 http://antisemitism.org.il/article/82729/%D7%A6%D7%A8%D7%A4%D7%AA-%D7%90%D7%A0%D7%98%D7%99%D7%A9%D7%9E%D7%99%D7%95%D7%AA-%D7%A2%D7%9B%D7%A9%D7%99%D7%95-%D7%91%D7%96%D7%A8%D7%9D-%D7%94%D7%9E%D7%A8%D7%9B%D7%96%D7%99 Accessed 1 July 2016.

Milner, I. *Kirey Avar* [*A Torn Past*] (Tel Aviv: Am Oved, 2003) [Hebrew].

Milo, H. 'Gvura umavet: humor shahor beshirey folklore shel hayalim yisraelim' ['Heroism and Death: Black Humor in Folk Songs of Israeli Soldiers'], *Humor Mekuvvan: Research Journal in Humor Studies*, 4 (December 2014), pp. 26-44 [Hebrew].

Milo, H. *Shirim medabrim: zehut, migdar veidioligia beshirei hayalim* [*Talking Songs: Identity, Gender and Ideology in Folksongs of Male and Female Israeli Soldiers*, a thesis submitted for the degree *Doctor of Philosophy*], University of Haifa [Hebrew].

Mishani, D. *Bechol hainyan hamizrahi yes eize absurd* [*The Mizrahi Debate is Absurd*] (Tel Aviv: Am Oved, 2006) [Hebrew].

Modan, R. *The Property* [*Haneches*] (Tel-Aviv: Am Oved, 2013) [Hebrew].

Molcho, A. 'Ta'anat hahaslala' ['The claim of subordination in Israeli Education'], *Israeli Sociology*, 13, 1 (2011), pp. 9-54.

Mor, S. 'Izuv moadei hazikaron shel medinat yisrael' ['Israel's Memorial Days: An Arena for Cultural Wrestling'], *Alei Moed* 27 (2009), pp. 25-29 [Hebrew].

Morreall, J. 'Humor in the Holocaust: Its Critical, Cohesive, and Coping Functions', *Holocaust TRC*, 22.11.2001; http://www.holocaust-trc.org/holocaust_humor.htm Accessed 2 October 2008.

Nativ, Y. 'Tishmeu bdiha' [Listen to a joke'], *Mako*, 24 September 2013 [Hebrew].

Ne'eman Arad, G. 'Israel and the Shoah: A Tale of Multifarious Taboos', *New German Critique* 90 (2003), pp. 5-26.

Nevo, O. 'Do Jews in Israel still laugh at themselves?' in A. Ziv (ed), *Jewish humor*, (New Brunswick and London: Transaction Publishers, 1998), pp. 191-202.

Newcomb, H. & Hirsch, P. 'Television as a Cultural Forum: Implications for Research,' in H. Newcomb (ed), *Television: The Critical View*, (New York: Oxford University Press, 1994).

Niv, K. *Ahaim yafim aval lo leyehudim* [*Life Is Beautiful but Not for Jews*] (Tel Aviv: N.B. Sfarim Hagut, 2000) [Hebrew].

Nofa, M. 'Zikaron basalon: letzayen et hashoah bezura kzat aheret' ['*Remembrance in the Living Room* - Remembering in a different way'], *City Mouse*, 12.4.2015 http://www.mouse.co.il/CM.articles_item,720,209,78320,.aspx Accessed 1.5.2016 [Hebrew].

Nora, P. 'Bein zicaron vehistoria' ['Between Memory and History'] *Zmanim* 43 (1993), pp. 5-13 [Hebrew]

Ofer, D. 'The Past That Does Not Pass: Israelis and Holocaust Memory', *Israel Studies* 14.1 (2009): pp. 1-35.

Ofer, D. 'We Israelis Remember, But How? – The Memory of the Holocaust and the Israeli Experience', *Israel Studies* (18, No. 2 Summer, 2013), pp. 70-85.

Ohana, D. & Wistrich, R. (eds), *Mitus vezikaron* [*Myth and Remembrance*] (Jerusalem: Van Leer, 1996) [Hebrew].

Olick, J. K. & Robbins, J. 'Social Memory Studies: from 'Collective Memory' to the Historical Sociology of Mnemonic Practices', *Annual Review of Sociology* 24, (1998), pp. 105-140.

Ophir, A. *Avodat hahove:Masot al tarbut Israelit bazman haze* [*Working for the present: Essays on Contemporary Israeli culture*] (Tel-Aviv: Hakibbutz Hameuhad, 2001) [Hebrew].

Oring, E. *Engaging Humor* (Illinois: Illinois University Press, 2008).

Oring, E. 'Jokes and the Discourse on Disaster', T*he Journal of American Folklore*, Vol 100. No. 397, (July-September, 1987), pp. 276-286

Oring, E. 'The People of the Joke: On the Conceptualization of a Jewish Humor.' *Western Folklore* 42.4 (1983), pp. 261–271.

Oster, S. 'Holocaust Humor', *UTNE Reader – The Best of the Alternative Press*, September-October 1999 http://www.utne.com/mind-and-body/holocaust-humor.aspx Accessed 21 May 2013.

Ostrower, H. *Lelo humor hayinu mitabdim* [*Without humor we would have killed ourselves*] (Jerusalem: Yad Vashem, 2009) [Hebrew].

Palmer, J. *The Logic of the Absurd: On Television Comedy* (London: BFI, 2003).

Parshani, R. 'Beregashot meoravim' ['With Mixed Emotions: the Empire Strikes Back'], *NRG*, 10 February 2015 http://www.nrg.co.il/online/47/ART2/675/259.html Accessed 5 March 2015 [Hebrew].

Peled, Y. and Shafir, G. *Mihu yisraeli* [*Who is an Israeli: the dynamics of complex identity*] (Tel Aviv: Tel Aviv University, 2005) [Hebrew].

Pfanzelter, E. 'At the crossroads with public history: mediating the Holocaust on the Internet', *Holocaust Studies. A Journal of Culture and History*, 21/4 (2015), pp 250-271 http://www.catsthatlooklikehitler.com/cgi-bin/seigmiaow.pl

Pfefferkorn, E. 'The Art of Survival: Romain Gary's 'The Dance of Genghis Cohn'', *Modern Language Studies*, Vol. 10, No. 3 (Autumn, 1980), pp. 76-87.

Pinto-Abecasis, N. *Hatavas, hamegohatz vehazi halsha* [*The Peacock, the Ironed Man and the Half-Woman*] (Jerusalem: Ben-Zvi Institute, 2014) [Hebrew].

Plotzker, S. 'Lehafsik lispor levanim veshhorim' ['Stop Counting Whites versus Blacks'], *Yediot Aharonot*, 15 January 2012, p. 21.

Popescu, D. 'Performance, Memory and Identity: The Israeli Third Generation in Yael Ronen's Third Generation Play (2009)', in: Jilovsky, E., Silverstein, J. & Slucki, D. (eds), *In the Shadows of Memory: The Holocaust and the Third Generation* (London: Vallentine Mitchell, 2016). pp. 209-226.

Porat, D. 'Arbaim shanim shel maavak: yomana shel anna frank umachhishei hashoah' ['Forty Years of Struggle: Anne Frank's Diary and Holocaust Deniers, 1958-1998'], in: *The Holocaust – the Unique and the Universal, essays presented in honor of Yehuda Bauer* (Jerusalem, 2001), pp. 160-183 [Hebrew].

Porat, D. *Café haboker barayach ashan: mifgashim shel hayishuv vahahevra hayisraelit im hashoah vanitzoleha*, [*The Smoke-Scented Coffee: The Encounter of the Yishuv and Israeli Society with the Holocaust and its Survivors*] (Tel Aviv and Jerusalem: Yad Vashem and Am Oved, 2011) [Hebrew].

Press, V.S,' Young Israeli social entrepreneur named 'leader of tomorrow' by TIME magazine', *Israel 21c*, 29.9.2014 http://www.israel21c.org/young-israeli-social-entrepreneur-named-leader-of-tomorrow-by-time-magazine/ Accessed 1 July 2016.

'PTSD', Diagnostic and Statistical Manual of Mental Disorders (5th ed.) (Arlington, VA: American Psychiatric Publishing, 2013). pp. 271–280.

Raav Meir, S. 'Yesh gvul' ['There is a limit'], *Yediot Aharonot, Hamusaf Leshabat*, 20 April 2012, pp. 18 [Hebrew].

Ravid, B. 'Netanyahu al neum sgan haramatcal yair golan: dvaraiv mekomemim vegormim lezilut hashoah' ['Netanyahu on the speech of the deputy chief of staff Yair Golan: his remarks are outrageous and cheapen the Holocaust'], *Haaretz*, 8 May 2016 http://www.haaretz.co.il/news/politics/1.2937286 Accessed 20 June 2016 Accessed 2 June 2016 [Hebrew].

Reading, A. 'Clicking on Hitler: The virtual Holocaust @ Home', in: Barbie Zelizer (ed.) *Visual Culture and the Holocaust* (Rutgers University Press, 2001), pp. 323-337

Refael, S. *Madrich laMevaker beBirkenau* [*A Visitor's Guide to Birkenau*] (Tel Aviv: Sifrei Iton 77, 2015) [Hebrew].

Reik, T. *Jewish Wit* (New York: Gamut Press, 1962).

Reimer, R. C. 'Does Laughter Make the Crime Disappear?: An Analysis of Cinematic Images of Hitler and the Nazis, 1940-2007,' September (2009) Issue 52, http://sensesofcinema.com/2009/feature-articles/does-laughter-make-the-crime-disappear-an-analysis-of-cinematic-images-of-hitler-and-the-nazis-1940-2007/ Accessed 8 February 2016.

Roccas, R. 'Kama mehasodot mitgalim' ['Some of the Secrets Are Revealed'], *Ha'aretz*, 9 April 2002. http://www.haaretz.com/israel-news/culture/leisure/some-of-the-secrets-are-revealed-1.48264Accessed 10 April 2002 [Hebrew].

Ronco, A. 'Hitler beyerushalaim' ['Hitler in Jerusalem'], *City Mouse Online*, 20 July 2008 http://www.mouse.co.il/CM.articles_item,610,209,25690,.aspx Accessed 2 April 2016 [Hebrew].

Rosen, R. *Live and Die as Eva Braun*http://roeerosen.com/tagged/Live-and-Die-as-Eva-BraunAccessed 1 March 2016.

Rosenberg, A. 'Holocaust Graphic Novels Give Israelis a Way to Connect to the Past Not Quite Theirs'. Tablet, 31 July 2013.HYPERLINK "http://www.tabletmag.com/jewish-arts-and-culture/139468/holocaust-graphic-novels%20Accessed%2020%20August%202013" http://www.tabletmag.com/jewish-arts-and-culture/139468/holocaust-graphic-novels Accessed 20 August 2013.

Rosenfeld, A. *The End of the Holocaust* (Indiana: Indiana University Press, 2013).

Rosenfeld, G. D. *Hi Hitler: How the Nazi Past Is Being Normalized in Contemporary Culture* (Cambridge University Press, 2015).

Rosenthal, P. & Rosenthal, S. 'Holocaust Effect in the Third Generation: Child of Another Time,' *American Journal of Psychotherapy*, October 34:4, 1980, pp. 572-580.

Roth, P. *The Ghost Writer* (Farrar, Straus and Giroux, 1979).

Sabo, S. 'Tkasim alternativim' ['Alternative Ceremonies'], *International Experts Seminar on Holocaust Education*, Massuah, 19 May 2016.

Sagi-Schwartz, A., van IJzendoorn M. & Bakermans-Kranenburg, M. J. 'Does Intergenerational Transference of Trauma Skip a Generation? No Meta-Analytic Evidence for Tertiary Traumatization with Third Generation Holocaust Survivors,' *Attachment & Human Development*, Vol. 10, No. 2, June 2008, pp. 105-121.

Sandel, M. *Liberalism and the Limits of Justice* (Cambridge University Press, 1982, 1998).

Sapir Weitz, C. 'Haperek shel zaguri' ['The Zaguri Episode Elicits the Question: Has the Commemoration of the Holocaust Also Been Privatized in the Israel of 2015?'], *Ma'ariv*, 12 February 2015 Accessed 5 March 2015 [Hebrew].

Sarig, R. *Chaim shtaim* (Jerusalem: Keter, 2005) [Hebrew].

Satloff R. *Among the Righteous: Lost Stories from the Holocaust's Long Reach into Arab Lands* (Public Affairs, 2006).

Scharf, M. 'The Trace of Trauma: Third-Generation Holocaust Survivors,' *Development and Psychopathology*, (Volume 19, Issue 02, April 2007), pp 603-622.

Scharf, M. &. Mayseless, O., 'Disorganizing Experiences in Second- and Third-Generation Holocaust Survivors,' *Qualitative Health Research*, November vol. 21 no. 11, 2011, pp. 1539-1553.

Schwabach, A. 'Reclaiming Copyright from the Outside In: What the Downfall Hitler Meme Means for Transformative Works, Fair Use, and Parody,' *Buffalo Intellectual Property Law Journal*, 2012

Segev, T. *Hamillion hashviyi* [*The Seventh Million*] (Jerusalem: Keter, 1991) [Hebrew].

Shalhevet, K. 'Zikaron basalon' ['*Remembrance in the Living Room*], *Local*, 19.4.2012 http://www.local.co.il/hod-hasharon/94415/article/ Accessed 1 July 2016 [Hebrew].

Shalom Chetrit, S. *Hamaavak hamizrahibey israel: bein dikui keshihrur, bein hizdahut lealternativa, 1948–2003* [*The Mizrahi Struggle in Israel: Between Oppression and Liberation, Identification and Alternative, 1948–2003*], (Tel Aviv: Am-Oved/Ofakim Series, 2004) [Hebrew].

Shani, A. 'Hoker hahumor hayehudi Arie Sover' ['Jewish Humor Researcher Arie Sover: Israeli Humor is less clever than the Jewish Humor'], *Haaretz*, 11 February 2016 http://www.haaretz.co.il/magazine/ayelet-shani/.premium-1.2848505 Accessed 12 February 2016.

Shapira, A. 'Lean halcha shlilat hagalut' ['The Denial of the Diaspora'], *Shvut* (2004), p. 13-61 [Hebrew].

Shapira, A. *Yehudim hadashim, yehudim yeshanim* [*New Jews, Old Jews*], (Tel-Aviv-Am Oved, 1997) [Hebrew].

Shenhar, A. 'Lihiyot sham: shirei mehaa shel hayalim bizman milhemet levabon' ['To be there: Protest songs by soldiers during the Lebanon War'], *Hetz*, A 1, 1989, pp. 34-41 [Hebrew].

Shifman, L. *Haars, hafreha vehaima hapolaniya* [*Televised Humor and Social Cleavages in Israel, 1968-2000*] (Jerusalem: Magnes Press, 2008) [Hebrew].

Shifman, L. 'An anatomy of a YouTube meme', *New Media and Society*, 14 (2) (2012), pp. 187-203.

Shifman, L. *Memes in digital culture* (Cambridge: MIT Press, 2013).

Shiloni, S. 'Zagury empire nafla bepach haotentiyut' ['The Zaguri Empire Fell into the Authenticity Trap'], *YNET*, 9 April 2014 http://www.ynet.co.il/articles/0,7340,L-4508186,00.html Accessed 1 May 2015 [Hebrew].

'Shoah bechol makom' ['Holocaust everywhere'], *Remembrance in the Living Room website*: http://www.zikaronbasalon.com/#!blank-6/frbrq Accessed 1 July 2016.

Shohat, E. *Mizrah umaarav* [*East and West in Israeli Cinema*] (Raanana, The Open University, 2007) [Hebrew].

Shohat, E. 'Zichronot asurim' ['Forbidden Memories'], *Keshet ha Mizrah* 2, Bimat Kedem le Safrut 13, 2010 [Hebrew].

Shragai, T. & Levi, H. 'Shoah – ma mazhik beze?' ['Holocaust: What's funny about that?'], *Walla!*, 18 April 2001 http://news.walla.co.il/item/54337 Accessed 2 May 2002 [Hebrew].

Shushan, A. 'Zaguri empire goremet nezek lemizrahim' [''Zaguri Empire' Is Causing Damage to the Mizrahim'], *YNET*, 1 February 2015 http://www.ynet.co.il/articles/0,7340,L-4620771,00.html Accessed 5 March 2015 [Hebrew].

Simpson, P. *On the Discourse of Satire: Towards a Stylistic Model of Satirical Humor*, (Amsterdam/Philadelphia: John Benjamin's Publishing Company, 2003).

Sliwa J. 'Jewish humor as a source of research on Polish-Jewish relations'. In Greenspoon, L. J., ed., *Jews and Humor* (West Lafayette, IN: Purdue University Press, 2011), pp. 67-82.

Slucki, D. 'Trivialization or Commemoration: Holocaust Humor in Australia,' in: Lederhendler, E. and Gabriel Finder, N. *A Club of their Own: Jewish Humorists in the Contemporary World*, (New York: Oxford University Press, 2016), pp, 204-229.

Smooha, S. 'Rav tarbutiyut bahevra haisrelit' ['Multiculturalism in Israeli society'], in: I. Yovel (ed), *Zman Yehudi Hadash* [*New Israeli Time*] (Jerusalem: Keter, 2007), 4, pp. 221-228 [Hebrew].

Solomon, Z. and Chaitin, J. (eds), *Yaldut bezel haShoah* [*Childhood in the Shadow of the Holocaust: Child Survivors and Second Generation*] (Tel Aviv: Hakibbutz Hameuchad, 2007) [Hebrew].

Solomon, Z. 'Haavara bein dorot shel hashoah' ['Transgenerational Effects of the Holocaust: The Israeli Research Perspective'], in Z. Solomon and J. Chaitin (eds.), *Children in the Shadow of the Holocaust* (Tel Aviv: Hakibbutz Hameuchad, 2007), pp. 304-336 [Hebrew].

Sorce, G. 'Hitler and Humor: Coming to Terms with the Past through Parody', *Global MediaJournal*, German Edition, Vol. 5, No.2 (Autumn/Winter 2015) http://www.db-thueringen.de/servlets/DerivateServlet/Derivate-32872/GMJ10_Sorce_final.pdfAccessed 2 February 2016.

Sover, A. *Bedarco shel haadam hazohek* [*The Pathway to Human Laughter*] (Jerusalem: Carmel, 2009) [Hebrew].

Sover, A. 'Jewish humor'. *Oxford Bibliographies* (2015). http://www.oxfordbibliographies.com/view/document/obo-9780199840731/obo-9780199840731-0117.xml?rskey=fmdMmn&result=32 Accessed September 30, 2015.

Spector, D. 'Hashoah ze passe', ('The Holocaust is Passe') *YNET*, 12 November 2001 http://www.ynet.co.il/articles/0,7340,L-1302168,00.html Accessed 20 February 2006 [Hebrew].

Steir-Livny, L. An interview with Clila and Hadassh Bau, 25 November 2016.

Steir-Livny, L. 'Anne Frank as a Comic Figure', *I'm Allowed..I'm Jewish* (Wayne State University Press, forthcoming).

Steir-Livny, L. 'Hacomback shel hagalut' ['The Comeback of the Jewish Diaspora in Israeli Culture'], in *Identity in transition in Israeli culture, A book in honor of Prof. Nurith Gertz* (Raanana: The Open University, 2013), pp. 461-481 [Hebrew].

Steir-Livny, L. *Har hazikaron yizkor bimkomi* [*Let the Memorial Hill Remember: Holocaust Representations in Israeli Popular Culture*] (Tel Aviv: Resling, 2014) [Hebrew].

Steir-Livny, L. 'Hitler Rants on YouTube Parodies in Hebrew', *The European Journal of Humour Research*, Vol 4, No. 4, pp. 105-121.

Steir-Livny, L. 'Holocaust humor, satire, and parody on Israeli television', *Jewish Film and New Media*, 3/2, (Fall, 2015), pp. 193-219.

Steir-Livny, L. *Shtei panim bamarah: Yezug Nitzolei haShoah baKolnoa haIsraeli* [*Two Faces in the Mirror: the representation of Holocaust survivors in Israeli cinema]* (Jerusalem: Eshkolot-Magness, 2009). [Hebrew]

Steir-Livny, L. 'Tam hatekes: hatekes haalternativy beteatron tmuna beerev yom hazicaron lashoah velagvura' ['Alternative Memory: Alternative ceremonies on Holocaust and Heroism Remembrance Day'], *Dapim Leheker Hasoah*, 28 (2016), pp. 131-150 [Hebrew].

Steir-Livny, L. 'The Link between the Holocaust and the Israeli-Arab Conflict in Israeli Culture, 1950s-1970s', in L. Aleksandrowicz-Pedich & M. Pakier (eds), *Jewish Identity in Pre- and Post-Holocaust Literature and Culture*, (Frankfurt: Peter Lang GmbHN Internationaler Verlag der Wissenschaften, 2012), pp.157-168.

Stier, O. B. *Holocaust Icons* (New Brunswick: Rutgers University Press, 2015).

Svirsky, S. *Hinuch beisrael [Education in Israel*] (Tel Aviv: Breirot, 1990) [Hebrew].

Svirsky, S. *Lo nehshalim ela menuhshalim* [*Not Backwards but Subordinated*] (Haifa: Machbarot leMechkar, 1981) [Hebrew].

Sznaider, N. & Levy, D. *The Holocaust and Memory in the Global Age* (Philadelphia: Temple University Press, 2006).

Trezise, B. *Performing Feeling in Cultures of Memory*, (Palgrave Macmillan Memory Studies, 2014), pp. 28-55.

Tsur, Y. 'Eimat hakarnaval' ['The Terror of the Carnival: the Moroccans and the ethnic problem in Young Israel'] *Alpaim* 19 (2000), pp. 57-82 [Hebrew].

Tydor Baumel-Schwartz, J. *Perfect Heroes: The World War II Parachutists and the Making of Collective Israeli Memory* (Wisconsin: University of Wisconsin Press 2010).

Walden, V. G. 'New Ethical Questions and Social Media: Young People's Construction of Holocaust Memory Online', *Frames Cinema Journal* http://framescinemajournal.com/article/new-ethical-questions-and-social-media-young-peoples-construction-of-holocaust-memory-online/ Accessed 1 June 2015.

Walzer, M. *On Toleration* (Yale: Yale University Press, 1997).

Ward, S. 'The Holocaust in North Africa and the Sephardic World', *The International Sephardic Journal* 1(1) (2004), pp. 72-86.

Wardi, D. *Nosei hahotam* [*Memorial Candles*] (Jerusalem: Keter, 1990) [Hebrew].

Wiesel, E. 'Art and the Holocaust: Trivializing memory', *The New York Times*, 11 June 1989, http://www.nytimes.com/1989/06/11/movies/art-and-the-holocaust-trivializing-memory.html?pagewanted=all Accessed 2 October, 2012.

Wisse, R. R. *No Joke: Making Jewish Humor* (Princeton: Princeton University Press, 2013).

Yablonka, H. *Harhek mehamesila: hamizrahim vehashoah* [*Off the Beaten Track: The Mizrahim and the Holocaust*] (Tel Aviv: Miskal-Yedioth Aharonot Books, 2008) [Hebrew].

Yosef, R. 'Ethnicity and Sexual Politics: The Invention of Mizrahi Masculinity in Israeli Cinema,' *Theory and Criticism*, 25, (Fall 2004), pp. 31-62.

Young, J. E. *The Texture of Memory: Holocaust Memorials and Meaning* (New Haven, CT: Yale University Press, 1993).

Yudelevitz, M. 'Metihat panim lashoah ['A makeover for the Holocaust'], *YNET*, 29 April 2003 http://www.ynet.co.il/articles/0,7340,L-2594315,00.html Accessed 1 May 2014 [Hebrew].

Yuran, N. *Arutz shtayim: hamamlachtiyut hahadasha* [*Channel 2: The New Statehood*] (Tel Aviv: Resling, 2001) [Hebrew].

Zand,S. *Kolnoa vehistoria* [*Cinema as History*] (Tel Aviv: Am Oved, 2002) [Hebrew].

Zandberg, E. 'Critical laughter: Humor, popular culture and Israeli Holocaust commemoration', *Media, Culture & Society*, (28(4), 2006), pp. 561-579.

Zandberg, E. ''Ketchup Is the Auschwitz of Tomatoes': Humor and the Collective Memory of Traumatic Events', *Communication, Culture & Critique*, 2014, pp. 1-16

Zertal, I. *Hauma vehamavet* (*The Nation and Death)* Tel Aviv: Dvir, 1993 [Hebrew].

'Zikaron 2:0: *Hashoah kamovila tarbutit*' ('Memory 2.0: Holocaust in culture'), *City Maus* 18 April 2012 http://www.mouse.co.il/CM.articles_item,610,209,67612,.aspx Accessed 3 September 2013 [Hebrew].

Ziv, A (ed), *Jewish humor* (Tel Aviv: Papyrus, 1986).

Ziv, A. 'Humor as a Social Corrective.' In: Laurence Behrens and Leonard J. Rosen (eds) *Writing and Reading Across the Curriculum* 3rd ed. (Glenview, IL: Scott, Foresman and Company, 1988), pp. 356-360.

Ziv, A. *Ishiut vehush humor* [*Personality and Sense of Humor*], (Tel Aviv: Papyrus, 1996) [Hebrew].

Ziv, A. 'Psycho-social aspects of Jewish humor in Israel and in the Diaspora.' In A. Ziv (ed), *Jewish humor* (New Brunswick and London: Transaction Publishers, 1998), pp. 47-74.

Zuckermann, M. *Shoah baheder haatum* [*Holocaust in the sealed room*] (Tel Aviv: Private pPblishing, 1993) [Hebrew].

Index